MARK TWAIN

A Study of the Short Fiction

Also available in Twayne's Studies in Short Fiction Series

Twayne publishes studies of all major short-story writers worldwide. For a complete list, contact the Publisher directly.

Twayne's Studies in Short Fiction

General Editors
Gary Scharnhorst, *University of New Mexico*
Eric Haralson, *State University of New York at Stony Brook*

Mark Twain.

Courtesy of the State Historical Society of Missouri, Columbia.

MARK TWAIN

A Study of the Short Fiction

Tom Quirk
University of Missouri–Columbia

TWAYNE PUBLISHERS

New York

Twayne's Studies in Short Fiction, No. 66

Copyright © 1997 by Twayne Publishers

Twayne Publishers
1633 Broadway
New York, NY 10019

Library of Congress Cataloging-in-Publication Data

Quirk, Tom, 1946–
    Mark Twain : a study of the short fiction / Tom Quirk
        p.   cm. — (Twayne's United States authors series ; no. 66)
    Includes bibliographical references and index.
    ISBN 0-8057-0867-7 (alk. paper)
    1. Twain, Mark, 1835–1910—Criticism and interpretation.   2. Short
story.   I. Title.   II. Series.
PS1338.Q57   1997
813'.4—dc21
                                                                97-3445
                                                                CIP

ACC Library Services
Austin, Texas

ninimum requirements of
:iences—Permanence of Paper
34. ∞ ™

Printed in the United States of America

For my brother

Contents

Acknowledgments

A book of this sort is the work of many hands. I want to thank Kevin Klingbeil for helping me in the research. I am grateful to the University of Missouri Press, the University of Pennsylvania Press, the Elmira College Center for Mark Twain Studies, and *Studies in American Humor* for granting permission to reprint the items contained in part 3 of this book. I am indebted to Gary Scharnhorst for his help, his patience, his judgment, and his goodwill throughout. I wish to thank Howard Baetzhold for his good advice and encouragement. A survey of the acknowledgment pages of Twain criticism and scholarship would prove that Louis J. Budd belongs to the Hall of Fame of Helpful Twainians; I know that I have been indebted to him before this and mean to be for a good long time to come. Last, I want to thank my wife, Catherine Parke, and my daughters, Laura and Ann, who make the whole thing worthwhile.

A Note on Texts and Abbreviations

I have tried wherever possible to cite texts of Twain's writings that are both reliable and readily available. The two-volume Library of America collection, *Mark Twain: Collected Tales, Sketches, Speeches, and Essays, 1852–1890* and *Mark Twain: Collected Tales, Sketches, Speeches, and Essays, 1891–1910*, edited by Louis J. Budd, serves that purpose admirably. The texts for a great many of the pieces printed there are those prepared by the Mark Twain Project, including tales and sketches that have not yet been published in the Iowa/California editions. In the case of writings that have not been prepared by members of the Mark Twain Project for the Works of Mark Twain, Budd typically, and quite rightly, selects as the most authoritative text the first American printing.

As complete as the Library of America collection is, however, I have discussed some pieces that do not appear there. For ease and convenience, quotations from Mark Twain's works are cited in the text with the following abbreviations:

> *CSS: The Complete Short Stories of Mark Twain*, ed. Charles Neider (New York: Doubleday, 1957).
>
> *CTS* I: *Mark Twain: Collected Tales, Sketches, Speeches, and Essays, 1852–1890*, ed. Louis J. Budd (New York: Library of America, 1992).
>
> *CTS* II: *Mark Twain: Collected Tales, Sketches, Speeches, and Essays, 1891–1910*, ed. Louis J. Budd (New York: Library of America, 1992).
>
> *ETS* I: *Early Tales and Sketches, 1851–1864*, ed. Edgar Marquess Branch and Robert H. Hirst (Berkeley and Los Angeles: University of California Press, 1993).
>
> *ETS* II: *Early Tales and Sketches, 1864–1865*, ed. Edgar Marquess Branch and Robert H. Hirst (Berkeley and Los Angeles: University of California Press, 1993).
>
> *MTHL: Mark Twain–Howells Letters: The Correspondence of Samuel L. Clemens and William D. Howells, 1872–1910*, ed. Henry Nash Smith and William M. Gibson, 2 vols. (Cambridge: Harvard University Press, 1960).

Notes on Texts and Abbreviations

MTL 1: *Letters, Volume 1: 1853–1866*, ed. Edgar Marquess Branch, Michael B. Frank, and Kenneth M. Sanderson (Berkeley and Los Angeles: University of California Press, 1988).

RI: Roughing It, ed. Harriet Elinor Smith and Edgar Marquess Branch (Berkeley and Los Angeles: University of California Press, 1993).

TA: Tramp Abroad (Hartford, Conn.: American Publishing, 1880).

Part 1

THE SHORT FICTION

Introduction

As a writer of short fiction, Mark Twain was, as he was in most things, various and variable. Simply put, when Twain wrote short fiction, he did not play by the rules. He knew the rules well enough. Anyone who could so effortlessly indulge in parody, satire, burlesque, and other forms of humor that rely upon a firm understanding of literary convention and so adroitly apply that understanding in his creations did not write out of literary ignorance. Twain's repeated professions of innocence or ineptitude in literary craftsmanship are not to be believed. He read widely and often acutely, and we know from the collection *Mark Twain's Library of Humor* and several stray comments on humorists that he was something of a literary historian and connoisseur of American humor.[1] However, his allegiances were not to established literary forms but to imaginative and humorous possibility.

Twain could adopt with apparent ease familiar comic forms and often extend or enlarge their literary potential. His familiar jumping frog story, for example, is a specimen of typical frontier humor, a frame, or "box," tale in which a genteel narrator introduces a vernacular narrator who in turn spins out his tall tale before the genteel narrator returns in the concluding paragraph. This story, although perfectly adapted to that established literary mode, goes beyond mere literary contrivance by departing from the quality of condescension detectable in the author that so often characterized the form and served American humorists well in entering Eastern publishing markets. Simon Wheeler and Jim Smiley are palpable. Their antics and earnestness are laughable, but they are not buffoons. They amuse, but because they are vivid and vividly possible, they also command our sympathy and respect as human creatures. As created characters, Simon Wheeler and Jim Smiley are self-sufficient and do not stand in need of translation or extenuation. The characters speak to us because they speak for themselves.

In part, the dignity Twain gave his vernacular yarn spinners such as Simon Wheeler derives from a refusal to interrupt, comment upon, or otherwise disrupt the narrator's tale. These tales might wander in their details, and the tellers may be comically unaware of the humor in their talk, but Twain was secure in the conviction that the vernacular point of view was adequate (verbally, morally, and emotionally) to depict the world his characters inhabit. The unruly freedom of this point of view may well be, as Henry Nash Smith has noted, "subversive" to the dominant culture and to received opinion, but I rather suspect that Twain himself held to a simpler faith—that he had served his muse well when, in Simon Wheeler and others, he had delivered the authentic voice of a man talking at his leisure. Even in the relatively fixed form of the frame tale, Twain frequently found simple variations and departures that gave his narratives a fresh vitality and resonance. For example, he sometimes declined to have his narrative persona round out the tale in the final paragraph, as was the custom, preferring instead to have his vernacular narrator have the last word. This is the case in "A True Story," a story in which Twain rather deliberately adapted the humorous form to his own experience and to serious moral purpose and as a consequence found literary opportunities in a rather shopworn mode that was widely regarded as "unliterary."

As different as they are, the jumping frog tale and "A True Story" (and many other tales as well) share the quality of sure artistic control and a sense of dramatic proportion. Nevertheless, any student of Twain's short fiction who concentrates too exclusively upon the formal excellences or deficiencies in his work is bound to be disappointed and, more important, to misapprehend the peculiar quality of his genius. His friend William Dean Howells grasped as well as anyone—and better than most—the special nature of that genius:

> Of all the literary men I have known he was the most unliterary in his make and manner. . . . He used English in all its alien derivations as if it were native to his own air, as if it had come up out of American, out of Missourian ground. His style was what we know, for good and for bad, but his manner, if I may difference the two, was as entirely his own as if no one had ever written before. I have noted before this how he was not enslaved to the consecutiveness in writing which the rest of us try to keep chained to. That is, he wrote as he thought, and as all men think, without sequence, without an eye to what went before or should come after. . . . He observed this manner in the construction of his sentences, and the arrangement of his chapters, and the ordering and disordering of his compilations.[2]

If Twain distributed his comic and dramatic effects as the opportunity arose (and he did), if he displayed a casual but knowing indifference to literary proprieties (and he did), and if, unlike Poe, he mined his material for manifold, not single, effects (and he did), it seems a mistake for the reader to strain for coherencies and unities that have been meticulously avoided. And it is equally a mistake to tie oneself too narrowly to a generic conception of Twain's short fiction. A more profitable method of investigation, and the one that is pursued in the following pages, is to inquire into the imaginative resources that combined with often original and seemingly spontaneous literary technique to produce a sizable body of short fiction, as remarkable for its unpredictable and uneven artistic achievement as it is for its sheer fun.

Such an approach to Twain's short fiction is consonant with Charles Neider's observation in his introduction to *The Complete Short Stories of Mark Twain:* "In almost any other writer's work it is easy to say, 'This is a short story, whereas that is not.' . . . But in Twain's case it is quite another matter. I have the sense that Twain wrote primarily to satisfy an audience rather than the requirements of a genre" (*CSS*, xiii). Justin Kaplan puts it rather differently in his introduction to *Mark Twain's Short Stories*, but the point is essentially the same: "The variety of short fictions he wrote practically exhausts the genre vocabulary: sketches, yarns, tales, fables, folk tales, tall tales, fairy tales, ghost tales, fantasies, allegories, incidents, anecdotes, hoaxes, domestic comedies, animal stories, and short short stories, in addition to short stories proper."[3] Such an abundance of forms tends to underscore their inconsequence, for Twain adapted his means to his ends, and those ends were, at his best, the knowing adjustment of creative inspiration to readerly delight and the expression of a personal loyalty to the internal logic of the tale to be told. For Twain, each story, properly rendered, was unique. As he remarked late in his life, "There is only one right form for a story, and if you fail to find that form the story will not tell itself. You may try a dozen wrong forms, but in each case you will not get very far before you discover that you have not found the right one—then that story will always stop and decline to go any farther."[4]

Neider and Kaplan have collected Twain's short stories in widely available anthologies. Walter Blair, in *Selected Shorter Writings of Mark Twain* (Riverside); myself, in *Mark Twain: Tales, Sketches, Essays, and Speeches* (Viking/Penguin); and most important, Louis J. Budd, in his two-volume *Collected Tales, Sketches, Speeches, and Essays* (Library of America), have offered other anthologies that readers may pick up in a bookstore or students may encounter in the classroom. As the titles imply, these anthologies avoid making strict generic distinctions, but seek instead to gather and distill Twain's remarkable and audaciously various attainments in his shorter works. Because this volume is meant to supplement the reading and enjoyment of these short works, whether they appear in one of the collections just named or elsewhere, and because imposing some formal or aesthetic scheme on Twain's short fiction may argue for the cleverness of the critic but ultimately only diminishes the author, I have attempted to locate our interest in an altogether different place—in Twain's imaginative originality and his creative attainments, however sporadic or momentarily sustained. In other words, I am less interested in performing literary analysis or interpretation of texts than in providing a descriptive account of Twain's imaginative energies and his literary development as they are revealed in his short fiction.

Even so, I have imposed some limitations on this study. Twain was a prolific and largely unpredictable writer. Samuel Clemens wrote a great deal before he adopted the pen name Mark Twain, and at the time of his death, he left a great many manuscripts incomplete and unpublished. Without question, many of those works (from the very early "The Dandy Frightening the Squatter" [1852] to the posthumously published "Little Bessie," "Letters from the Earth," the three *Mysterious Stranger* manuscripts, and many others) are of great interest and, unfinished or fragmentary as some of them are, aesthetically rewarding. Many of those writings have been or will be published by scholars involved in the Mark Twain Project or by other able Twain scholars. For reasons of economy and focus, however, I have chosen to begin my study with the short fiction published after Samuel Clemens became "Mark Twain" in 1863 and to treat only those stories published before his death in 1910. The reader will discover soon enough that those limitations are not severe and that there is sufficient richness and variety in the more than 60 tales published during this period to give an adequate and, I hope, satisfying portrait of the man and his work.

As an artist, Twain was something of a conjurer. The incantations of his imagination called forth wild, almost cartoonlike images of human and animal behavior, but always tinged with realistic detail. And he heard voices. Or rather, he listened to the voices of innumerable men and women, and he remembered. He remembered the cadences and hesitations, the dialects and homespun figures of speech, and his remembering in its turn reproduced on the printed page the flavor of speech itself. As Walter Blair has acutely remarked, Mark Twain addressed himself to the "mind's ear."[5] Twain both judged others' writing and meant for his own to be judged by reading the prose aloud.

A wag once noted that a popular but second-rate poet wrote poetry for people whose lips moved when they read. But Twain went much further—he wished to be read, of course, but he also wished to be heard. The secret of the "high and delicate art" of rendering a humorous tale, as Twain identified it in "How to Tell a Story," lies not in the subject matter but in the manner of the tale's telling. If the tale is properly told, the result is something "delicious and charming." "How to Tell a Story," reprinted in part 2 of this volume, sheds interesting light on many of his tales and sketches, but one should remember that Twain's essay concerns how to "tell" a story, not how to write one. At least half of the art of Twain's published stories is to be found in his dramatic management of the fiction, what he referred to in his essay on Howells (also reprinted in part 2) as "stage directions": "those artifices which authors employ to throw a kind of human naturalness around a scene and a conversation, and help the reader to see the one and get at meanings in the other which might not be perceived if intrusted unexplained to the bare words of the talk" (*CTS* II, 727).

As with most conjurers, Twain was sometimes possessed by spirits. He often referred to himself as the "amanuensis" to his own art: The voices of his characters would speak their lines in authentic speech if only he would submit to the natural informing principle of the tale to be told.[6] Left alone to work in his imagination, the tale would realize itself at last; for this reason, Twain sometimes spoke of his imagination as a "tank" that, if it ran dry, would refill itself in its own way and in its own good time. Eventually, the "right" way to tell a tale would declare itself and reaffirm the distinctive quality that made it uniquely interesting. Though he might have devalued his role as author to some sort of mediumship, Twain was also an artist: He was willing to consign hundreds or even thousands of pages of manuscript to oblivion if the prose was forced or inauthentic, and he was a tireless, if not always meticulous, reviser, whose experience as a typesetter and journalist created in him a certain practical and professional detachment from his own work.

Even as a conscious artist, however, he was a conjurer. In the act of creation, he conjured up the improbable and the fantastic, the hilarious and the bittersweet. The apparent spontaneity of his best short pieces (patiently preserved and intensified through revision) is actually the result of careful craftsmanship. The illusion of immediacy is infectiously conveyed to the reader, and one tends to respond to Twain's imaginative exfoliations and verbal extravagance more as an agreeable participant and a present witness than as a judging onlooker.

In this sense, much of Twain's fiction has the quality and feel of dream. If the author suspends an allegiance to "consecutiveness," to use Howells's word, the reader cannot second-guess the story as to plot, consequence, or narrative mode. Instead he or she watches with a certain cordial intimacy and innocent trust as events and figures of speech unfold, as speculation, anecdote, and remembrance disappear as unexpectedly as they came. Consider this passage from "The Story of the Old Ram":

> Seth Green was probl'ly the pick of the flock; he married a Wilkerson—Sarah Wilkerson—good cretur, she was—one of the likeliest heifers that was ever raised in old Stoddard, everybody said that knowed her. She could heft a bar'l of flour as easy as I can flirt a flapjack. And spin? Don't mention it! Independent? Humph! When Sile Hawkins come a-browsing around her, she let him know that for all his tin he could'nt trot in harness alongside of *her*. You see, Sile Hawkins was—no, it warn't Sile Hawkins, after all—it was a galoot by the name of Filkins—I disremember his first name; but he *was* a stump—come into pra'r meeting drunk, one night, hooraying for Nixon, becuz he thought it was a primary; and old deacon Ferguson up and scooted him through the window and he lit on old Miss Jefferson's head, poor old filly. (*RI*, 362–63)

This passage is representative of the whole, and one can see easily enough why some critics have detected modernist qualities in the story. Jim Blaine's spontaneous association and his unsegmented narrative (the entire story is a single paragraph) have led some to see in the tale a prefiguring of stream of consciousness techniques one finds in Joyce or Faulkner. Moreover, the narrative is structured around the anticipation of a subject (the ram) that will never appear. But it would be a mistake to see in the rustic Jim Blaine, sitting on an empty powder keg with a clay pipe in his hand, a premonitory Molly Bloom, and despite the story's absurdist features, it is hardly a backwater *Waiting for Godot*. Blaine's haphazard narrative is not stream of consciousness but social soliloquy. The old ram story bears greater resemblance to Aeschylus's *Prometheus Bound* (where the title figure, through augury and recollection, creates a wide-ranging verbal world, but at the same time answers to the complaints and questions of a very real polis) than it does to any disclosure of the riotous human heart. The old ram story is not the dramatic projection of a private and interior consciousness but the hazy and unaccustomed awareness in the speaker that he has the apparently respectful attention of others.

Perhaps, in order to see the delicacy of Twain's art, it is worthwhile and instructive to mutilate this passage by untangling it and giving it the sense of proportion and narrative continuity it so steadfastly refuses. Even in this brief snippet, we have the ingredients of a succinct narrative. We know from the beginning that Sarah Wilkerson has married Seth Green and that he is the "pick of the flock" of Greens, but we get nothing of their courtship or of the qualities that Green possesses that make him acceptable. Instead, we get snapshots of the fellows Sarah rejected, or rather one fellow under two names—Sile Hawkins and Filkins, whose first name has been "disremembered." In any event, we know that Sarah Wilkerson was generally held to be the "likeliest heifer" in Stoddard ("everybody said that knowed her") and therefore deserves only the best. We know as well that she is strong (she can "heft" a barrel of flour), accomplished in such domestic arts as spinning ("Don't mention it!"), and independent ("Humph!"). She is impatient with artifice and brassiness and won't put up with Hawkins's "tin." And we may infer that neither Sarah Wilkerson nor Jim Blaine has any use for a man who comes to camp meeting drunk and hooraying for Nixon.

This is all the more amusing, of course, because due to Twain's careful dramatic management, Blaine's cabin suddenly becomes a candlelit amphitheater on the frontier where he weaves his tale in garrulous inebriation. We know nevertheless that Blaine is mindful of the proprieties and supremely admiring of such upright figures as Sarah Wilkerson and Seth Green. Blaine describes these characters in an idiom appropriate to his farmer background—Seth Green, Sarah Wilkerson, and even Miss Jefferson are likened to sheep and horses and other worthy and useful farm animals, but Hawkins (or is it Filkins?) is something of a mongrel and a cur. Sarah comes from good stock, we are told, and will have nothing to do with a man such as Hawkins, whose attentions are questionable at best. (One can easily imagine that Twain might have had Hawkins "sniffing" around her before changing the word to the less vulgar "browsing.") As a miniature tale of romance, or rather as a Western romance, flirtation and courtship are expunged, and our heroine has little use for sentimental frippery or posies. The marriage she has in mind is almost literally a yoking of equals; she will choose to "trot in harness" with someone who is forthright and respectful. And we may infer, as well, that after the marriage she continued to heft her barrel, while her husband, like Jim Blaine, might "flirt" the flapjacks.

This filling in the blanks in order to make a continuous narrative out of the passage is gross surmise on my part, of course, but the point is that however disjointed the story may be, there is an emotional, social, and tonal coherence that abides throughout. Blaine's tangled recollections do not add up to a plotted narrative, but they do dramatize a steadfast loyalty to principles of conduct and an appreciation of upright, which is to say moral, character. Certain values and forms of behavior are acceptable; others are not. Certain kinds of men and women command our admiration; others, our contempt. But such a coherence is the background to the verbal play that is the tale itself. When Deacon Ferguson tosses Filkins out the window and he lands on Miss Jefferson's head, the narrative ricochets in another direction. And so Jim Blaine rambles on until drink gets the better of him, and he winds down, and at last falls asleep. The tale ends not with a bang or a whimper but with a snore, and Twain, as narrator, realizes quite belatedly that he had been set up from the beginning.

"The Story of the Old Ram" was published as chapter 53 of *Roughing It* (1872) and was probably interpolated into the manuscript at a late stage of production. As with many of his tales included in longer works, there is a self-sufficiency to this piece that makes its appearance in *Roughing It* almost incidental, and this fact is corroborated by Twain's frequent use of the tale on the lecture circuit. Late in his life, Twain explained that the purpose of this story was "to exhibit certain bad effects of a good memory . . . which has no sense of proportion, and can't tell an important event from an unimportant one, but preserves them all, states them all, and thus retards the progress of a narrative, at the same time making a tangled, inextricable confusion of it."[7] However, Twain's comments notwithstanding, this story is not merely the case study of a certain sensibility, nor is it a demonstration of an associationist psychology run riot.

True, Jim Blaine lacks the narrative gift of a sense of proportion, but while we may be amused by his rambling tale and by the fact that the putative subject of the story never appears, Twain has carefully insured Blaine against the reader's condescension. For one thing, though Blaine's "story" is famous, he is not a natural storyteller but an apparently timid man who needs to be "tranquilly, serenely, symmetrically drunk" in order to loosen his tongue and to trigger his random recollections. For another, it is not Jim Blaine but Mark Twain, the tenderfoot, who is the butt of the joke. The "boys" have repeatedly told him that he really ought to hear this compelling tale until Twain's curiosity is "on the rack to hear the story," and he has watched for Blaine's intoxication with "absorbing interest." Of course, no one has ever heard the story of the ram because Blaine has never gotten beyond the first sentence before he starts to wander, and the embarrassing defeat of Twain's anxious interest is the true occasion for the boys to gather round Blaine. Twain, of course, perceives that he is "Sold!" in the end, but the humiliation is merely temporary, and the more durable result is that Twain has become one of the "boys" himself, one who may well participate in setting up, in good-humored fashion, the next tenderfoot who comes to camp.

One should not underestimate the craft that disposes us to give over, even for so brief a time, a natural critical reserve. This is especially so when we know full well that some joke, hoax, or unanticipated reversal is coming and that we, too, stand a good chance of being "Sold!" One of the mysteries of Twain's fiction is the faith we, as readers, instinctively place in him. Howells observed that Twain possessed a "fine, forecasting humor," and that the reader, "knowing some joke must be coming, feels that nothing less than a prophetic instinct can sustain the humorist in its development."[8] More interested in sustaining, and sometimes straining, the reader's attention to his narrative, Twain appears to exhibit a grand indifference to received literary convention and a comic oblivion to a reader's expectations.

Twain does not insist on the willing suspension of the reader's disbelief in his incredible narratives; in fact, he rather depends on that disbelief. Part of the charm of the tall tale resides in the full awareness that the storyteller is stretching the truth without ever snapping it, and the knowing reader measures impossibility and exaggeration against a commonsense view of the actual and the possible. For that reason, tall-tale humor is almost always a blend of the actual and the imaginary. Blue jays don't talk, but if they did, they would talk like Jim Baker's blue jays. And we feel this because Baker's blue jays cock their heads and hop back and forth and otherwise behave just like real blue jays. Of course, the narrator seems to believe that he is giving us the unvarnished truth, while the listeners are choking back the laughter. As Harold H. Kolb observed of the tall tale, it is a story told as truth and heard as fiction,[9] and the reader who would get full comic value for his or her attention must be alert to the difference.

The literary comedian is a trickster, fond of the hoax, the joke, or the unanticipated reversal, and, as such, is naturally suspect. Even competent readers, fearful that they will soon be made fools, are apt to too closely scrutinize the joke or try to second-guess the humorist. The gifted humorist's somewhat paradoxical task is clear: to overcome readers' suspicions while at the same time defeating their expectations. Twain is such a humorist, for time and again he manages to insinuate himself into our good graces, and the willing suspension of the reader's distrust, or at least suspicion, of the narrator is essential to his humor. In order for his humor to work on us, we must feel that though the narrator may, almost certainly will, mislead or trick us, he will not betray us. The trust that readers have customarily placed in Twain derives in part from some sense of the author's affably earnest character and of his congenial good faith, and in part from his self-evident contempt for pretense and sham. Is it any wonder, then, that Twain would characterize himself as principally a moralist, more interested in delivering a sermon than a joke?

Twain's imagination ran in both directions: He could and would expose counterfeits as readily as he would reveal in such base coin as Tom Sawyer and Huckleberry Finn basically decent boys with good hearts. At the same time, in "A Curious Dream," he might rail at the citizens of Buffalo who were unashamed of the unkempt graves in the North Street cemetery. In tales such as "The Christmas Fireside: The Story of the Bad Little Boy That Bore a Charmed Life" or the "The Story of the Good Little Boy Who Did Not Prosper," he debunked the nationally popular myth of the providentially ordained success of unsullied virtue. The satire in the most formally perfect of his stories, "The Man That Corrupted Hadleyburg," is strident and almost relentless. In its exposure of the piousness and hypocrisy of small-town America, this story occupies an important place in the tradition of the "revolt from the village" literature. Whether Twain's humor extolled the virtues of unknown folk in remote outposts or carved up one or another nationally sacred cow, the cogency and popularity of it depended upon a perceived sense of the author's upright moral character coexisting with his sense of good-natured fun.

Whether or not Samuel Clemens possessed the sorts of qualities that install this sort of trust in us, Mark Twain, as a literary persona, did. The creation of that persona was its own form of genius, for as a creation, "Mark Twain" is not a fixed entity but a fluent and fluid perspective. To be sure, this persona is a literary device, but it was likely a great deal more for its creator. Samuel Clemens was not merely a literary ventriloquist who might speak his piece through a manipulated dummy, though it is certainly true that he sometimes spoke sentiments through his persona that he dared not utter in his own person. As often, however, Mark Twain, as a literary personality, seems to announce his own purposes and to pursue his own ends. At all events, in the public mind, then as now, Mark Twain lived a life strangely independent of the life of Samuel Langhorne Clemens. It is an even question, for example, whether it was Mark Twain or Sam Clemens who wore his white suit out of season and gave interviews in his nightshirt. It was Samuel Clemens who got himself in financial trouble, but it was the lecturing feats of Mark Twain that bailed Clemens out. When Henry Huttleston Rogers undertook to straighten out Clemens's money troubles in the 1890s, Rogers insisted that Clemens settle accounts with his debtors down to the last penny. Rogers knew, whether Clemens did or not, that the good "character" of Mark Twain was a wise investment and would pay dividends in the long run. Rogers was right; Clemens recouped his fortune because Twain paid his debts. This is merely an instance of a general principle—that Twain's authority to speak and to amuse was grounded in an unannounced covenant of trust between writer and reader.

I have already said that much of Twain's short fiction possesses the quality of dream. I recall once hearing a philosopher observe that the only difference between the waking world and the dreaming world is that in the waking world, one makes plans, whereas in the dreaming world, one does not. One cannot "plan" for the effects of the typical Twain story—one cannot predict the comic reversals or the mild and affectionate jokes, and one cannot brace against bitter insight or sudden, unanticipated, and indignant condemnation. One cannot prepare for the lavish figures of speech or the outlandish situations (comic, grotesque, or both); one can only submit with delight to the cadences and the predilections of the narrative voice. Because that voice is part and parcel of a full-blown and ever-shifting literary persona named Mark Twain, much of the so-called success of his literary work has been prepared beforehand by cultivating our glad acceptance of a literary personality.

Twain often qualified his feats of imaginative improvisation with disarming simplicity. Through sometimes preposterous "stage directions," Twain found the means to liberate his fancy. Simon Wheeler is one of a multitude of credulous narrators who seem to believe the tales they are telling; Jim Blaine is drunk when he begins his rambling story; "Barnum's First Speech to Congress," we are to understand, was conveyed to Twain by "spiritual telegraph"; the grotesque story of "Cannibalism in the Cars," we learn in the last paragraph, was nothing but the "harmless vagaries of a madman"; "A Curious Dream" is, of course, the recounting of a dream; "A Ghost Story" is a supposed experience that has happened in the twilight state of interrupted sleep; and "Jim Baker's Blue Jay Yarn" is prefaced by the admission that the narrator has been reading so much in German legend and fairy tale that he "was beginning to believe in the gnomes and fairies as realities." These are merely a few instances of Twain's relatively simple management of the conditions of his tales in order to give his humor free play.

The "found" manuscript, mental telegraphy, confessions of a madman, dream visions, these and other literary conventions were common to earlier writers such as Walpole, De Quincey, Poe, Coleridge, Mary Shelley, and others who meant to give their narratives an exotically gothic credibility. Twain often used the same conventions, but his dramatic framing was allied to the Southwestern humor tradition. Far from compelling our belief in a narrator who is an initiate into some dreadful and often arcane knowledge and in converse with demonic powers, Twain's vernacular narrators require us merely to believe that they believe the yarns they spin. In "Jim Smiley and His Jumping Frog," the story that launched Twain's career as a "literary person," he craftily prepares us for the story that follows. He instructs us in the tone of the tale, the cadence of the prose, and, importantly, in the manner and the character of the narrator, Simon Wheeler: "all through the interminable narrative there ran a vein of impressive earnestness and sincerity, which showed me plainly that so far from his imagining that there was anything ridiculous or funny about his story, he regarded it as a really important matter, and admired its two heroes as men of transcendent genius in finesse" (*CTS* I, 171–72). Jim Smiley and the mysterious stranger who bests him are, in Wheeler's eyes, mythic heroes. By recounting their exploits, Wheeler functions as the unofficial historian of a largely local oral culture.

The publication and popular reception of the jumping frog story marks a moment not only in Twain's career but also in the history of American humor. It has been observed before that this story represents both a beginning and an ending: It is the culmination of an oral tradition of tale telling that flourished in whaling ships, bunkhouses, trading scows, and taverns, a tradition that was part of, and indeed helped define, the American experience. But at the same time, because Twain and others had transcribed those narratives and voices, and thus had moved them from an oral to a text-centered culture, these writers had dramatically shifted the focus from an actual communal experience where men and women gathered to swap yarns to the illusion of that shared experience.

In other words, the oral tale, as a spoken art form delivered in a community, had been uprooted from its natural environment and removed to the private experience of reading. The successful Twain story retains the sense of gesture, spontaneity, direct address, and dialect at the same time that it frees us from the necessity of the gathered occasion or being a witness to the event. Frontier humor, like local-color writing and other forms of regionalism, is charged with sustaining a vivid paradox. Regionalist writers wish to dramatize and preserve culturally specific occasions, customs, habits, and idioms at the same time that they undertake to broadcast and popularize those cultural characteristics on the basis of universal appeal and commonly held values and truths. This apparent dilemma supplies yet another reason for Twain's reliance upon a perceived moral perspective and a sense of shared humanity that ultimately transcends cultural and regional boundaries.[10]

In time, frontier humor became a cultural commodity that could be infinitely reproduced and disseminated from New York to New Orleans, from Philadelphia to San Francisco. What is more, it became a distinctly American mode of cultural expression, capable, or so it seemed, of expressing a national ethos. As Henry Wonham has shown, the tall tale was not an indigenous cultural product, but it grew in the soil of a democratic society because it best dramatized the incongruities between the idealistic promise of America and the less-than-ideal actuality of everyday experience. Mark Twain became the teller of tall tales, par excellence, but for many readers, he seemed to be preserving and returning to Americans what was already theirs, a democratic point of view and a distinctly native art form.

Mark Twain—never mind Samuel Clemens—came to stand for some important feature of a distinctive American character and, in some minds, for America itself. Clemens did not apply for the job, however; to a degree, it was forced upon him by a ready and widespread responsiveness to him in his readers. Unlike Walt Whitman, who interceded on behalf of the American multitudes and by means of passionate conviction and a personal poetic metaphysics made himself part and particle of the masses, Mark Twain became a representative man almost by accident. But he accepted the role and played it well. In his preface to *The Innocents Abroad* (1869), for example, he declared that the purpose of his book "is to suggest to the reader how *he* would be likely to see Europe and the East if he looked at them with his own eyes instead of the eyes of those who traveled in those countries before him." In point of fact, however, Twain's vision was so antically original that as a rule, readers were more than willing to look at the world through his spectacles and to believe that his point of view was their own. For the same reason, however, he was sometimes taken for a literary clown and little more. With some difficulty, he outgrew the typecasting as the nation's "funny fellow," but however much he wished to be taken seriously, he did not try to become some other kind of writer.

Twain's genius resides, in part, in his acceptance, rather than his rejection, of what came naturally to him. He did not try to emulate the literary masters; he did not wish to become an American Shakespeare (as did Melville) or an American Flaubert (as did Henry James) or an American Tolstoy (as did William Dean Howells). To put it another way, Twain did not succumb to that ordinary and frequently debilitating ambition to do something extraordinary. He sometimes claimed that he was merely the humble servant to his own creative impulses and once identified himself as a "jack-leg" novelist, but such evident self-effacement is misleading. As Louis J. Budd has acutely observed, Twain's humor derived from an "instinctual energy" embedded in his deepest self, a humor that confirmed a liberating sense of selfhood. The dynamic and essential quality in Mark Twain is, in Budd's terms, one of "ecstasy": Only the word *ecstasy* expresses Twain's "élan of self-liberation from arbitrary rules." When speaking of Twain's humor, we need such a word "to carry the headiness of cutting through to the malleability of experience, to celebrate the delight of exploding the rigidities of wisdom. In contrast to the mystic's privatized trance, the humorist's transcendent ecstasy is directed outward, is transactional, is made social."[11] Twain's gifts as a humorist drew their reserves of power from an interior life that refused—not by rebellion, but by imaginative transformation, extravagance, and comic negotiation—the restrictions that socialized life would impose upon him. At the same time, that self realized it fullest expression in socialized life. Privately, Twain's humor was a liberation, an indulgence, and a privilege, but publicly, it was a social calling, expansive and responsible in its application and democratic in its loyalties.

The following three sections of part 1 of this volume divide Twain's career into three fairly distinct phases. "The Early Years" deals with Twain's literary beginnings as an itinerant journalist and literary comedian. "The Middle Years" presents Twain at the height of his creative powers, sure of an eager readership and in control of an established literary personality. "The Late Years" describes a writer whose personal circumstance created a sorrow and cynicism reflected in the tone and subject matter of his fiction. These divisions are as much a matter of convenience as anything else, and I do not insist on their strict accuracy. Twain was a man capable of a wide range of sometimes contradictory feelings and attitudes. Short fiction (as opposed to the novel or the travel narrative) is by its very nature more likely to register and dramatize these vacillations of feeling and make them intelligible, particularly when practiced by a man who often wrote quickly and out of some immediate and perhaps evanescent stimulus or annoyance.

In any event, these divisions are at least suggestive enough to describe the contours of Twain's career. It is not possible, and would not be fruitful even if it were, to try to examine all of Twain's short fiction in so short a space. In the following pages, I linger over some of the more interesting or important pieces of short fiction, touch lightly upon several others, and omit some altogether. My treatment here is meant to be suggestive and comprehensive, not exhaustive; the purpose of this series is to supplement, rather than displace, the understanding and enjoyment of the short fiction of notable American writers. Twain himself observed that "nothing is half so good as literature hooked on Sunday on the sly" (*MTHL* I, 438). Modern students of Twain's short fiction may well be cheated out of the guilty pleasure of violating the Sabbath by reading his tales, but readers will learn soon enough that such enjoyment as they may have is its own warrant and opportunity.

Probably the most important feature of the early period in Samuel Clemens's literary development was his decision to adopt the pen name and persona of "Mark Twain," for his early fiction relies upon the artfully managed voice of a tale-teller, through which he might relate and improve upon stories he had heard along the river or on the Western slope and coordinate otherwise disparate or fantastic fictional incidents. This period also includes the publication of the jumping frog story, which propelled him into national prominence, and shows the author experimenting with vernacular humor (as in "Buck Fanshaw's Funeral" or the "Story of the Old Ram") alongside many other comic modes— parody and political satire, visual and orthographic humor, inverted moral parables, and literary burlesque. Many, if not all, of these modes of humorous fiction were familiar to Twain's readers, and his early career is largely derivative and imitative. However, as in many of his other occupations, Clemens was an alert and quick student of literary humor, one who mastered forms and techniques quickly and brought some individual and distinctive quality to otherwise formulaic tales or sketches that his literary competitors did not.

The short fiction of the early years describes a segment in the arc of Twain's career. The second section, "The Middle Years," begins with an examination of "A True Story" (1874)—the first piece Twain published in the *Atlantic Monthly* and the first time he had used a vernacular narrator to tell a socially and morally serious story. For most Americans, the *Atlantic Monthly* magazine meant "literature," and publication there also meant, at least for Twain, a sudden and unaccustomed respectability and an attendant social responsibility. The jumping frog story brought Twain popularity, but the *Atlantic Monthly* gave him literary and cultural authority. Twain was gratified by Howells's acceptance and praise of "A True Story," though the irony of the fact that the majority of the story was told in the very un-Bostonian voice of a black woman could scarcely have been lost on him.

These middle years, often considered the period of Twain's literary maturity and finest achievement, are characterized by a deep personal ambivalence that is transformed in his fiction into sustained artistic tension and ambiguity. Many of the more interesting pieces of short fiction deal with complexities of social identity and moral responsibility as they have been conferred upon a man who often yearned for the irresponsibility of youth or felt a personal shame for what he considered his Southern and frontier origins. Sometimes he dealt with these problems in antic and fantastic ways ("Encounter with an Interviewer," for example, or "The Facts Concerning the Recent Carnival of Crime in Connecticut"), and sometimes he adopted the familiar form of the inverted parable of moral rectitude and providential reward ("Edward Mills and George Benton: A Tale" is an instance).

The most famous example of Twain's humiliation and feelings of social inadequacy came out of his disappointing experience with the "Whittier Birthday Speech," but he seems to have indulged in a muted form of self-justification, if not revenge, when he wrote "Jim Baker's Blue Jay Yarn" a few years later. Often, through a created narrator or character, Twain cast an eye backward to his own formative experiences as a schoolboy, a miner, a journalist, a soldier, or, most memorably, the apprentice riverboat pilot in "Old Times on the Mississippi." The salutary effects of such nostalgic remembrance was to represent in his fiction an almost tactile quality of blamelessness, but these tales and sketches also represent a fall into adulthood and an awareness of the burdens of social responsibility. This period in Twain's career ends with the publication of "The Private History of the Campaign That Failed" (1885), an autobiographical fiction that served as a public extenuation of his military desertion in the Civil War as well as a private translation of lived experience that, through his imaginative management of the tale, justified his behavior on individual moral grounds instead of on the unquestioning performance of patriotic duty.

The final section, "The Late Years," treats Twain's short fiction in fairly familiar terms: as the imaginative product of the author's despair and bitterness. That bitterness came out of financial failure and shame combined with the sorrow brought about by the death of his daughter Susy in 1896, of his wife, Olivia, in 1904, and, only a few months before his own death, of his daughter Jean in 1909. But the monotony of a comic temperament gone sour, observable in the later fiction, is more than offset by a creative vitality and literary experimentation that are remarkable for an established writer entering old age. Although the last years of Twain's life as a writer betray an imaginative faltering (there are many examples of unfinished manuscripts and false starts on ill-conceived novels and stories), these years also bear witness to a creative ingenuity and a seemingly inexhaustible variety of fictional forms.

The originating and creative energy evident in Twain's so-called bad mood period has been undervalued, I think. It is true that his themes typically have to do with greed and venality, vain desire for public approval, the insurmountable influences of habit and environmental conditioning, and, more generally, a pervasive deterministic philosophy that disputes notions of honor, courage, and nobility. These recurrent themes are dramatized in such stories as "The $30,000 Bequest," "The Man That Corrupted Hadleyburg," and the three versions of the *Mysterious Stranger* manuscripts. But Twain also made interesting experiments in point of view, writing "A Dog's Tale" from the perspective of a dog whose pup is vivisected in her presence and "A Horse's Tale" from the point of view of Buffalo Bill's horse. He supplied "extracts" from Adam's diary and Eve's diary, and he recorded the dream vision of Captain Stormfield, who sailed for heaven but entered at the wrong port. He also parodied Arthur Conan Doyle in "A Double-Barreled Detective Story." In short, Twain's late short fiction is amazingly diverse. However monochromatic was his philosophical vision, however unrelenting his cynicism and despair, the imaginative exuberance of the late writings suggests that the creative act remained for him a public charge and a private satisfaction.

The Early Years, 1863–1873:
Oral Tradition and the Individual Talent

Perhaps the most famous pen names in Western literary history are Voltaire and Mark Twain. Both names conjure in the popular mind images of moral outrage, democratic sympathies, wry humor, cantankerous irreverence, and satiric bite. Beyond these shared qualities, all useful comparison ceases. François-Marie Arouet adopted his nom de plume in 1718 in Paris after his first literary triumph; Samuel Clemens acquired his under rather more obscure and remote circumstances. In February 1863, when he was in the Nevada Territory, Sam Clemens indulged in a bit of claim jumping and struck the richest lode he would ever strike. Believing that the riverboat captain Isaiah Sellers had used the name "Mark Twain" and therefore had rights to it, and believing, too, that Sellers had recently died and forfeited his claim to the persona, Clemens published three letters in the *Territorial Enterprise* and signed them with that alias. It so happened that Sellers was not dead, and there is no extant evidence that Sellers ever published anything under that name. However, Clemens was looking for a new nom de plume, and he gave himself so eagerly and so completely to the Twain persona that it is tempting to believe that he had tried on this sobriquet in the imagination well before he made the name his own.

The "letters" from Carson City appeared successively on February 3, 5, and 8, 1863. The original appearance of Mark Twain as a literary persona in these letters is interesting because one can see a comic personality, which is also a literary device, developing in situ, so to speak. The jokes and other fictional elements are essentially narrative embroidery for a journalistic report on the doings of Carson City—a party, a wedding, a special session of the Territorial Legislature, and a record of recent certificates of incorporation. But the letters achieve a certain dramatic continuity through the fictionalized rivalry between the narrator, Mark Twain, and a man he called the Unreliable (actually his friend Clement Rice).

The Unreliable is charged with all manner of social and domestic crimes—he rifled through Twain's wardrobe in Washoe City and appropriated several articles of his clothing and a gold-plated pistol; he gluttonously carries a codfish under one arm and dips his fingers in a borrowed plug hat filled with sauerkraut; he attempts to exit the wedding party through the back door carrying 17 silver spoons, a New Testament, and a gridiron. But in the process of making the Unreliable the object of his scorn and the butt of his jokes, the narrator discloses his own shortcomings with a seemingly accidental and innocent inconsequence. He and the Unreliable "guard" the punchbowl together until it "evaporates," and the dance and the dancers soon become blurry: "The dance was hazier than usual, after that. Sixteen couples on the floor at once, with a few dozen spectators scattered around, is calculated to have that effect, I believe" (*ETS* I, 196). The reader recognizes soon enough that there is more than one Unreliable in the sketches. The narrator himself is a likable hypocrite, at once graced with a cordial obtuseness and a steadfast loyalty to the proprieties, at least as their violation is detectable in the man who borrowed his clothes and his money.

The humor here, as it does in much of Twain's humor, simultaneously addresses itself to several levels of the reader's understanding. At one level, the narrator deceives himself about his own conduct, and his disgust with the Unreliable is in its own way as humorous as his rival's social transgressions. At another level, the readers of the *Enterprise* understood this journalistic fiction to be a vehicle for the hard facts of local news; moreover, the author expected many of his readers to be able to identify the actual parties as Clemens and Rice and to distinguish fact from fiction, persona from person, and pretended enmity from a demonstration of boisterous and comic camaraderie. Humor of this sort seeks its own level of readership. Either one gets the joke or one does not. If not, the reader is not hurt by the exclusion, merely ignorant of the depth and precision of comic intent. Nearly everyone can find some particle of the fun that allows them to feel superior to the occasion or the folks that inhabit the dramatic incident. However much or little one is "in on the joke" matters less than that one has become an insider to some degree and thus a participant in a community of fun and excess.

The comic incongruities in these letters perform two opposing functions—they both uphold and demolish notions of the proper and thereby recommend, without ever advocating or demonstrating, a sense of proportion and good sense. The image of the Unreliable sweeping the parlor "like a pestilence"—wearing a one-tailed evening coat with a fish in his pocket, crowding himself into a double quadrille and making all the young women wilt from his breath until someone persuades him to drink some kerosene to tone it down a bit—does violence to a decorous occasion, but it throws into dramatic relief the absurdity of pretended gentility as well.

Humor of this sort is particularly easy to manufacture. Put a codfish in a tuxedo pocket and there is laughter, but only because we as readers have a sense of proportion bred by experience and privately recognize and share, more or less, the commonsense sensibility operating behind the voice of the narrator. Only by virtue of having broad acquaintance with measured conduct and social convention are we allowed to perceive disjunction and excess. To violate common expectation is a species of what we might call Mr. Potato Head humor and requires no more than alert observation and a certain imaginative audacity. The literary persona of Mark Twain instantly supplied Clemens with a protective coloring and freedom of view that, in turn, permitted him to indulge in a natural mischief and audaciousness. But the means Clemens found to yoke the engine of his humor to the car of literary and imaginative purpose is at the heart of his distinctive achievement. This fusion of comic strategies and serious moral purpose sets him apart from the multitude of nineteenth-century American literary humorists and the wholesome variety of unknown tale-tellers in mining camps and on riverboats whose idle times were spent preserving and dispensing an oral tradition of folk wisdom, anecdote, and story.

Late in his life, Twain himself reflected in his "Autobiography" upon the curious fact that he had survived while so many humorists had had their brief success and then vanished from memory. Talented humorists faded, Twain remarked, because they were "mere humorists." Humor by itself is only a "fragrance" or a "decoration." Lasting humor serves as accompaniment to a solid and incontestable moral point of view: "Humor must not professedly teach, and it must not professedly preach, but it must do both if it would last forever."[12] However acute, Twain's explanation of the reasons for his own success is partial. Mark Twain's comic appeal has lasted a good deal longer than that of his contemporaries, and surely part of that appeal has to do with the infectious creative joy that so often permeates his fiction. Humor is a responsibility, of course, but it is also and at the same time a liberating and socializing force. Moreover, for whatever reasons, whether he is playing the dandy, the buffoon, or the innocent, Twain seems to speak for some large and heterogeneous segment of the nation itself.

Bret Harte detected in Twain distinctive and original qualities while his career was still very much in the making. In his 1874 lecture "American Humor," Harte disputed common British opinion that Artemus Ward was the "flower" of American humor. Harte found a "want of purpose" in the man and, respectable figure though he was, found it doubtful that Ward "bears any resemblance to any known American type."[13] Instead, Harte acknowledged Mark Twain as the "most original humorist America has yet produced. He alone is inimitable." Even so, for Harte, the "true" American humorist had not yet come into existence: "when he does come he will show that a nation which laughs so easily has still a great capacity for deep feeling, and he will, I think, be a little more serious than our present day humorists."[14] These may or may not have been prophetic words, but however coincidentally, they chart the course Twain would pursue and the sobering and serious conclusions he would eventually reach.

Sadly, in his last years, Twain's seriousness sometimes outstripped his humor, and a corrosive feeling often remained after the laughter had subsided. In 1863, however, the appropriation of a new and, as it would turn out, permanent cognomen was liberating. The editors of the Iowa/California edition of Twain's *Early Tales and Sketches* note that there is a special appropriateness in the fact that the first letter from Carson City begins with the narrator awaking from a long sleep. It would be too much to say that Mark Twain roused Sam Clemens from his slumbers, but the nom de plume was undoubtedly the most valuable possession he took with him when he left Nevada in 1864 and traveled first to San Francisco and then for a brief time to California's Western Slope.

For the next two years, Clemens moved about, writing for newspapers and literary magazines—the San Francisco *Morning Call*, the *Golden Era*, the *Enterprise*, and the *Californian*. As a consequence, he made the acquaintance of several talented and influential literary humorists— Bret Harte, Artemus Ward, Charles Henry Webb, and many others. Clemens carried with him his adopted persona, "Mark Twain," a name that was already beginning to receive some recognition as far east as New York. Evidently he took the literary persona with him from San Francisco to Jackass Hill in Calaveras County, where, with his friend Jim Gillis, Clemens halfheartedly practiced a bit of pocket mining, when the weather permitted, and loafed and talked and listened. In Angel's Camp, Clemens heard a rather obtuse man named Ben Coon tell pointless stories without ever betraying the slightest awareness that he was rambling to no purpose or that there was any humor in his tales. It was Sam Clemens who listened to Ben Coon tell the story of the jumping frog, but it was Mark Twain who absorbed the story and was particularly fascinated by the manner of the telling.

The jumping frog story was locally familiar, but it was new to Clemens, and he knew from the beginning that there was something literary in it. He recorded a telegraphic outline of the tale in a notebook: "Coleman with his jumping frog—bet a stranger $50—stranger had no frog, & C got him one—in the meantime stranger filled's C's frog full of shot & he couldn't jump—the stranger's frog won" (*ETS* II, 263). Later, when he and Gillis were mining, Clemens adapted a phrase from Coon's story to their immediate circumstance and relived the humor of it. As Albert Bigelow Paine notes, Clemens might remark to Gillis, "I don't see no p'ints about that frog that's better'n any other frog," and Gillis might reply, "I ain't got no frog, but if I had a frog I'd bet you." Or on the slopes while mining, Clemens might stupidly observe, "I don't see no p'ints about that pan o' dirt that's any better'n any other pan o' dirt," and the two would laugh at the versatile application of the phrase.[15] The tale, as disconnected as it was, had the force of a vernacular parable—it put dramatic humor into monotonous toil, thus lightening the load of everyday life, and it commented aptly on a miner's (or a gambler's) dreams of success as they combined with workaday routine. The published story, as Twain reshaped it, retains that original interest, and one may turn from Simon Wheeler's fantastic account armed with a resilient—which is to say a humorous—attitude toward all things ordinary and common. But it was not until Artemus Ward requested a story from Twain for a collection Ward was putting together that Twain sat down to write the tale, and when he did, he made a sudden leap into the literary life.

Evidently, the story did not come easily; manuscript evidence indicates at least two false starts and a certain consternation about how he might effectively join the natively humorous possibilities of his narrator, Simon Wheeler, with the story of the jumping frog.[16] Twain succeeded admirably, however, and the form, as opposed to the substance, of the tale is especially remarkable for its seemingly easy sophistication. To tell his story, Twain adopted the mode of the frame tale so common to Southwestern humorists, but unlike so many other humorists, Twain refused to condescend to his frontier storyteller or to make him little more than a amusing buffoon. Instead, through his narrative persona, the first and final butt of the joke is Twain himself.

As John Gerber has pointed out, Clemens's comic poses as Mark Twain took many forms—as the Gentleman, the Innocent, the Sentimentalist, and so forth—and even in their several combinations, he was able to project through this mask an attitude toward the world that was far less complicated than Clemens's own.[17] The opening paragraph of the jumping frog story presents us with a stilted and pompous narrator, rather ripe for a comeuppance: "In compliance with the request of a friend of mine, who wrote me from the East, I called on good-natured, garrulous old Simon Wheeler, and inquired after my friend's friend, Leonidas W. Smiley, as requested to do, and I hereunto append the result." The result, of course, is the tale itself, but it is equally clear from the stiff and elevated diction of the opening that the experience and the fun of the tale have been lost on the narrator.

If Ben Coon and, by extension, Simon Wheeler were unaware of the humor of their narratives, so too is the refined narrator, who finds the story he is about to give both "tedious" and "useless." Moreover, in this story, as he would do in subsequent tales, Twain supplied the reader with a user's manual in order to suggest, if not preserve, the oral quality of a rambling tale taking shape before the reader's eyes. Of Wheeler's narrative manner, Twain observes, "He never smiled, he never frowned, he never changed his voice from the gentle-flowing key to which he tuned his initial sentence, he never betrayed the slightest suspicion of enthusiasm—but all through the interminable narrative there ran a vein of impressive earnestness and sincerity" (*CTS* I, 171). Significantly, once Wheeler begins his story, the narrator never interrupts him. This, too, was a departure from literary convention, for it was more customary to comment upon the coarseness of the backwoods character or sometimes to extenuate his vulgarity or stupidity.

Wheeler's recollection of Jim Smiley begins in haphazard association. One soon learns that Smiley was an inveterate gambler who would bet on anything and everything, and to ensure that the wager would take place, he would take either side. But one learns of his qualities, too, though they are cast in a tall-tale tradition that makes them as exaggerated as his exploits. He is persistent enough to follow a straddle-bug to Mexico to settle a bet; he is perceptive enough to recognize in his bull pup Andrew Jackson, a dog that "hadn't no opportunities to speak of," a valiant and durable warrior; he is patient enough to spend three months "educating" his frog, Daniel Webster, in the secrets of jumping; and he is hospitable enough to splash around in a swamp to find a frog for the stranger who is willing to make a bet. The reader is apt to find these gestures preposterous, but within Wheeler's frame of reference, Jim Smiley and the mysterious stranger who bests him are, indeed, admirable "men of transcendent genius." But for the narrator, who is intent on locating the Reverend Leonidas W. Smiley and benefiting from his improving company, the tale is doubly deficient. The qualities Wheeler admires are invisible to the narrator, and unlike his readers, who are, or should be, enormously amused, he finds the story tiresome.

Jim Smiley approaches the stranger with feigned indifference and a casual canniness. When the stranger asks Smiley what he has in the box, "Smiley says, sorter indifferent-like, 'It might be a parrot, or it might be a canary, maybe, but it ain't—it's only just a frog' " (*CTS* I, 175). Soon enough, a bet of $40 is arranged, and Smiley sets out in search of a frog for the man. Meantime, the stranger ponders his opportunities and then fills Daniel Webster with quail shot; he wins $40 and the contest of wits. Jim Smiley, we suppose, has learned something from the experience; not so Twain as narrator, who remains indifferent to the tale-teller's gifts or the object of his admiration. At the end of the story, Wheeler is called away for a moment and then returns, ready to tell the story of Smiley's "yaller one-eyed cow that didn't have no tail" (*CTS* I, 177), but Twain is not interested in the afflicted cow and takes his leave. And so the story ends, or rather breaks off, leaving Wheeler anxious to tell the story of the cow and most readers ready to hear it.

The jumping frog story is one of Twain's most tightly controlled tales and reveals a sure artistry in a still relatively young writer, but the structural coherence serves a double purpose that has less to do with formal mastery than with a liberation, in Clemens, of an otherwise unruly creative resource. First, the form allows Twain to corral an exuberant, even riotous, imagination and to indulge in various stylistic maneuvers that amount to a blend of vernacular poetry and almost surreal transformations. Jim Smiley's mare is an unlikely racehorse—she had distemper, asthma, and consumption—but in the home stretch, out of mere desperation or excitement, she came alive, "cavorting and straddling up, and scattering her legs around limber, sometimes in the air, and sometimes out to one side amongst the fences, and kicking up m-o-r-e dust and raising m-o-r-e racket with her coughing and sneezing and blowing her nose," but crossing the finish line ahead of the rest. Andrew Jackson, the puny bull pup, is a fiercely proud fighter who has a jaw "like the for'castle of a steamboat" and grips the hind legs of his competitors like a vise (*CTS* I, 173). He meets his match, however, when he tears into a dog that has no hind legs. Andrew Jackson loses the fight, but he is not mortally wounded. Instead, he dies of shame and gives Smiley a look that spells betrayal. Daniel Webster, a frog educated in the ways of jumping, merely requires a punch in the behind before he launches himself into the air, turning one, sometimes two, somersaults in midflight, "whirling in the air like a doughnut" and landing "as solid as a gob of mud" (*CTS* I, 174). These fantastic similes have the feel of unmediated originality because the author has so managed the dramatic presentation that Simon Wheeler seems earnestly to spin out his yarn with spontaneous association and halting confusion. However, it is more significant that Twain instinctively recognized that the foundation of humor is rooted in the social. As the stiff and highfalutin persona in search of respectable company, the narrator is the first and final object of fun. Because he adopted a persona with whom he might identify, at least in part, yet still reserve sufficient detachment to treat the figure with comic energy, Twain avoids condescending to his created characters. As persona, Twain may look down on Wheeler, but as author, he does not want his readers to. As mixed up as he is, Simon Wheeler is a good-natured soul whom the reader is apt to warm to as a fascinating and genial companion.

It requires confidence and sure artistic purpose to begin a tale by announcing how tiresome the ensuing narrative will be and then to so engross us that we are eager to hear Wheeler's tale of the one-eyed cow, though at the same time somehow unresentful that we must exit with a narrator who has had enough. The net effect of the story is like the narrative itself, something of an initiation rite. We are immersed in the homespun idiom of the frontier, and the dramatic structure of the story gives us the illusion of the immediacy of the spoken tale, not so much because the genteel narrator has been displaced by the vernacular narrator, but because we prefer Wheeler's company to his.

The jumping frog tale is moral, then, not because the author has endeavored to preach or to teach. His own comments notwithstanding, Twain separated himself from other literary comedians by creating a vivid interest and sympathy in his created characters. He does not simply give us a slice of life from the provinces, a practice typical of Southwestern humorists who published their tales with established literary markets firmly in mind. Instead, by redirecting the humor toward his literary persona, Twain absorbs the contempt—or at least the reader's laughter—into himself so that Wheeler, and that part of the American character he represents, may speak in his own voice without embarrassment.

It is not at all clear that Twain recognized his own achievement in this story. He sent the piece to Artemus Ward, but it arrived too late to be included in the collection Ward was assembling. Instead, the story was forwarded to the *Saturday Press*, where it was first published on November 18, 1865, and then picked up in newspapers throughout the country. The story was an instant success, and its author was carried along in the wake of its popularity. At first Twain resisted the celebrity thrust upon him, but he eventually acceded to popular opinion, and the tale became a signature piece. (He republished it more than once, used it frequently on his lecture tours, and published a pamphlet in which his original tale and a French translation were printed side by side before he "clawed" the story back into English.)

Eventually, Twain learned to respect the admiration of the common reader, and popular approval became his muse. He stated late in his life that he always depended on the sanction of his "submerged clientele" over and above the opinions of the literary establishment. For the moment, however, he depreciated his achievement; in a letter to his mother, he dismissed the piece as a mere "squib." Nevertheless, a few months after the national acclaim of the jumping frog tale, he wrote his brother Orion that he was satisfied enough with the role of comedian to settle on a vocation: "I *have* had a 'call' to literature, of a low order—i.e. humorous. It is nothing to be proud of, but it is my strongest suit. . . . I would long ago have ceased to meddle with things for which I was by nature unfitted & turned my attention to seriously scribbling to excite the *laughter* of God's creatures. Poor, pitiful business!"[18] He resolved to play his trump suit, and for the next 40 years he devoted himself to the "pitiful" business of humor.

Only a month after the jumping frog story appeared, Twain published in the *Californian* "The Christmas Fireside: For Good Little Boys and Girls. By Grandfather Twain. The Story of the Bad Little Boy That Bore a Charmed Life." Five years later, in May 1870, he published in the *Galaxy* "The Story of the Good Little Boy Who Did Not Prosper," a tale that Twain called a "fair and unprejudiced companion-piece" to "The Christmas Fireside." Both tales invert the abundant and cherished homiletic stories for America's youth designed to install grateful virtue in obedient children and to fortify unquestioning belief in a benevolent, all-just Providence and in the preordained material and social success of those who cheerfully toe the line and never tell a lie.

The tradition of this sort of literature stretches back at least as far as eighteenth-century conduct books (of which Benjamin Franklin's *Autobiography* is an especially original and particularly American version) and novels such as Susanna Rowson's *Charlotte Temple*. The novels of Elizabeth Stuart Phelps, Horatio Alger, Marie Corelli, and others extended the tradition. Such easy assurance and sentimental moralizing survive today in William Bennett's thick anthology *A Book of Virtues* and Nancy Reagan's slender maxim "Just say no." But satire of the genre and the sentiment is nearly as old as the form itself. Such satire can be found in Melville's "China Aster Story" in his novel *The Confidence Man*, in Stephen Crane's *Whilomville Tales* (which, apart from the devastating story "The Monster," are mildly parodic sketches), and in Nathanael West's *Miss Lonelyhearts*. In Flannery O'Connor's *Wise Blood*, 15-year-old Sabbath Lily Hawks writes "Dear Mary" to ask whether she should neck; "Dear Mary" tells Sabbath that she is not adjusted to the modern world and recommends that she read some books on "Ethical Culture." Sabbath's reply is cogent: "Dear Mary, What I really want to know is should I go the whole hog or not? That's my real problem. I'm adjusted okay to the modern world."[19] More familiar rebuttals to this fastidious ethos are to be found in the movie *Animal House* or in the comic monologues of Richard Pryor and Whoopi Goldberg.

In such company, Twain's companion stories do not fare all that well; they are neither trenchant nor rollicking, but merely droll. The previous summer, he had published "Advice for Good Little Boys" and "Advice for Good Little Girls," two sketches that, although they departed from Sunday school sentiments, were benign enough to be published in the San Francisco *Youth's Companion*. "The Christmas Fireside" and "The Story of the Good Little Boy Who Did Not Prosper" are far more cynical than these earlier sketches, but not much more subtle, for the author's intent is uncomplicated and unmistakable. Nevertheless, there is a degree of sophistication in his management of the narrating persona and his artful location of his audience that deserve comment.

By identifying himself in "The Christmas Fireside" as "Grandfather Twain," the 35-year-old Clemens abruptly abandoned the tenderfoot persona of the jumping frog story. Grandfather Twain is the voice of a man who is apparently confused by the story he narrates and the moral it imparts but nonetheless maintains the avuncular tone of a kindly elder who is mystified by the experience of little Jim. Everything about Jim (not "James," as bad boys are always named in the "Sunday school books") contradicts the received wisdom of adults, whom Grandfather Twain represents. The straightforward story of the boy's life is punctuated by negatives: he didn't have a sickly and pious mother; he stole jam, but he was not plagued by a guilty conscience; he stole apples from Farmer Acorn's tree, but the limb did not break; he went hunting on the Sabbath but did not shoot two or three of his fingers off; he committed all manner of transgressions but was not struck by lightning, and he wasn't drowned.

The narrator is incredulous at the tale he tells, a tale presumably told to children by the Christmas fireside. Nothing that happens in "those mild little books with marbled backs" seems to happen to Jim, and grandfather Twain finds this oversight a complete "mystery." Twain increases in seriousness in the final paragraphs, however: Jim grows up, runs away from home, and returns years later "drunk as a piper." He marries, has children, and kills them all with an ax. Retributive justice is swiftly nonexistent—Jim grows wealthy through his swindles and becomes a member of the legislature. Grandfather Twain, without realizing that he is calling Sunday school wisdom, and perhaps Providence itself, into question, finds the story of this bad little boy a remarkable "streak of luck."

Unlike so many of Twain's better tales and sketches, "The Christmas Fireside" is not meant to be heard, but overheard. That is, the unrealized poignancy of the tale depends on an adult perspective of the events as they are rendered to children. This form was not without dramatic possibilities. The late story "Little Bessie" (written in 1909, but not published during Twain's lifetime) is powerful to the degree that the uncomprehending girl is caught between two very different forms of adult wisdom. Bessie is perceptive enough to recognize contradictions and old enough to frame questions that her mother cannot answer, but Bessie is too young to weigh the consequences for her own innocent future. It has been noted as well that "The Christmas Fireside" contributed something to the formulation of *The Adventures of Tom Sawyer* (1876), but the story also participates in the bifocal vision of *Huckleberry Finn*, a novel that Twain claimed was not for children but for adults who used to be children. Huck's untutored perceptions and conclusions speak powerfully to adults as the caretakers of youth and at the same time realistically convey Huck's bewilderment.

"The Story of the Good Little Boy Who Did Not Prosper" is more humorous than "The Christmas Fireside," but it is less inventive, too. Young Jacob Blivens aches to be the model boy and to be put in a Sunday school book: "He wanted to be put in, with pictures representing him gloriously declining to lie to his mother, and she weeping for joy about it; and pictures representing him standing on the doorstep giving a penny to a poor beggar-woman with six children, and telling her to spend it freely, but not to be extravagant, because extravagance is a sin . . ." (*CTS* I, 375). The narrator's impatience with Jacob is obvious, and the tone of the story is sardonic. Jacob's honesty is "ridiculous," and his resistance to childhood amusements is irrational. The other boys conclude that young Blivens is "afflicted" and protect him as they would any other idiot, but the narrator simply says that "there was a screw loose somewhere" (*CTS* I, 376).

"The Story of the Good Little Boy Who Did Not Prosper" is deficient in a number of ways. For one thing, it is never entirely clear whether Jacob Blivens is the object of, or the vehicle for, Twain's satire. Herman Melville had experienced similar indecision in his creation of the title character in his novel *Pierre; or the Ambiguities* (1852). Pierre Glendenning is described as a "fool of virtue," and the author's impatience with his created character is evident particularly in the second half of the novel; nevertheless, Melville was able to get considerable metaphysical and psychological mileage out of his narrative. Twain, too, is clearly unsympathetic with his boy, who is likewise a fool of virtue and wants to be enshrined in the Sunday school books, but unlike Melville, Twain does not explore the mental and social machinery that has created such a caricature of childhood.

Jacob's desire is complicated by the evident fact that he will have to die before he gets into a book, where his goodness will become illustrative and illustrated. He loves life and knows that it is "not healthy to be good." He resolves to do the best he can—"to live right, and hang on as long as he could, and have his dying speech ready when his time came" (*CTS* I, 375). As a case study in demented virtue, mixed with some jocular version of the death wish, the story of Jacob Blivens has the makings of a potent American fable. However, in this instance, Twain the humorist got the better of Twain the moralist, and the author settled on cheap laughs.

The misguided and deformed injunctions of Sunday school literature were widespread enough for Reverend Henry Ward Beecher to publish an essay in the *New York Times* observing that the lives of real boys had yet to be written and describing these petty idealizations of forced piety as "monstrous." A few years later, Twain would give his readers a real boy in Tom Sawyer, but Jacob Blivens was slated for annihilation. The funniest part of the story of the good little boy is his demise: Jacob Blivens sits on some nitroglycerin and begins to admonish the bad boys who have been taunting dogs. Alderman McWelter happens by and, mistaking Jacob as the culprit, swats the boy on the rear:

> in an instant that good little boy shot out through the roof and soared away toward the sun. . . . And there wasn't a sign of that Alderman or that old iron foundry left on the face of the earth; and as for young Jacob Blivens, he never got a chance to make his last dying speech after all his trouble fixing it up, unless he made it to the birds; because, although the bulk of him came down all right in a tree-top in an adjoining county, the rest of him was apportioned around among four townships, and so they had to hold five inquests on him to find out whether he was dead or not, and how it occurred. You never saw a boy scattered so. (*CTS* I, 378)

Twain admitted in a note that this final catastrophe was "borrowed" because it was a suitable "doom" for a boy who needed to be sent out of the world with "*éclat*." However, as a means of ending his tale, Twain resorted to standard comic fare. One of the easiest ways to get a belly laugh is to blow things up, or rather to instantly turn a living creature into so many detachable parts. The device is monotonously familiar to us in the humor of cartoons such as the "Roadrunner." Twain used the tactic often, perhaps most notoriously (and, for some readers, most problematically) in the "Battle of the Sand Belt" at the end of *A Connecticut Yankee* (1889).

But conclusions are always something of a problem for a humorist. Plotless narratives and other forms of comic disruption constantly slip the yoke of the Frietag triangle and refuse Aristotelian catharsis and resolution. The stories of the bad little boy and the good little boy (along with the unpublished burlesque of the same period, "Mamie Grant, Child Missionary") rely upon the reader's familiarity with the conventional form but work through a series of erasures of that mode. That is, Jim and Jacob Blivens are involved in experiences roughly parallel to those of the class of narratives to be burlesqued but receive neither the punishments nor rewards that give the experience a point. Humorous narratives tend to end by evasion, not resolution—the narrator dozes off or lights out for the territory; the mysterious stranger leaves as abruptly as he came; the little boy is blown to smithereens or grows up and gets elected to the state legislature.

Indeed, for Twain, plot itself is the stuff of comic innovation. "The Christmas Fireside" and "The Story of the Good Little Boy Who Did Not Prosper" are examples of condensed novels, even though the stories are not broken into constituent brief chapters to accent their comic resemblance to longer romances. The typical condensed novel ran from 500 words to 2,500 words and was segmented into perhaps a half-dozen chapters replete with intricacies of plot, mistaken identity, and thwarted romance. Condensation was itself a satirical technique, for the burlesques demonstrated by virtue of their very compactness the absurdity of the popular romance and the smallness of its large passions and grand proclamations. As Franklin Rogers has shown, this kind of burlesque was popular with the San Francisco Bohemians (including Bret Harte and Charles Henry Webb) and constituted an important part of Twain's comic repertoire during the years he associated himself with them. Twain used the same techniques (although they were not, strictly speaking, burlesques), for other purposes in two of his miniature "romances," "The Legend of the Capitoline Venus" and "An Awful— Terrible Medieval Romance."

Both of these stories were published in the Buffalo *Express*, the first in October 1869, the second in January 1870. "The Legend of the Capitoline Venus" consists of seven chapters that develop an extremely foreshortened melodramatic plot. The penniless American sculptor George Arnold is in love with Mary, but her father forbids their marriage until George has made $50,000 and gives him six months to do so. George has nothing to his name save his creation, a statue he calls "America." He is desperate, but his boyhood friend John Smith upbraids him—calling him "Idiot! Coward! Baby!"—and says he will raise the money for him. John takes up a hammer and mangles "America" (breaking off her nose, several of her fingers, and her left leg) and carts the statue down the street. Six months later, the Italian newspaper, *Il Slangwhanger di Roma*, announces the discovery by one "John Smitthe" of the ancient Capitoline Venus. John claims to have discovered the statue on the grounds of George Arnold, and a commission composed of art critics, antiquaries, and cardinal princes determines the value of the piece to be 10 million francs, half of which is due by law to the owner of the property, George Arnold. Chapter 6 occurs 10 years later, with George, now a millionaire and married to his beloved, standing before the statue in the Roman Capitol. George declares to his wife that John is the "Author of all our bliss" before complaining, "Do you know what that wheeze means? Mary, that brat has got the whooping cough. Will you *never* learn to take

33

care of the children!" The romance ends with a warning to the reader—
"when you read about gigantic Petrified Men being dug up near Syracuse in the State of New York, keep your own counsel,—and if the Barnum that buried them there offers to sell to you at an enormous sum,
don't you buy. Send him to the Pope!" (*CTS* I, 324).

There are at least a dozen jokes, both public and private, hung upon
this deliberately creaky plot. The immediate satirical point is to poke
fun at the recent unearthing of the so-called Cardiff Giant, actually a
piece of sculptured gypsum, near Syracuse, New York. But Twain had
himself contrived a similar hoax in 1862 when he published a piece in
the Virginia City *Territorial Enterprise* called "The Petrified Man." He
thought the article about the discovery of a mummified man with his
fingers making an impudent gesture was a transparent joke, but the
gullible public accepted the story as petrified fact. Clemens may have
been poking fun at himself as well. The year before the publication of
this story, he had been courting Olivia Langdon and, due to his unre-
fined origins and lack of stable employment, had been initially deemed
an unsuitable match for her. A few years later, Twain lampooned his own
ardent courtship of Olivia in *Tom Sawyer* when he had Tom perform
ridiculous antics to impress Becky Thatcher. He may have been remind-
ing himself that his romantic aspirations and his impending marriage
(wedding invitations were sent out in January 1870, and he and Olivia
were married in February) invited self-deception and would dissolve
soon enough into the annoyance of a child with the whooping cough.
Finally, the tale participates in the same comic mood that pervades *The
Innocents Abroad*. The statue, epitomizing a new and vigorous country
and aptly titled "America," is virtually worthless, but with a bit of
instant aging, a change of name, and the consensus approval of art critics, it suddenly becomes a revered masterpiece. Even in early short stories such as this one, Twain displayed a fascination with history and
antiquity, not merely because any comparison of the past to the present
was likely to provide grist for his satiric mill, but because his defense
(and censure) of the living present over and against the dead hand of
the past contributed to an articulation of essentially American and
democratic values.

Emerson, in *Nature* (1836), might characterize the age as "retrospective" and complain that while we "build the sepulchres of the fathers,"
we forfeit our own claim to a "poetry and philosophy of insight and not
of tradition." But Mark Twain knew that history works itself out in such
devilish detail that it is not easy to throw off caste, legacy, injunction,

superstition, and the rest. In this sense, "An Awful—Terrible Medieval Romance" is a triple redundancy. In Twain's view, any medieval romance is apt to be awful or terrible or both, plagued by hairbreadth escapes, masquerade, curses, prophecies, and other intricacies of development all tending to no instructive end. Twain's miniature romance has a self-devouring plot, and the burlesque follows the irrefutable logic of his premises to their inevitable and ridiculous irresolution.

Set in thirteenth-century Germany, the story concerns the rivalry for the throne between two brothers, the Lord of Klugenstein and Ulrich, the Duke of Brandenburgh. Their father had decreed that the line of succession should pass to Ulrich's son unless he had no son, in which case the son of the Lord of Klugenstein should occupy the throne. If neither brother had a son, then the daughter of Ulrich should reign, provided she was a virgin; if not, the daughter of the brother should inherit the throne. As it so happens, neither brother had a son, but both had daughters. However, the Duke of Brandenburgh had raised his daughter as a son, naming her Conrad and killing all those who knew the child's sex.

Twain pursues the plot of this story religiously, casually introducing further complications as the five-chapter condensed novel progresses— on penalty of death, no woman may sit upon the ducal chair before she is crowned; Ulrich's daughter has become pregnant by the villainous Detzin; Detzin has departed, and meantime Lady Constance has fallen in love with Conrad, who has already begun to administer his uncle's affairs, always careful not to sit upon the throne; Conrad must pass judgment on Lady Constance, who must die unless she names the father of the child; Conrad, by law, must sit on the royal chair when he makes his judgment; Constance, full of hatred for Conrad because she feels he has scorned her, names him as the father; and Conrad cannot prove his innocence except by proving that he is a woman, but to do so is to pass a death sentence on himself because he sits upon the ducal chair.

Ulrich swoons, and Mark Twain enters in bracketed paragraphs to pronounce this paradoxical situation unsolvable: "The truth is, I have got my hero (or heroine) into such a particularly close place that I do not see how I am ever going to get him (or her) out of it again—and therefore I will wash my hands of the whole business and leave that person to get out the best way that offers." The story itself, in other words, is yet another hoax and dramatizes the author's impatience with romances of this sort at the same time that it embodies his fascination with a reader's gullibility. In fact, Twain ends the piece on the latter note when he remarks that *Harper's Weekly* or the New York *Tribune* may reprint these initial chapters of this awful medieval romance in their pages at the usual rates, "provided they 'trust' " (*CTS* I, 339). Of course, it is the reader's trust that has just been violated, in a good-humored way; like the narrator in the old ram story, we have been "sold."

We have already considered the comic strategies of the old ram story in the first chapter. The old ram story discloses a comic invention quite unlike that used in "A Medieval Romance," but taken together, the two stories map out opposing routes to comic absurdity. In the first instance, the narrator states his topic and absentmindedly wanders away from it through a deadpan disclosure of irrelevant but apparently accurate recollections. In the second, absurdities are presented as facts, and their logic is strictly adhered to. Seth Green may have in fact married Sarah Wilkerson, but what their marriage has to do with the old ram, we will never know. The death penalty for a woman sitting in the ducal chair before she has been crowned has no rational justification other than it thickens a plot that is doomed from the beginning. This taboo codified into law brings the narrator to such an impasse that he simply walks away from the narrative and tries to sell the damaged goods to another newspaper.

Comedians are ever alert to absurdities, and experience, history, and the daily newspapers obligingly cough them up in abundance. When he learned that P. T. Barnum was running for Congress, for example, Twain saw an opportunity for comedy as ripe as if one today were to learn that Rush Limbaugh had left his radio talk show to take up ice dancing. Unlike the sketch "Buck Fanshaw's Funeral," which paired two mutually unintelligible modes of discourse in a riot of noncommunication, "Barnum's First Speech to Congress" fused the bloated rhetoric of Congress with the spiel of a sideshow barker: "Because the Wonderful Spotted Human Phenomenon, the Leopard Child from the wilds of Africa, is mine, shall I exult in my happiness and be silent when my country's life is threatened? No! Because the Double Hump-backed Bactrian Camel takes his oats in my menagerie, shall I surfeit with bliss and lift not up my voice to save the people? No!" (*CTS* I, 210). In this sketch, Twain makes it an even question whether the idea of Barnum as a congressman is any more absurd than the idea of Congress as a museum of curiosities. But Twain knew, as every humorist knows, that Congress convenes annually in order to supply comedians with new material. "Cannibalism in the Cars" (first published in *The Broadway* in November 1868) and

"The Facts in the Case of the Great Beef Contract" (first published in the *Galaxy* in May 1870) are two specimens of Twain's ability to domesticate and bureaucratize the tall tale.

The first story, as Edgar M. Branch has convincingly shown, is a masterful blend of the author's personal experience and his reading in newspapers.[20] Briefly, the published origins of the story are the following: In 1855, Sam Clemens's brother Orion published in his newspaper an item titled "Three Hundred People in a Snow Bank," detailing one railway passenger's account of being snowbound in Illinois for a week. It so happens that the train carried a number of state legislators eager to reach the state capital of Springfield. Moreover, a St. Louis newspaper reported that the passengers ate dogs to keep from starving. Clemens, then living in St. Louis, no doubt saw these newspaper items, and perhaps others as well. But it was not until 13 years later, evidently in a flurry of writing activity, that he retrieved these items of information from his think tank and combined them with other experiences as he wrote "Cannibalism in the Cars."

He had recently been serving as a Washington correspondent and was more than a little familiar with congressional maneuvering and rhetoric. Although Clemens himself had not been snowbound in a train, he had experienced similar feelings of captivity and isolation, and particularly in the West, he had seen how irritable men behave under such duress. For several reasons, according to Branch, Twain was in a "savage disposition" during the likely period of composition of this tale—he was negotiating for permissions and contracts related to the writing and publication of *The Innocents Abroad,* and when he was not chained to his writing desk, he was traveling. The several strands of past experience and reading and his immediate circumstance came together in a story Branch rightly calls a "brilliant tour de force."

"Cannibalism in the Cars" is cast in the familiar frame tale form, but it is divested of a Western vernacular flavor and a frontier setting. Instead, Twain poses as a traveler bound for St. Louis who comes in contact with a stranger who is obviously conversant in the ways of Washington. When the stranger's memory is prompted by the stray remark of another train passenger, thoughtfulness and melancholy are detectable in the stranger's face, and he offers to tell Twain a "secret chapter" of his life. That chapter, the inset piece called "The Stranger's Narrative," is neatly divided into halves. The first half is largely descriptive scene setting and an account of how 24 male passengers become snowbound on a train on its way to Chicago in 1853. After seven days without food,

the happy party has become desperate and is presented with an unspo-
ken but commonly understood and unavoidable option—that they must
eat one another in order to survive until help arrives.

The second half of his narrative is predominantly dialogue shaped by
the idiom of legislative process. The macabre comic effect of the narrative's second half is the consequence of casting the urgency of the passengers' situation in the language and process of a group of Washington
insiders. The result could not be more grotesquely humorous if one
were to rewrite *Robert's Rules of Order* from the point of view of a
Wyoming survivalist:

> MR. HALLIDAY, of Virginia: "I move to further amend the report by
> substituting Mr. Harvey Davis, of Oregon, for Mr. Messick. It may be
> urged by gentlemen that the hardships and privations of a frontier life
> have rendered Mr. Davis tough; but, gentlemen, is this a time to cavil
> at toughness? is this a time to be fastidious concerning trifles? is this a
> time to dispute about matters of paltry significance? No, gentlemen,
> bulk is what we desire—substance, weight, bulk—these are the
> supreme requisites—not talent, not genius, not education. I insist
> upon my motion."
>
> MR. MORGAN (excitedly): "Mr. Chairman,—I do most strenuously
> object to this amendment. The gentleman from Oregon is old, and fur-
> thermore is bulky only in bone—not in flesh. I ask the gentleman from
> Virginia if it is soup we want instead of sustenance? if he would delude
> us with shadows? if he would mock our suffering with an Oregonian
> spectre?" (*CTS* I, 273–74)

A summation of the proceedings follows. Halliday's amendment fails,
a substitute motion nominating Mr. Harris ensues, and after six ballots,
Harris is elected. The relentless march of the author's periodic sentences, the series of rhetorical questions, the impassioned pleas for consensus, even acclamation, hover above, and at times displace, the grisly
severity of the business at hand. We do not see Harris taken to the
kitchen, and there is no violent resistance; instead the stranger remarks
upon the passengers' ingenuity in improvising makeshift tables, and the
emphasis falls on the travelers' gustatory satisfaction. Twain improvises,
once again, unexpected narrative turns and twists. The "secret chapter"
in the stranger's life becomes not a disclosure of perverse human barbarity but a sweet recollection: "That I know was the cheeriest hour of
my eventful life. . . . I liked Harris. He might have been better done,
perhaps, but I am free to say that no man ever agreed with me better

than Harris, or afforded me so large a degree of satisfaction. Messick was very well, though rather high-flavored, but for genuine nutritiousness and delicacy of fibre, give me Harris" (*CTS* I, 273).

It is not until this point that the direction and the true subject of the stranger's narrative dawns on Twain. He begins to ask the stranger a question and is rebuffed: "Do not interrupt me, please. After breakfast we elected a man by the name of Walker, from Detroit, for supper. He was very good. I wrote his wife so afterwards." The narrative then swiftly moves to its conclusion as the narrator recalls the entrees in succession—Davis; Doolittle; Hawkins; two Smiths; Bailey, who had a wooden leg ("which was a clear loss, but he was otherwise good"); an Indian boy; an organ-grinder; and obnoxious Buckminster, who "wasn't any good for company and no account for breakfast. We were glad we got him elected before relief came" (*CTS* I, 276).

The stranger concludes his narrative with a happy ending—John Murphy lived to marry the widow of Harris and is happily married still. Recollection of the events and particularly of this union makes the stranger nostalgic: "it was like a novel, sir—it was like a romance" (*CTS* I, 276). After confessing his affection for his companion, a favor Twain finds rather "perilous," the stranger departs at his station, and Twain learns from the conductor that the man is a harmless lunatic, a "monomaniac." The man had in fact formerly been a congressman, and he was once snowbound in a train and so suffered frostbite and deprivation that he became sick "out of his head." Ever since, the stranger has inflicted his story upon any passenger who will listen.

This story seems to express the author's mood at the time and unquestionably possesses a personal element (five of the passengers named in the stranger's narrative were friends of Clemens). Twain may have felt that he was himself being devoured by the obligations of travel, writing, and negotiations of one sort or another, and he may have felt the strain of a forced and artificial amiability. As was often the case, however, he seems to have found the imaginative means to deal with aggravation with comic flair. But beyond the personal, the story is a witty, if grotesque, satire.

However, as a satirist, Twain is often difficult to pin down; the satirical impulse here is straightforward and sustained, though the satirical object seems oddly out of focus. To be sure, "Cannibalism in the Cars" satirizes political posturing and oratory and appears to dramatize a basic human savagery that no appeal to parliamentary process can erase. But there is a marvelous democratic efficiency about it all, as well. The several arguments and nominations are conducted without regard to section, condition, or class (the organ-grinder is among the last to be consumed). Instead, the questions comically concern "nutritiousness" and "flavor," though the narrative again takes a devious twist when the stranger recalls feasting on Morgan of Alabama: "He was one of the finest men I ever sat down to,—handsome, educated, refined, spoke several languages fluently—a perfect gentleman—he was a perfect gentleman, and singularly juicy" (*CTS* I, 274).

Of course, the elements of the narrative acquire a radical shift of perspective when we learn that they are the "harmless vagaries of a madman, instead of the genuine experiences of a bloodthirsty cannibal" (*CTS* I, 277). But this revelation hardly helps us grasp the special character of the stranger's monomania. The story begins in a mood of thoughtfulness and gloom, but before it is over, the stranger is recollecting the happiest and tastiest events of his life. If there is a monomania operating here, it has less to do with reliving actual memories (because the event never happened) than it does with storytelling itself. At the outset, the stranger feels compelled (like one of Poe's narrators) to make a full confession of some dark secret, but before the story is over he (like one of Twain's narrators) is contentedly nostalgic about the whole business. His "earnestness" and the "dreadful details" of the story throw Twain into "hopeless confusion" (*CTS* I, 277), but when he learns that the events never took place except in the stranger's feverish hallucinations, he is deeply relieved.

This disclosure serves more as a means to finish the tale than it does as explanation, however. Somewhat like "A Medieval Romance," though less conspicuously, "Cannibalism in the Cars" does not conclude so much as it simply quits, the author having milked the comedy for about as much as it is worth, and no more. The genius of this story does not reside in any formal consistency of purpose or direction; in fact, there are inconsistencies of detail and unaccountable shifts in mood and tone. And, of course, the story that has just engaged us and Twain turns out to be a nonstory, a demented farce.

In recent years, it has been common to describe Mark Twain as an early metafictionist, and this story does seem to be concerned more with fiction making itself than with its putative subject. The stranger's narrative tells the story of something that never occurred; Twain, as persona, is taken in by the story; and in turn, Twain supplies the narrative of his own confusion and mystification, even as he takes the reader in in the process. However, such a reading makes "Cannibalism in the Cars" into a kind of vaudevillian version of Henry James's "The Real Thing." A self-reflexive reading of this story may convey some sense of Twain's cleverness, but it says virtually nothing about his peculiar genius or his spirited sense of playfulness. Neither as unequivocal satire nor as a specimen of narrative thimblerigging, then, does this story command and sustain our interest. The brilliance of this tale is to be found in the several opportunities for humor Twain permitted himself and in the variety of ways he capitalized on them.

Twain's comic ingenuity can be seen in its bare-boned riotousness in a thematically related story, "The Facts in the Case of the Great Beef Contract," first published in the *Galaxy* in May 1870. The story hangs upon a simple gimmick—the ill-fated attempt to collect on a bill for 30 barrels of beef purchased by General Sherman in 1861. The beef contractor, John Wilson Mackenzie, in his attempts to deliver the merchandise, chases Sherman to Washington, then Manassas, through Atlanta and to the sea, always a few days behind his customer. Mackenzie hears a rumor that the general traveled to the holy land on the *Quaker City* steamer (as Twain himself had actually done the previous year) and sets out after him. In Jerusalem, Mackenzie learns that Sherman had in fact gone to the Western Plains and then sets out for the Rocky Mountains. Mackenzie eventually gets within four miles of Sherman, when the Indians attack, appropriate the barrels, and tomahawk the supplier. In a subsequent raid, Sherman's army captures one of the barrels, so the contract might be said to have been fulfilled to the extent of that single barrel, though by this time the bill for the beef, including transportation costs, amounts to $17,000. Twain treats this final barrel as a kiosk upon which he can post all manner of jokes.

As David E. E. Sloane and others have observed, the 1860s and 1870s were a period when Twain experimented with a variety of comic forms and explored the flexibility and adaptability of his literary persona.[21] One consequence of this experimentation is that Mark Twain, as a persona, is not so much a point of view as he is a full-fledged personality whose vacillations of thought and feeling occur from one tale to the next, but also within individual stories. This is the case with "The Great Beef Contract." For most of the story, Twain speaks as the victim of a legacy, but in the end, he becomes comically aggressive.

The beef contract seems to have a death hex on it. After Mackenzie's scalping, the contract passes through no fewer than 13 hands before it reaches Twain, each person dying shortly after receiving the cursed contract. Twain receives the document from a relative named Bethlehem

Hubbard: "He had had a grudge against me for a long time; but in his last moments he sent for me, and forgave me everything, and weeping gave me the beef contract" (*CTS* I, 368). This is the mask of Twain as an innocent buffoon, perfectly unaware that his relative's favor is made as satisfaction for the grudge he bears him still. By the end of the tale, however, Twain has become wry and sardonic himself and finally bequeaths the contract to an obnoxious young man who has treated him with bureaucratic indifference. Twain's apparent graciousness and affection toward the man are worthy of Bethlehem Hubbard's deathbed bequest: "Young man, you love the bright creature yonder with the gentle blue eyes and the steel pens behind her ears—I see it in your soft glances; you wish to marry her—but you are poor. Here, hold out your hand—here is the beef contract; go, take her and be happy!" (*CTS* I, 373). Shortly thereafter, the young clerk dies.

The narrative that occurs between the time Twain receives the contract and the time he gets rid of it constitutes the funniest part of the story. He means to give an account of himself and his part in the beef contract matter that, he says, has acquired so widespread a reputation. The author takes the literary techniques of frontier humor into the Washington, D.C., city limits, and there he rings some changes on satirical treatment of government bureaucracy. He starts at the top, taking the $17,000 bill straight to the President, and from there begins his descent into what, adapting a phrase from Dickens, he eventually describes as the "Circumlocution Office of Washington." He is referred to the Secretary of State and then to the Secretary of the Navy, the Secretary of the Interior, the Postmaster General, the Agricultural Department, the Speaker of the House, the Commissioner of the Patent Office, and at last the Treasury Department. Within the Treasury Department, he is directed to a series of auditors and then on to the "First Comptroller of the Corn-Beef Division." He moves from Corn-Beef to the Claims Department, the Mislaid Contracts Department, the Dead Reckoning Department, and, at long last, to the Commissioner of Odds and Ends, who happens to be out of the office at the moment. It is the Fourth-Assistant-Junior Clerk of the Commission of Odds and Ends who, after finishing his newspaper, informs Twain that in order to collect on his contract, he must prove that the original contractor, Mackenzie, is actually dead. And to do that, Twain must produce the tomahawk that killed Mackenzie and the Indian that wielded it. If these items of proof are sufficient, Twain is told, he *may* be able to collect on his contract, but only for the one barrel Sherman's army captured and for none of the transportation costs. In other words, he may be able to collect a total of one hundred dollars.

This story is hardly nuanced, but it is hilarious. As Twain descends the ladder of bureaucratic hierarchy, the terms of his address mount to the heavens. He addresses the President as "Sire," the Secretary of State as "Your Royal Highness," the Secretary of the Navy as "Your Imperial Highness," and so on. But by the time Twain reaches the Corn-Beef Division, his patience has worn thin. He confesses that he has learned to wait with endurance and is now able to shift his weight from one foot to the other no more than two or three times every four or five hours. His address of the young clerk betrays his annoyance: "Illustrious Vagrant, where is the Grand Turk?" he asks (*CTS* I, 371), but the Grand Turk being out, Twain has to deal with the clerk, whom he now addresses as "Renowned and honored Imbecile." The clerk is the glad recipient of the contract, which by this time has acquired the potency of a virulent disease and has caused the death of some 13 people.

Slight in itself, "The Great Beef Contract" nibbles at the edges of the sort of modern, gothic humor we find in Faulkner's *As I Lay Dying* or Kafka's *The Trial*. The travels of those barrels of beef are as strange and grotesque as those of Addie Bundren's coffin, and whatever crime Joseph K. has committed cannot be more serious than the reasons for Bethlehem Hubbard's grudge against Twain; in either case, the sins are more than atoned for by the characters' weird adventures in government bureaucracy. But, again, one should not push this sort of comparison too far. Twain was capable of summoning in the imagination the ingredients for absurdist comedy; temperamentally, however, he tended to pursue other, more comprehensible ends. "The Facts in the Case of the Great Beef Contract" epitomizes one of the patterns of experience, and thus of narrative development, Clemens often adopted for his literary persona. The Twain of the "Great Beef Contract" is representative of one facet of the so-called American character that, in our own time, is perhaps best embodied in the cinematic performances of Jack Lemmon in films such as *The Apartment, The China Syndrome*, or *Save the Tiger*—a responsible, obliging, rather timid, unaffected, and above all patient man is made fierce, sometimes by trivial annoyance and sometimes, more seriously, by unconscionable circumstance.

This is also the case in "My Watch—An Instructive Little Tale," published in the *Galaxy* for December 1870. In this story, Twain takes his fairly new watch to a jeweler's to be set. He endures the manifold repairs and "improvements" to his watch for some days. But when the repairman observes that the watch "makes too much steam, you want to hang the monkey-wrench on the safetyvalve!" his reaction is swift and just: "I brained him on the spot, and had him buried at my own expense" (*CTS* I, 499). The same pattern is more successfully developed in "How I Edited an Agricultural Newspaper Once," published the *Galaxy* for June 1870. Twain published this tale when he was a one-third owner of the Buffalo *Express* and was making some editorial decisions of his own. In this tale, he poses as the temporary editor of an agricultural newspaper, and he is almost immediately regarded by the town as a curiosity and a laughingstock. The reasons for his sudden fame derive from his printed observations on the care and feeding of plant life; for example: "Turnips should never be pulled—it injures them. It is much better to send a boy up and let him shake the tree" (*CTS* I, 413). The preposterous comedy of the story escalates. We learn in his columns that "The guano is a fine bird, but great care is necessary in rearing it," that "The pumpkin is the only esculent of the orange family," that ganders spawn and cows moult, that horse chestnuts are gaining favor as an article of commerce, that polecats are good ratters, and that clams "will lie quiet if music be played to them" (*CTS* I, 414–15).

To this point, Twain is pictured as a complete buffoon, and the regular editor returns from holiday to upbraid Twain for his incredible stupidity and the commotion he has caused. But turnabout is fair play. The editor admits that there has been a sudden increase in the paper's circulation, but that does not soften his angry rebuke. At last, he asks why Twain did not confess that he did not know anything about agriculture, and Twain turns aggressive:

> "*Tell* you, you cornstalk, you cabbage, you son of a cauliflower! . . . I tell you I have been in the editorial business going on fourteen years, and it is the first time I ever heard of a man's having to know anything in order to edit a newspaper. You turnip! Who write the dramatic critiques for the second-rate papers? Why, a parcel of promoted shoe-makers and apprentice apothecaries, who know just as much about good acting as I do about good farming and no more. Who review the books? People who never wrote one. . . . Who edit the agricultural papers, you—yam? Men, as a general thing, who fail in the poetry line, yellow-covered novel line, sensation-drama line, city-editor line, and finally fall back on agriculture as a temporary reprieve from the poor-house. . . . Sir I have been through it from Alpha to Omaha, and I tell you that the less a man knows the bigger noise he makes and the higher salary he commands." (*CTS* I, 416)

Twain's rejoinder has the feel of angry and personal authenticity—the world may take him for a fool, but it does so out of its own cheerless and literal-minded ignorance and at its own peril. The story also demonstrates his authoritative acquaintance with the journalistic life, and Clemens's professional experience was not confined to journalism alone. He once observed that until he was 37 years old, his life consisted of a series of "apprenticeships." When he came to write short fiction, he retrieved from his several vocations an occupational savvy that might be put in the service of his humor, even if that savvy wore the mask of ignorance. Whether an insider's know-how came from mining ("Dick Baker's Cat"), riverboat piloting ("Old Times on the Mississippi"), journalism ("Journalism in Tennessee"), soldiering ("The Private History of a Campaign That Failed"), or editing ("How I Edited an Agricultural Newspaper Once"), Twain often used an appropriate technical vocabulary as well as a narrowly occupational perspective on events to give a factual vividness and a comic specificity to his work. In other words, he was transforming the facts of his experience into material for his fiction, all the while adapting that experience to his plastic and variable persona.

The period between 1868 and 1871, as Jeffrey Steinbrink has perceptively and persuasively charted it, was a time that Samuel Clemens spent "getting to be Mark Twain."[22] During this period, as we have already noted, Clemens's experiments with his persona had more to do with discovering a variety of literary techniques than with how he might present himself to the world. As his reputation spread, and as the Twain label began to acquire and to cultivate in his readers an appetite for certain distinctive characteristics, Clemens could indulge himself more freely in a naturally antic point of view. To know that the work one was reading was by Mark Twain was also to know that sooner or later, as Howells remarked, some sly joke or abrupt reversal was coming. Twain's readers, rapidly growing in number after the publication of *The Innocents Abroad*, approached his work without the customary expectations that announced genres and practiced literary conventions satisfy; instead they were ready for some sort of unanticipated, but surely humorous, form of entertainment. But a reputation as merely a funny fellow was ashes in the mouth, and it was during this time (not from the very beginning, as he recollected in his autobiography) that he began self-consciously to mix preaching and teaching with his mirth and mischief.[23]

No doubt part of his reshaping of his literary identity had to do with marrying into a well-to-do and respectable New York family and with keeping company with what he considered a better class of folks than he had in Virginia City or San Francisco. During this period, he was continually professing that his behavior was on the mend and that he was a redeemable fellow after all. This circumstance helps to explain the high moral ground he takes in a tale such as "Curious Dream," with its baldly stated subtitle, "Containing a Moral," in which he scolds the citizens of Buffalo for failing to keep their cemeteries neat. But surely his own pride had something to do with the way he was revising and stabilizing his literary identity. In "Political Economy" (1870), for example, he presents himself not as a knockabout traveler but as thoroughly domesticated man engaged in writing a tract on political economy when a lightning rod salesman visits and manages to sell him 150 rods, including one for the cow.

From this point of view, "A Mysterious Visit" (1870) is a rather more complicated story than it may at first appear. In it, Twain is approached by a man who presents himself as an assessor for the Internal Revenue Department, a branch of government Twain has not heard of. The joke of the tale is that because Twain does not wish to appear ignorant, he naively volunteers the very information the assessor most wants to know. Twain takes a condescending attitude toward the assessor—"My son, you little know what an old fox you are dealing with" (*CTS* I, 341)—and boasts that his recent income from lecturing amounts to $14,750; from the Buffalo *Express*, $8,000; and from sales of *The Innocents Abroad*, $214,000. Twain actually inflates the figures in order to impress the stranger, who meanwhile is making meticulous notes in his little book.

These published financial disclosures would have likely been regarded by his in-laws, the Langdons, as simply vulgar, but Clemens seems rather more intent on justifying himself, for personal reasons, almost entirely on the grounds of his material success instead of his good character. He shifts his ground a bit in the concluding paragraphs, however, when he confesses that through the assistance of an opulent friend, he discovers "deductions" and swears to lie after lie about his financial situation. In the end, Twain avoids the income tax except on a paltry $250, but at the same time, he manages to stoop to the ways of the "very best of the solid men in Buffalo." Twain confesses that his soul is covered with perjury and his self-respect is gone forever, but he is not ashamed, for he has joined the most "respected, honored, and courted men in America" (*CTS* I, 344).

"A Mysterious Visit" is a wonderful example of having your cake and eating it, too. In a few short pages, Twain has managed to (1) boast of his fame and his income, (2) claim membership in the most respected class in the nation, (3) satirize that same class for its conniving, (4) publicly indulge in the delicious satisfaction of being ashamed of himself, and (5) announce that he has learned his lesson and will in the future keep his mouth shut and "eschew fire-proof gloves, lest I fall into certain dreadful habits irrevocably" (*CTS* I, 344). In this story, Twain is victimized by the government and, in a different way, by his prosperous friend; yet, in the end, he appears triumphant economically, socially, and morally.

The comedy of victimage is a relatively easy form of humor and provides nearly unlimited opportunities for laughter. At least half of the appeal of famous comic victims such as Oliver Hardy and Stan Laurel, Harold Lloyd, Charlie Chaplin, and Buster Keaton stems from their brilliant ability to act out physically their status as victims. If verbal comedy can somehow be said to participate in physical comedy, then "A Day at Niagara" (1869) and "Journalism in Tennessee" (1869) are exquisite examples of physical comedy. In the first story, an innocent traveler to the falls suffers robbery, a beating, a dunking, and six "fatal" injuries at the hands of "Irish" Indians. In the second, Twain travels to Tennessee for his health and takes a berth on the *Morning Glory and Johnson County War-Whoop* and finds that Tennessee journalism is rough business. He leaves the state for the same reason he came—for his health—but before he does, he receives assaults meant for his boss, loses two teeth and a finger, chips a knuckle, suffers a cowhiding, and takes bullets in the arm and thigh. These are rather raw examples of one aspect of Twain's comic genius: he willingly makes himself vulnerable to the fictive events of his tales and is implicated in the comedy itself. He absorbs into himself the calamities, the sins, and the petty vanities that he would laugh out of existence.

The six short stories he included in *Roughing It* (1872) reveal a distancing of Twain as a participant in the comedy he dramatizes. At the same time, he seems often to authorize and legitimize the reader's interest in his created fictions by speaking from the position of a representative of the established culture whose own sympathies and fascination have been aroused. Those six stories—"The Great Land-Slide Case" (chapter 34), "Buck Fanshaw's Funeral" (chapter 47), "Capt. Ned Blakely" (chapter 50), "Jim Blaine and His Grandfather's Ram" (chapter 53), "Dick Baker and His Cat" (chapter 61), and "A Letter from Horace Greeley" (chapter 70)—occur in the latter half of the book. And, as Henry Nash Smith observed, in the second half of *Roughing It* (in Smith's estimation, the decidedly inferior half), Twain speaks not as a tenderfoot but somewhat ambivalently, now as one of the "boys," now as a representative of the dominant culture.[24] How much this observation applies to these stories, as stories, is questionable. It is true, neverthe-less, that Twain often speaks not as the comic protagonist but as the witness, the raconteur, or the reporter.

"The Great Land-Slide Case" is another hoax story, though it has an interesting twist. Twain had published two earlier versions of this tale before he interpolated it into his travel narrative. Unlike other hoax sto-ries, such as "The Petrified Man" (1862), the joke is not on a gullible community but on a man who believes himself to be above those around him. The citizens of Virginia City prepare an elaborate bit of hazing for General Buncombe, a man who has taken a post as attorney general for Nevada and considers himself a "lawyer of parts," eager to demonstrate his natural superiority. When Dick Hyde informs Buncombe that Tom Morgan's ranch has slid down on top of Hyde's own in a landslide and that Morgan now claims ownership of Hyde's property, Buncombe gladly takes the case. He musters witnesses, gathers evidence, makes an impassioned closing argument, quoting from "poetry, sarcasm, statistics, history, pathos, bathos, blasphemy," and winds up with a tribute to the "Glorious Bird of America and the principles of eternal justice" (*RI*, 224–25).

Buncombe thinks he has the case in his pocket until the presiding judge, ex-Governor Roop, after much meditation, declares that Hyde has been deprived of his ranch by a "visitation of God" and rules in favor of Morgan. It takes Buncombe two full months before it dawns on him that he has been the victim of a wild joke. The model for General Bun-combe was Benjamin Bunker, a man Twain did not particularly like, but the satire has less to do with a personal animus than with the commu-nity's ability to take a supercilious person down a peg or two. However, at least thematically, this story also shares with "A Mysterious Visit" and "A Letter from Horace Greeley" a preoccupation with false pride and the consequences of maintaining one's vanity at the expense of a sense of reality.

"Capt. Ned Blakely," sometimes reprinted under the title "The Trial," is one of several pieces in which Twain inscribed his affection and admiration for Captain Edgar (Ned) Wakeman. Before he appeared as Ned Blakely, Twain had called him Captain Waxman, and in later works, Wakeman would appear as Captain Hurricane Jones and, most significantly, as the title character of "Extract from Captain Stormfield's Visit to Heaven." The traits particularly emphasized in the Ned Blakely story have to do with a no-nonsense attitude toward justice. When Bill Noakes shoots Blakely's black mate in the back, the case for Blakely is cut-and-dried: He captures Noakes and invites neighboring captains to a nine o'clock hanging the next morning. Then Blakely faces a series of obstacles and patiently, if inelegantly, endures most of them. The other captains insist that Noakes must have a trial; fine, says Blakely, right after the hanging and the burying. No, he must be tried first, and then hanged. All right, then, a trial it is, and Blakely will harangue Noake's conscience while they try him. No, the defendant must be present at the trial. At last the trial is convened, and the jury finds the accused guilty. Blakely is satisfied, but when the court says that a sheriff must be appointed to do the hanging, Blakely, a man of "boundless wrath," has had enough, and the subject is dropped. Blakely marches Noakes off to a canyon to hang him, but before he does so, Blakely reads to Noakes from the Bible—"There. Four chapters. There's few that would have took the pains with you that I have" (*RI*, 337).

"A Letter from Horace Greeley" is good-natured satire. The story gets its fun out of two widely known facts about Greeley—that he was an amateur farmer who published his agricultural views widely, and that his handwriting was notoriously illegible. Greeley had taken a good deal of kidding in the newspapers on both scores. Around these two details, Twain drapes the preposterous story of a mother's concern for her son, whose life's ambition is to make the turnip a growing vine. The son is yet another version of the good little boy whose earnestness is ridiculous, even fatal, and his failure to train his beloved turnip plants is causing him to waste away. The mother writes to a Michigan minister named Simon Erickson for help. Erickson turns to Greeley for advice and receives a letter in a script that looks more like turnip vines than handwriting. Erickson deciphers the note several times, with such wide variations in the opening clause as "Polygamy dissembles majesty," "Bolivia extemporizes mackerel," and "Potations do sometimes wake wines" (*RI*, 484–86). The minister pridefully wrestles with the script for several days. At last Erickson relents and writes Greeley another letter; this time he receives a clerk's translation of the advice: "Potatoes do sometimes make vines; turnips remain passive; cause unnecessary to state. Inform the poor widow her lad's efforts will be vain" (*RI*, 487). But the information arrives too late—the widow's boy has perished, and Erickson goes crazy and removes to the Sandwich Islands to recuperate.

The most interesting stories are the three vernacular pieces, the old ram story (discussed in the opening chapter), "Dick Baker's Cat," and "Buck Fanshaw's Funeral." Each of these three tales has an individual coherence, but they are related to one another thematically as well. Twain seems to be sponsoring the vernacular narrators' rights to our interest and insisting that they receive a generous hearing and sympathetic judgment. Gregg Camfield has pointed out, though from a rather different perspective than the one I am taking here, that it is misleading to see Twain as a cultural outsider waging war against a dominant, essentially genteel culture. Instead, according to Camfield, Twain was dedicated to, and worked from within, that culture and "followed the fracture lines of his culture's ideas and pursued them to the extremes out of the depth of his commitment."[25] This may be too sober a way of stating the point I wish to make here, however. Twain's marvelously antic parody, "A Map of Paris" (1870), for example, was the product of one of those "spasms of humorous possession" that his imagination was prey to and that his talents were trained for. But, as Jeffrey Steinbrink has noted, there is something adolescent about "A Map of Paris"; the sketch's "general silliness aptly reflects [Twain's] knack for finding imaginative freedom and release from the draining cares of adulthood through childish forms and perspectives."[26] By contrast, the narrative stance Twain takes toward his *Roughing It* stories is more authoritative than many of his earlier pieces and seems to derive both from an artistic firmness (born out of several years of experience in the literary game) and a felt social and moral responsibility (brought about in part by his personal domestic circumstance and in part by the recognition that he had acquired a literary reputation to protect).

In these stories, at any rate, Twain characterizes the frontier figures he is about to introduce in a way that both informs his readers about where their sympathies should lie and establishes Twain's own authority to make those sorts of judgments about the characters. Thus we learn that Scotty Briggs "had a warm heart, and a strong love for his friends, and never entered into a quarrel when he could reasonably keep out of it" (*RI*, 310); that Jim Blaine, who never gets around to the story of his grandfather's old ram, is also a "stalwart" and earnest man; and, most profusely, that Dick Baker, who affectionately reminisces about his cat, was "one of the gentlest spirits" that ever lived, "earnest, thoughtful, slenderly educated, slouchily dressed, and clay-soiled, but his heart was finer metal than any gold his shovel ever brought to light" (*RI*, 416). In a word, though these men (because they are isolated, poor, or uneducated) do not belong to the dominant culture, they nevertheless epitomize the very values that that culture loudly espouses but so often quietly disregards—patience, honesty, gentleness, courage, simplicity, and modesty. In his *Roughing It* stories, Twain undertakes to introduce his social pariahs into the precincts of respectable society—that is, into the sympathies of his readers—by entering not at the kitchen door but through the main entrance. And Twain accomplishes this social feat by, in effect, saying to the exclusionary butler of cultural democracy, "Not to worry. He's with me."

I do not wish to overemphasize the sometimes improbable moral authority Twain casts over his fictions or to give him too much credit for the social responsibility he only intermittently accepted when he realized that he had gained a hearing from a large segment of American society. After all, Twain was perpetually subject to "spasms of humorous possession" and felt great personal joy when he freely indulged a natural sense of whimsy and outrageous comedy. These rival points of view—the adolescent and the adult, the renegade and the magistrate, and the outsider and the insider—seemed never to have coalesced into a single perspective. How could they? But Twain did find various ways to coordinate them and, at least in *Huckleberry Finn*, was able to fuse the vision of a child with the worries and disappointments of an adult. In "Dick Baker's Cat" and "Buck Fanshaw's Funeral," there are the marks of incipient attempts to reconcile these points of view.

Dick Baker is introduced as a poor and lonely man who has patiently endured his deprivations on the Pacific slope for some 18 years: "Whenever he was out of luck and a little down-hearted, he would fall to mourning over the loss of a wonderful cat he used to own (for where women and children are not, men of kindly impulses take up with pets, for they must love something). And he always spoke of the strange sagacity of that cat with the air of a man who believed in his secret heart that there was something human about it—maybe even supernatural" (*RI*, 416). The story Baker tells of his cat, Tom Quartz, is exuberantly and extravagantly funny, all the more so for the narrator's thoughtful earnestness. The cat's sagacity and its sense of injured dignity may be the preoccupation of Baker, but the reader's immediate interest is sustained by the slangy humor of it all.

When Baker and his partner take to "pick'n 'n' blast'n instead of shovelin' dirt on the hillside" they fail to inform Tom Quartz of the change in procedure. As a consequence, the cat is blown out of the shaft and comes down a bit altered in look and attitude:

> Well, I reckon he was p'raps the orneriest lookin' beast you ever seen. One ear was sot back on his neck, 'n' his tail was stove up, 'n' his eye-winkers was swinged off, 'n' he was all blacked up with powder an' smoke, an' all sloppy with mud 'n' slush f'm one end to the other. Well, sir, it warn't no use to try to apologize—we couldn't say a word. He took a sort of disgusted look at hisself, 'n' then he looked at us—an' it was just exactly the same as if he had said—"Gents, maybe *you* think it's smart to take advantage of a cat that ain't had no experience of quartz-minin', but *I* think *different*"—an' then he turned on his heel 'n' marched off home without ever saying another word. (*RI*, 418–19)

Unlike Jim Smiley, whose meandering recollections veer away from the stated subject, Dick Baker is absorbed by his memory of his cat, the object of his love and the symbol of his loneliness. Twain's stated reaction to the tale is surely meant to shape the reader's understanding of Baker's situation: "The affection and the pride that lit up Baker's face when he delivered this tribute to the firmness of his humble friend of other days, will always be a vivid memory with me" (*RI*, 419). "Firmness," a sense of purpose and dignity preserved in the face of inhospitable circumstance or compromised condition, seems to have been one of Twain's central preoccupations during this period and informs, in greater or lesser degree, much of *Roughing It* as well as the stories within the book.

What we know of Scotty Briggs's history makes him as much a "rough" and a "stalwart" as Ned Blakely or Buck Fanshaw, the man whose funeral Briggs means to arrange. As a "committee of one," deputized to call on the local minister, Briggs is a representative of the community. Indeed, "Buck Fanshaw's Funeral" is representative in any number of ways: The story and its principal characters are a conflation of several people Twain had known and several events he had witnessed or heard about. And the vernacular, or slang, that is the stuff of the humor of the piece is itself a rich compound: "as all the peoples of the earth had representative adventurers in the Silverland, and as each adventurer had brought the slang of his nation or his locality with him, the combination made the slang of Nevada the richest and the most infinitely varied and copious that had ever existed anywhere in the world, perhaps" (*RI*, 308–9).

It is probably a mistake to see in the conversation between Scotty Briggs and the unnamed minister a contest between two forms of discourse. The exchange, though Scotty continually invokes comparisons to a poker or billiard game, is neither competitive nor aggressive—each man would gladly give up his native tongue if he could speak the other's. As much as he is capable, Scotty has adjusted his speech to the occasion, and is deeply apologetic, for example, when a "d——d" escapes his lips. Both men are sensitive to the rhetorical decorum of the meeting, but it is a decorum without mutually intelligible terms or protocols. Moreover, Scotty's speech is not culturally or regionally specific but an amalgamation of slang from every quarter of the nation. The language he speaks is highly idiomatic, but it is the sort of language one might construct if one were to rebuild the Tower of Babel brick by idiomatic brick. The resulting structure, we can be sure, would not resemble its monolithic original so much as it would one of Gaudi's fantastic and brightly colored constructions.

Nor does it seem particularly important or profitable to try to determine whose side Twain is on in this linguistic pinball game. Our sympathy runs toward Scotty Briggs, but not because the minister is antipathetic. Rather, the "stalwart" fireman, in the presence of the minister, finds himself in an alien condition, but Briggs had expected that. He is dressed, as he always dresses for "weighty official business," in his fireman's uniform, with spanner and revolver attached to his patent leather belt and his pants stuffed into his boots. He looks ridiculous, of course, and he feels ridiculous. But the point is that this man is on an uncomfortable errand and, willingly and to the best of his ability, is on his best behavior because of his deep affection for the departed friend, Buck Fanshaw.

The terms of Scotty's admiration for Fanshaw are hilarious and affecting:

> "But pard, he was a rustler! You ought to seen him get started once. He was a bully boy with a glass eye! Just spit in his face and give him room according to his strength, and it was just beautiful to see him peel and go in. He was the worst son of a thief that ever drawed breath. Pard, he was *on* it! He was on it bigger than an Injun!"
>
> "On it? On what?"

"On the shoot. On the shoulder. On the fight, you understand. *He* didn't give a continental for *any*body. *Beg* your pardon, friend, for coming so near saying a cuss-word—but you see I'm on an awful strain, in this palaver, on account of having to cramp down and draw everything so mild. But we've got to give him up. There ain't any getting around that, I don't reckon. Now if we can get you to help plant him—" (*RI*, 312)

Fanshaw does eventually get planted, and in high style: "for years afterward, the degree of grandeur attained by any civic display in Virginia was determined by comparison with Buck Fanshaw's funeral" (*RI*, 317).

Whether the cause for the transformation was the funeral ceremony or his conversation with the "duck who runs the gospel-mill," Scotty Briggs becomes a changed man. He converts to Christianity and takes to teaching Sunday school to the pioneer children in a language they can comprehend. Twain closes down the story in a way he had done before, by leaving the reader wanting more. Twain says he had the privilege once of hearing Scotty tell the story of Joseph and his brothers "without looking at the book," but he "leaves it to the reader to fancy what it was like" (*RI*, 317).

The *Roughing It* stories dramatize in various ways notions and moods that Clemens was experiencing as a man who had recently acquired a certain unaccustomed respectability and who had embarked (several times) on plans for self-improvement. He was concerned with how one maintained one's dignity under compromised circumstances, as the feline Tom Quartz had done; he was aware of the difference between a sense of dignity and a false and self-satisfied sense of pride of the sort that made General Buncombe a laughingstock and Simon Erickson mad; he obviously admired men such as Ned Blakely and Buck Fanshaw, whose no-nonsense views of justice were backed by swift and unmistakable courage and purpose; he was alert to the seemingly endless ways men and women could misunderstand one another; and, in a rather more partisan fashion, he insisted on behalf of Scotty Briggs, but may well have been engaging in self-justification, that "inborn nobility of spirit was no mean timber whereof to construct a Christian" (*RI*, 317).

Clemens may or may not have joined the flock himself, but if we are to judge from his *Roughing It* stories, his religious views in 1872 were really not much different from the views he expressed to his brother Orion in the same letter of 1865 in which Clemens announced his calling as a humorist: "I have a religion—but you will call it blasphemy. It is that there is a God for the rich but none for the poor."[27] By the early 1870s, he had developed literary techniques, the most important having to do with the management of his literary persona, that enabled him to "sermonize" in his fiction whether jokes applied for admission or not. Moreover, he discovered certain stage directions that permitted him to introduce his readers to the less fortunate or refined of God's creatures without creating in his audience a sense of condescension. It was well for Twain, and for us, that the jokes, an apparently endless variety of them, continued to make application to his imagination. But the next phase of his career was launched with a story that was both true and very serious.

The Middle Years, 1874–1890:
Literary Respectability and
Social Responsibility

Roughing It was published in February 1872. For the next two years, Clemens's time was hectically but profitably divided between traveling, writing, lecturing, and acting the part of businessman. An authorized English edition of *The Innocents Abroad* was published in 1872, and the jointly authored novel *The Gilded Age* in 1873. A play based on a character from that novel, *Colonel Sellers*, opened in 1874 and proved to be a long-standing success and, eventually, one of the most prosperous children of Twain's imagination. By this time, he had also begun writing *Tom Sawyer* and had planned a book on England and the English. His "Self-Pasting Scrap-Book" was patented in June 1873 and generated a good deal of money for the next several years, though, from Twain's point of view, not enough. He became a director of the American Publishing Company the same year.

What is more, during this period, Twain proved himself to be a most clubbable fellow—he was made an honorary member of the London literary clubs the Whitefriars and, later, the Temple Club; he also became a member of the Lotos Club in New York City. During a visit to England, he met, among other notables, Wilkie Collins, Robert Browning, Herbert Spencer, George MacDonald, and Anthony Trollope; and Twain found that he had to spend extra time preparing after-dinner speeches for one occasion or another. All the instruments that measure success seemed to agree—Mark Twain had arrived.

But Twain was always ambivalent about his fame. He was pleased, and even a bit surprised, by the attention and approval he received, but he was irritated, too, by the constant interruptions and the several demands placed on his time and his good nature. At this time, he was trying to settle into a comfortable and secure domestic life. He bought a lot in the Nook Farm area of Hartford, Connecticut, in 1873 and made arrangements for the construction of a house there. When the Clemenses moved in a year and a half later, the house was still not finished. But that was mere annoyance compared with the happy additions and the sad subtractions in his life—his daughter Olivia Susan (Susy) Clemens was born in March 1872, and his daughter Clara two years later; but his 18-month-old son Langdon died of diphtheria on June 2, 1872, and Clemens unfairly blamed himself for the boy's death.

The unsettled and busy life that Clemens and his wife, Olivia, were leading must have made their stays in Elmira, New York, all the more agreeable, even necessary. Sometimes they stayed in the Langdon house downtown and sometimes with Olivia's adopted sister Susan Crane and her husband Theodore at Quarry Farm, high on a hill overlooking the town in the Chemung Valley. In 1874, when Susan had an octagonal study built for Clemens on the premises, the refuge was complete, and Twain was to do some of his best work there. The Cranes and the Clemenses got along splendidly, and summering at Quarry Farm became something of a habit for years afterward. But there must have been some uneasiness, too, and there were probably many opportunities for Twain to explain his native point of view to a family whose training and background were so different from his own.

One of those differences was sectional. The Langdon family had been active abolitionists; Twain's father-in-law, Jervis Langdon, had helped found the antislavery church in Elmira and had done important work for the underground railroad in the area. Clemens's family, by contrast, had at one time or another owned slaves, but Sam seemed to believe that close acquaintance with blacks during his childhood spoke in his favor. Specifically, Clemens had more than once claimed that because he had lived among and had known blacks in his native Missouri, he was better acquainted with their customs and desires.[28] Evidently, Susan Crane was unconvinced by Clemens's authoritative pronouncements on his understanding of racial matters. In any event, she urged her brother-in-law more than once to have their cook, "Auntie" Mary Ann Cord, tell him her story. And more than once Clemens politely demurred. However, one summer evening in 1874, when the Clemenses and Cranes were sitting on the porch of the farmhouse, Samuel Clemens casually asked Auntie Cord about her history and her seemingly inexhaustible good humor. After some hesitation, she agreed to tell her story. The literary result of this exchange was one of Twain's finest sketches, "A True Story, Repeated Word For Word As I Heard It," published in the *Atlantic Monthly* the following November. A more immediate result, in Clemens, must have been not only a sudden awareness of his own ignorance of African-American experience but the recognition that he had been tricked into a new understanding by Susan Crane. In other words, Clemens, like his literary persona in tales he had written before, must have known that he had been set up.

In substance, the sketch he published was indeed a true story. Mary Ann Cord (in the tale, she is called Aunt Rachel to give her separation from her children a certain biblical significance) was in fact born in Maryland and raised in Virginia, and she was separated from her family when she was sold at auction to a man from North Carolina. Her favorite son was named Henry, he did manage to escape to freedom when he as about 13 years old, and he did become a barber in Elmira. More important, during the war, Henry did join the Union troops (though perhaps not as a soldier) and kept alive what must have been a desperate hope that he might find his mother somewhere in the South. Finally, against all odds, the two were reunited in rather dramatic fashion.[29]

The story Aunt Rachel tells, then, is autobiographical and therefore personal to her; but it is representative, too. As Philip Foner long ago observed, Twain managed to compress in this brief story much about the humanity of blacks, their liberating role in the Civil War, and their postbellum attempts to find their families, as well as to suggest the barbarity of slavery alongside an unvanquished dignity in the slaves who survived it.[30] Despite the pathos of Aunt Rachel's story, it is not tragic, however; for every Mary Cord who lived to see at least one of her children again, there were a hundred mothers who did not. That Aunt Rachel knows full well that she is one of the lucky ones only adds to her dignity. Her concluding remarks to "Misto C——" suggest none of the qualities she so obviously possesses—love and forgiveness, defiance and patient suffering, courage, nobility, and pride. Instead, her remarks affirm her prayerful gratitude: "De Lord God ob heaven be praise', I got my own ag'in! Oh, no, Misto C——, *I* hain't had no trouble. An' no *joy!*" (*CTS* I, 582).

When John W. DeForest, the novelist and former Union captain, read "A True Story" in the *Atlantic*, he freely confessed to William Dean Howells that the story brought tears to his eyes. The story retains its affective power even today, but the critical emphasis upon Aunt Rachel's story and the studied authenticity of her dialect has tended to obscure other, though quite different, affecting and artistic qualities in the tale. Twain's subtitle, "Repeated Word For Word As I Heard It," was likely inserted in part to call attention to the vividness of dialect he had worked hard to achieve and in part to forewarn readers that the story was not just another comic production. However, the subtitle is misleading in several ways. Although the story Aunt Rachel tells is substantially "true" in most of its details, it has been shaped to achieve a double purpose—first, to dramatize Mary Cord's dignified humanity, and second, to make "Misto C——" not merely foolish but culpable.

After hearing Mary Cord's story, Twain told it to John Hay and was encouraged to write it up. As with so many of Twain's oral performances, the story was probably altered with each subsequent telling, and when he came to write the piece, it likely received still other improvements. From a letter he wrote to Howells, we do know that Twain knew he was working unfamiliar territory and changed the sequence of the telling: "I enclose also 'A True Story' which has no humor in it. You can pay as lightly as you choose for that, if you want it, for it is rather out of my line. I have not altered the old colored woman's story except to begin it at the beginning, instead of the middle, as she did—& traveled both ways" (*MTHL* I, 22). Somewhat to Twain's surprise, though Howells rejected the comparatively slight piece that accompanied it, "Some Learned Fables for Good Old Boys and Girls," he accepted "A True Story" and paid Twain well for it.

Twain had adopted the mode of the frame tale for this story, but he made the form serve serious purposes. In violation of nearly all the rules he would outline in "How to Tell a Story" (1895), he deliberately avoided the aimlessness that is so amusing in the jumping frog and old ram tales. Moreover, although Aunt Rachel is earnest, she shares very little else with Twain's vernacular narrators. She does not speak in a monotone, she does not ramble, and she is not self-absorbed in the telling—if anything, she is rather canny in the way she involves Misto C—— in the narration. And Clemens's own persona in the story is clearly altered to enhance Rachel's dignity and to emphasize his own unfeeling stupidity.

By appearing as "Misto C——" (an only slightly disguised version of Mr. Clemens) instead of Mark Twain, the author has removed the armor of his literary persona in order to absorb more completely the guilt and humiliation that properly belong to him. Moreover, the author does not sponsor the good character of his vernacular narrator, as he had done in the *Roughing It* stories. Instead, he is manifestly wrong about Aunt Rachel, or rather his appreciation of her is altogether misplaced and self-deceived: "She was a cheerful, hearty soul, and it was no more trouble for her to laugh than it is for a bird to sing. She was under fire, now, as usual when the day is done. That is to say, she was being chaffed without mercy, and was enjoying it" (*CTS* I, 578). To reread the opening paragraph after having read the story is to see clearly and feel strongly the sting of a basically well-meaning but clearly self-satisfied bigotry. In the end, by giving the last words to Aunt Rachel, the author invites us to imagine more fully the shame that Misto C—— has brought upon himself by the unwanted recognition of the cook's dignity and of his own insufficiency.

"A True Story" is rightly regarded as a vernacular tour de force and rivals even the most powerful speeches Jim delivers in *Huckleberry Finn*. But the tale is remarkable, too, for the stage directions Twain gave to the piece, which were likely a matter of invention rather than recollection. The story begins with Aunt Rachel "sitting respectfully below our level," when Misto C—— blunders into asking her, "Aunt Rachel, how is it that you've lived sixty years and never had any trouble." Rachel becomes serious and scrutinizes him. She asks, "without even a smile in her voice," "Misto C——, is you in 'arnest?' " The sudden seriousness sobers Clemens's manner, and she has given him an opportunity to get out from under the onus of his question. Misto C—— falters but nervously gives her the entering wedge to continue her story: "Why, I thought—that is, I meant—why, you *can't* have had any trouble. I've never heard you sigh, and never seen your eye when there was n't a laugh in it" (*CTS* I, 578).

Twain had often implicated himself in his humorous tales and thus made himself vulnerable to the laughter he provoked. But this was a serious story, told without the defenses of an established persona. Through the dramatic management of the piece, he made sure that Aunt Rachel's story would embody her natural dignity and humanity, but for Twain, the story also served as self-accusation, even indictment. Within only a few hundred words, Twain moves the cook from below his level (spatially, socially, and morally) to considerably above it. As Rachel continues her story, she gradually rises and "now she towered above us, black against the stars" (*CTS* I, 579).

More to the point, Rachel's story, though it casts its eye backward to her condition as a slave in the antebellum South and brings the narration forward to the reunion with her son just after the war, is delivered with a disturbing presentational immediacy. Rachel compares the stand where she and her family were auctioned off to the porch where Misto C—— and, by implication, the Clemenses and Cranes, too, are sitting. And she not only tells but vividly performs her tale. The narration is punctuated with "so" to indicate accompanying physical gestures. Rachel holds the little Henry "clost up to my breas' so"; before the

Union officers, she "drops a kurtchy, so, an' I up an' tole 'em 'bout my Henry, dey a-listenin' to my troubles jist de same as if I was white folks"; she reenacts her fierce anger, "my soul *alive* but I was hot! My eye was jist a-blazin'! I jist straightened myself up, so,—jist as I is now, plum to de ceilin'"; and she charges the black soldiers who have invaded her kitchen, "Well, I jist march' on dem niggers,—so, lookin' like a gen'l,—an' dey jist cave away befo' me" (*CTS* I, 579–82).

Clearly, Aunt Rachel is not a woman to be trifled with, and if Misto C—— was at first confounded by her unanticipated earnestness, we imagine him now surprised by, perhaps even fearful of, her fierce dignity. The presumably jolly Aunt Rachel now presses her advantage with a shrewd seriousness. It seems unlikely that Mary Ann Cord, a black servant who had known Twain only a few months before she told him her story, should have assumed the physical familiarity she does in the concluding paragraph. Instead, the stage directions were probably Twain's invention and designed to bring her words home with unmistakable force. At any rate, she acts out the recognition of her son in ways that would make anyone squirm:

> I was a-stoopin' down by de stove,—jist so, same as if yo' foot was de stove,—an' I'd opened de stove do' wid my right han'—so, pushin' it back, jist as I pushes yo' foot . . . I see a black face come aroun' under mine, an' de eyes a-lookin' up into mine, jist as I's a-lookin' up clost under yo face now; an' I just stopped *right dah*, an' never budged! just gazed, an' gazed, so. . . . an' I grab his lef' han' an' shove back his sleeve,—jist so, as I's doin' to you,—an' den I goes for his forehead an' push de hair back, so. (*CTS* I, 582)

To convey something of the power of this scene, one need only recall a more recent anecdote. When John F. Kennedy was running for president, he arranged for a meeting with Jackie Robinson, hoping to obtain his political support and, as a consequence, help secure the black vote. Robinson refused his support for a simple reason—during their lengthy meeting, Kennedy never once looked Robinson in the eye. Aunt Rachel makes Misto C—— look her in the eye, and her gaze fixes his guilt and his shame with unmistakable clarity and power.

Twain's rendering of this "true story" surely exceeded whatever Susan Crane had in mind when she urged him to hear Mary Cord's tale. For if Aunt Rachel's story is both personal and severely representative (of both the past and the present), Misto C—— is representative, too, not merely of the antebellum South but of a continuing and pervasive white guilt. If one understands the story in this way, one wonders whether the Union veteran Deforest's tears were shed for Aunt Rachel's sake alone or for his own lingering shame as well. Somewhat more certain is the fact that when Twain harnessed the devices of his humor to his capacities as a serious moralist, he was accepting a social responsibility as the fee simple for his gifts as a storyteller.

"A True Story" appeared in the November 1874 issue of the *Atlantic Monthly*. For the first time, Twain had broken into that prestigious Boston-based periodical, and as Justin Kaplan rightly observes, the story's publication represented Twain's " 'literary' literary debut."[31] The *Atlantic* meant literature and literary respectability. Twain could identify with Aunt Rachel's situation to the extent that he knew laughter might disguise solemnity and a sense of wounded pride and that perpetual good humor did not accurately register one's true depth of feeling. At any rate, Twain was surely gratified to be counted among the *Atlantic* authors who gathered at a dinner in Boston that December, and he intended to extend the association, for he had already begun to write "Old Times on the Mississippi," which would appear in the *Atlantic* in seven installments beginning in January 1875.

When Howells reviewed *Mark Twain's Sketches, New and Old* (1875), he identified "A True Story" as the best piece in the collection (perfect in the "rugged truth" it conveyed), but he lamented that most of the notices of the story saw it as yet another humorous sketch. Howells firmly corrected this misapprehension, but more generally, he also detected in the volume as a whole "a growing sense of seriousness of meaning in the apparently unmoralized drolling, which must result from the humorist's second thought of political and social absurdities."[32] This observation was no doubt gratifying to Twain, and he apparently associated Howells's perceptiveness with the readers of the magazine he edited. In a letter to Howells dated December 8, 1874, Twain noted his responsive attraction to the *Atlantic* audience: "It isn't the Atlantic audience that distresses me; for *it* is the only audience that I sit down before in perfect serenity (for the simple reason that it don't require a 'humorist' to paint himself stripèd & stand on his head every fifteen minutes)" (*MTHL* I, 49).

This remark is all the more poignant when one remembers that not long after that letter, Twain wrote the first of his three domestic farces about the McWilliams family, each story picturing a man going through just these sorts of antics. "Experience of the McWilliamses with Membranous Croup" was first published in *Sketches, New and Old*. Twain wrote two other McWilliams sketches a few years later—"Mrs. McWilliams and the Lightning" was published in the *Atlantic Monthly* for September 1880, and "The McWilliamses and the Burglar Alarm" appeared in a Christmas supplement to *Harper's Monthly Magazine* in 1882. All three stories are built upon the same dramatic situation: Mortimer McWilliams, a New York gentleman, falls into conversation with Twain, and sooner or later, the subject turns to the narration of a recent domestic episode. Mrs. McWilliams is a fearful woman—fearful that their children may come down with the croup, that lightning will enter the bedroom and strike them dead, or that the house will be invaded by burglars. Mr. McWilliams is an accommodating husband who cannot reason with his wife; he cannot convince her that their daughter should not chew a pine stick, that Mrs. McWilliams needn't hide in the closet during a thunderstorm, or that a burglar alarm is not a wise investment.

Slight in themselves, the stories seem somehow to replicate and comment upon the Clemens's own domestic situation, though critics divide over the significance of the sketches. Some see the pieces as proof of Twain's submission to a bourgeois, genteel culture and of his emasculation at the hands of Olivia. Others find the tales a sly form of revenge for daily household concessions to a largely irrational, or at least fussy, domestic routine. Howells, on the other hand, thought the stories were representative, "a bit of *genre* romance which must be read like an abuse of confidence to every husband and father."[33] In any event, the McWilliams stories prefigure Thurber's more accomplished, but also more aggressive, comic pictures of the battle between the sexes. Mrs. McWilliams may be a fretful woman, and in the eyes of her husband an irrational one, but Mr. McWilliams is a buffoon. His conversations with "Mr. Twain" serve as both mild complaint and parodic confession.

In "Mrs. McWilliams and the Lightning," Mortimer announces that "fear of lightning is one of the most distressing infirmities a human being can be afflicted with" and that this fear is "mostly confined to women." He prepares us for his domestic tale of woe by adding that a woman's "fright is something pitiful to see" (*CTS* I, 753). In point of fact, however, we do not see Mrs. McWilliams at all; when the booming starts (presumably from lightning, though it turns out to be cannon fire), she hides in the boot closet and stays there. What we do see instead is Mr. McWilliams making ridiculous accommodations to her worry. In a series of negatives, she advises him from the closet in the customary precautions against lightning—don't stay in the bed; don't light a match; don't stand in front of the fireplace or the window; don't wear wool or turn on the water. And in a series of prescriptions she attempts to secure his well-being against the lightning—do shut up the cat; do stand on a chair in the middle of the room; put the legs of the chair in glass tumblers; put on your fireman's helmet and your saber and spurs; and ring the dinner bell with all your might. The ringing brings several men in the neighborhood, who throw open the shutters and see Mr. McWilliams in nightshirt and helmet standing on the chair ringing his bell. Two of the men die laughing.

Because McWilliams is such a preposterous sight, it is difficult to see how this tale functions as a piece of revenge upon Twain's wife. Because McWilliams's behavior and dress are so far from being buttoned up and proper, it is difficult to imagine how the picture suggests submission to Victorian mores. Howells was surely right. Twain gives us a privileged glimpse into the absurd circus of domestic life, and his "abuse of confidence" of all husbands and fathers who, of their own free will, have been similarly compromised consists in his so thoroughly painting the husband as the clown.

The growing sense of moral "seriousness" Howells discerned in Twain's fiction does not apply to the McWilliams sketches, but it does to a tale he wrote in January 1876 and published in the *Atlantic Monthly* the following June. "The Facts Concerning the Recent Carnival of Crime in Connecticut" was, from the beginning, designed to make a serious point. Twain prepared the story for presentation to fellow members of the Monday Evening Club, a group of some 20 notable citizens of Hartford. His previous contributions to this discussion group were relatively proper productions, but with this story, Twain meant to examine "an exasperating metaphysical question . . . in the disguise of a literary extravaganza."[34] The question itself had to do with the nature and function of conscience, and the metaphysical quality of the piece derived in large part from Twain's recent reading of W. E. H. Lecky's *History of European Morals from Augustine to Charlemagne* (1869).

Lecky's book would exert a lifelong, though somewhat contradictory, influence upon Twain, who wrestled with and commented upon the book's argument in the margins of his copy. Lecky had divided the history of morals into two opposing camps—the intuitionists and the utilitarians. He advocated the intuitionist view that one's sense of good and evil is innate and harshly criticized the utilitarian position that denied an innate moral sense and argued instead that one's feelings and actions depend on the degree to which they contribute to individual happiness. Twain was deeply ambivalent about Lecky's argument. On the whole, Twain leaned toward the utilitarian view, increasingly so in his later years, but seemed to agree with Lecky's view of conscience.

Howard Baetzhold observes that "A Carnival of Crime" "parallels Lecky's discussion almost exactly." Baetzhold nicely summarizes Lecky's position:

> Conscience is more often a source of pain than of pleasure, and if happiness is actually the sole end of life, then one should learn to disregard the proddings of conscience. If a man forms an association of ideas that inflicts more pain than it prevents, or prevents more pleasure than it affords, the reasonable course would be to dissolve that association or destroy the habit. . . . Therefore, a man who possessed such a temperament would be happier if he were to "quench that conscientious feeling, which . . . prevents him from pursuing the course that would be most conducive to his tranquility."[35]

Twain's wry and antic story of a man who would kill (or "quench") his conscience was largely founded on Lecky's sardonic extension of the utilitarian argument, and the author's reading of the tale was duly appreciated by the Monday Evening Club. Joseph Twichell recorded in his journal the same night he heard the story that the piece was "serious in its intent though vastly funny and splendidly, brilliantly read." A few years later, Howells paid Twain a greater compliment in the pages of the *Century Magazine,* writing that the story "ought to have won popular recognition of the ethical intelligence underlying his humor. . . . Hawthorne or Bunyan might have been proud to imagine that powerful allegory."[36]

The story is the work of a passionate and acute ethical intelligence, of course, but one should not overrate its philosophical heft. As a philosopher, Twain would have made a good third baseman; as a metaphysician, a first-rate pastry chef. When Twain identified the metaphysical question of conscience as "exasperating," he was registering his own annoyance with a nagging sense of guilt that had dogged him all his life—for he was temperamentally disposed to feel remorse and, sometimes, to claim responsibility for events he could not possibly have controlled or prevented. When Twain confessed that the question was disguised as a "literary extravaganza," he was reaffirming a humorist's customary allegiance to hyperbole and incongruity, however grotesque a turn the tale might take, not so much to make light of a serious matter as to make its painful gravity endurable.

The "Carnival of Crime" begins and ends in calm and blessed joy. For this reason, it is unlikely that this tale represents, as some critics have claimed, either a rebellion against an oppressive superego or an exorcism of an inherited Puritan past. The story opens with the narrator lighting a cigar, feeling "blithe, almost jocund" (*CTS* I, 644). Ever since the narrator has become immune to his Aunt Mary's nagging, particularly about his smoking, "the one alloy that was able to mar my enjoyment of my aunt's society was gone" and her visits have become a "tranquil satisfaction" (*CTS* I, 644). Conscience in the form of external influence, symbolized by the aunt, has already been defeated before the story ever begins, but the narrator's lies to tramps and budding authors still trouble him a bit. Unlike Aunt Mary, the mossy and ill-formed dwarf who appears, as if summoned by the casual claim that Twain is willing to right any wrong committed against his worst enemy, is an internal agent whose perverse business is to torture the narrator for no other purpose than the satisfaction of it.

Through a series of cagey maneuvers, the narrator manages to kill this figure, this "dim suggestion of a burlesque upon me, a caricature of me in little" (*CTS* I, 645). The dwarf is, of course, the narrator's conscience, and the death of the little man brings "Bliss, unalloyed bliss" (*CTS* I, 660), though his contentment is rather different from the earlier tranquil satisfaction. The difference between these two states of happiness has little to do with any profound distinction Twain was trying to make between an intuitionist's or a utilitarian's view of conscience. This brassy dwarf does not appear as a recognizable moral sense in any of the manifold shapes it might take—a Quaker inner light, a Calvinistic reminder of innate depravity, a Poesque imp of the perverse, or a transcendentally rational categorical imperative. Instead, the dwarf is a nuisance and a trial.

The conscience, Twain seems to be saying, checks our basest impulses by making us agonize and worry but not by mending our flawed human nature, and the toll it takes is worn on the face and experienced in the vitals. The narrator observes that once he had destroyed his conscience, he was free to indulge in his grotesque and whimsical carnival of crime. Since that day, he has been on a delicious rampage. "I killed thirty-eight persons during the first two weeks.... I burned a dwelling that interrupted my view. I swindled a widow and some orphans out of their last cow.... I have also committed scores of crimes of various kinds, and have enjoyed my work exceedingly, whereas it would have formerly broken my heart and turned my hair gray, I have no doubt" (*CTS* I, 660).

Although the social consequences of loosing a man without a conscience upon the world are both funny and disturbing, Twain betrays little interest in determining the ontological nature of conscience or its spiritual function. The middle part of the story is an interrogation of the repulsive figure, but if the story poses a metaphysical question, the answer remains a surly and grotesque mystery. The narrator is "suffering" to ask his conscience some questions, and he does: Having at last appeared before me, how long will you be visible to me? "Always!" Why can't a conscience punish a man just once for an offense and then let him alone? "Well, *we* like it; that suffices." Do your continual tortures indicate an "honest intent" to improve me? We are "disinterested agents," and we torture you because it is business. "It is our trade." Is there any way to appease the "malignant invention" that goes by the name of conscience? "Well, none that I propose to tell *you*, my son" (*CTS* I, 652–54). The relation between the narrator and his conscience is identified as one between a slave and a master, and the dwarf's proud mastery is as cryptic, dismissive, and tyrannically cruel as he pleases it to be.

"The Facts Concerning the Recent Carnival of Crime in Connecticut" is not really a metaphysical inquiry at all. And as autobiographical as the story sometimes is, it is not solely expressive of Twain's feelings of restraint and regret. Most of the narrator's concerns have to do with comparative judgments. He accepts the information that Robinson and Smith's consciences are taller and more comely than the hideous dwarf that represents the narrator's conscience, and he is willing to believe that his Aunt Mary's conscience "lives in the open air altogether, because no door is large enough to admit her" (*CTS* I, 657). But he is gratified to know that Hugh Thompson's conscience is a small, misshapen figure who sleeps in a cigar box and is absolutely delighted to find out that the conscience of a publisher who once cheated him was put on exhibit under a powerful microscope, though the curious still could not see him.

In other words, the narrator is primarily motivated by a local sense of self-esteem; he measures himself against his neighbors and relatives. His place within the great chain of consciences is a middling one, with a few below him and several above him. The real tyranny of conscience, however, is that he will forever be equally reminded of past sins alongside courteous lies and forgivable misjudgments, for a conscience seems to have no sense of proportion. "Every sentence was an accusation, and every accusation a truth," he recalls. "Every clause was freighted with sarcasm and derision, every slow-dropping word burned like vitriol" (*CTS* I, 648). Nothing so exasperates the narrator, however, as the awful prospect that the dwarf will continually remind him of himself. The dwarf's pertinacity makes the narrator indignant because it is an "exaggeration of conduct which I myself had sometimes been guilty of in my intercourse with familiar friends" (*CTS* I, 645). His language was "hardly an exaggeration of some that I have uttered in my day." And most disconcerting of all, the dwarf's ready accusations are, and henceforth will ever be, "delivered in a tone of voice and with an exasperating drawl that had the seeming of a deliberate travesty of my style" (*CTS* I, 646).

Here in germ is the basis for Twain's later philosophizing in such pieces as "Corn Pone Opinions" (1901) and *What Is Man?* (1906). In "Corn Pone Opinions," for example, he locates the universal impulse to conform in the "inborn requirement of Self-Approval" (*CTS* II, 508), but the source of one's self-esteem always comes from the outside, from the approval of other people. However, it would be a mistake to view the "Carnival of Crime" as a prolegomenon to the fiction belonging to Twain's darker and more cynical period. The story might more accurately be described as an apologia for the humorist as citizen and moralist. As we have already seen, Clemens often had Twain play the fool and absorb the first wave of laughter and contempt in order to win over his readers and thereby more forcibly laugh the sin, if not the sinner, out of court. This tendency in his short fiction may or may not dramatize his own self-loathing, but it surely figures as one of his redeeming and most effective comic strategies.

When he delivered this piece before the Monday Evening Club, Twain deliberately engaged in a form of self-mockery and self-accusation that included a satire of the very drawl that club members were hearing as he read the tale. He intentionally made himself foolish and vulnerable in this story, but the dwarf wields the same weapons that the humorist keeps in his arsenal—burlesque, satire, exaggeration, and caricature. The dwarf of conscience merely holds up the altered and grotesque image of the man and makes his shortcomings comically obvious, but the grotesqueness is not of the dwarf's making. Moreover, although the dwarf is invisible to everyone but the narrator, his being and conduct are implicated in the social order. Insofar as the narrator's conscience works in concert with other consciences to harass their victims, and because Twain's conscience has become misshapen according to his own diminished conduct in a world of living men and women, this comedy of conscience is rooted in a social community. As a citizen, Samuel Clemens accepted his part in that community and took a vital, if sometimes haphazard and eccentric, interest in the laws, policies, and attitudes that regulate the national life. As a humorist, however, he was much like the dwarf, a disinterested agent who merely exaggerates existing transgressions and absurdities in order to make us see them more clearly and feel them more completely.

Twain's ethical intelligence underlying the humor on display in this story and others is neither self-righteous nor condescending. Nor does it respect class or condition. Samuel Clemens might hobnob with Hartford's elite, he might even pick up the tab, but the source of his humor, and his morality too, was distinctly plebeian. Enclosed within his Hartford circle, the humorist as moralist had no choice but to bore from within, to appear at once as scapegrace and scapegoat, but not as martyr. Before Howells dramatized his notion of "moral complicity" in his novels *The Minister's Charge* (1887) and *A Hazard of New Fortunes* (1890), Twain had expressed in the coordinated strategies of his humor a willingness to play the fool and to serve as the compromised accomplice to a nation's transgressions and folly. He freely acknowledged his guilty place in the social order, even though the social order had fixed him as a mere humorist. But he was proud, too, and that pride was most eloquent in his sly insistence that like Aunt Rachel, despite appearances, he was not simply jolly but serious too, not exceptional but representative. Publicly, Twain was willing to play the part of an ass, for virtue's sake; privately, he might console himself with the pert observation of a dwarf—"I am not an ass; I am only the saddle of an ass" (*CTS* I, 654).

For the next few years, Twain was preoccupied with a number of projects. He began "Huck Finn's Autobiography" in the summer of 1876 and would work on it intermittently for the next seven years; he collaborated with Bret Harte on the play *Ah Sin* (1877) and began work on *A Tramp Abroad* (1880) and *The Prince and the Pauper* (1882). Although Twain wrote a few short stories during this period, they are notable more for the patent absurdity of their conception than for the merit of their execution. "The Canvasser's Tale" was published in the *Atlantic Monthly* for December 1876. It tells of a man who encourages his uncle in the European custom of collecting "*objets de vertu.*" The uncle successively collects cowbells, brickbats, primeval tools, Aztec inscriptions, and stuffed whales but fails each time to corner the market. At last he determines to acquire a complete set of echoes and squanders the family fortune as a result.

Twain and Charles Dudley Warner had named their times "the gilded age," but this satire of material acquisitiveness is better described by Thorstein Veblen's phrase in *The Theory of the Leisure Class* (1899)—"conspicuous consumption." The theme of "The Canvasser's Tale" was a potent one at any rate. In *The Portrait of a Lady*, Henry James achieved in his Europeanized American and fastidious collector, Gilbert Osmond, a disturbing picture of cold and egoistical cruelty; and in *McTeague*, Frank Norris's depiction of the misers Trina and Zerkow suggests an erotic and fearful obsession, even madness. But Twain's treatment of the subject is genial and ordinary. The "sad-eyed" nephew who must pay for his uncle's indiscretions has become just another canvasser trying to sell intangible trifles.

Two years later, Twain concocted a romantic tale he called "The Loves of Alonzo Fitz Clarence and Rosannah Ethelton" and this time made the lovers themselves intangibles. Alonzo Fitz Clarence, on the telephone with his aunt, hears in the background a young woman singing "In the Sweet By-and-By" and falls in love with the voice. A telephonic courtship of some duration follows, and the romance is complicated by the deceitful intervention of Sidney Algernon Burley, the vile suitor for Rosannah's hand. Burley's plot is spoiled, and the couple is married over the telephone—Rosannah in Hawaii and Alonzo in New York. A few weeks after the marriage, the couple is brought together for the first time. The tale is overlong, and the essential joke of the story is repeated throughout. Clearly, Twain enjoyed the story more than his readers ever will, though a generation familiar with the encouragement of telephone companies to "reach out and touch someone" and with the resources of Internet romance, computer dating, and 900 numbers may be more responsive to the story's comedy than I am.

Twain was both fascinated by and skeptical of improvements, technological and other. In 1879, he installed a telephone in his home, but he also wrote "A Telephonic Conversation," a brief domestic farce about hearing only one side of a conversation. Years later, in *A Connecticut Yankee in King Arthur's Court* (1889), he would import all manner of technological improvements (bicycles, telephones, newspapers, soap, and gunpowder) to Camelot and derive a lot of comedy from the incongruities. But Hank Morgan imported democratic reforms as well, and those sorts of improvements and their unlooked-for consequences were predicted in another story Twain wrote in 1879, "The Great Revolution in Pitcairn." In that tale, an American named Butterworth, a visitor to the tranquil and primitive British colony of Pitcairn, sows the seeds of discontent in the community, and before long the total population of 90 citizens has divided into factions. But division is merely the preliminary to his cry for "unification" and independence. Butterworth becomes emperor, randomly passes out titles of nobility, and establishes an army and a navy. Soon a community that had previously had no currency at all is saddled with taxes and a national debt. The people revolt. They hoist the British flag and reject political independence, preferring the mild yoke of colonial indifference to the urgent and debilitating reforms of social improvement and political autonomy.

In 1880, Twain published three short stories. "Edward Mills and George Benton: A Tale" was published in the *Atlantic Monthly* for August 1880. "The Man Who Put Up at Gadsby's" and "Jim Baker's Blue Jay Yarn" first appeared in *A Tramp Abroad* (1880). The first two stories extended themes Twain had explored before, but the blue jay yarn signaled a return to the frontier qualities and the creative verve that had made the jumping frog tale a miniature classic.

"Edward Mills and George Benton" is another good little boy/bad little boy story, though in this instance Twain followed the lives of his characters beyond boyhood into maturity and eventually to the grave. Edward and George are distant cousins who are brought up as foster brothers by a childless couple, the Brants. The boys' upbringing in godly virtue may be summarized by the advice the Brants repeatedly give: "Be pure, honest, sober, industrious, and considerate of others, and success in life is assured" (*CTS* I, 747). Edward lives out this creed with pious devotion; George, however, resists it to the last. The doting couple, and eventually the community at large, leave Edward unassisted in his virtue because godliness seems to be his "natural bent" (*CTS* I, 748). George receives special consideration and dispensation his whole life; he gets more candy and swimming and berrying than his brother, and when the Brants die, George receives their estate because he "needs" it, whereas Edward can rely upon "bountiful Providence" to provide for him.

Providence seems to have a perverse sense of humor, however. The woman who loves Edward throws him over so that she might "reform" poor George. Edward marries another woman, and George abuses his wife and child. Edward is a dutiful husband and businessman; George is a tippler and a gambler. Edward honors his foster parents' wish that he take care of his brother and enters into a business partnership with him, but George's gambling ruins the enterprise. Edward becomes a social disgrace, but George is taken out of the gutter by members of a temperance organization and given a good situation. George backslides continually, and each time, he is rescued with hand-wringing popular acclaim. He is sent to prison for forgery, but the Prisoner's Friend Society obtains a pardon for him and a job with a good salary. Meantime Edward has steadfastly earned his way in the world and has become a cashier in a bank. When he refuses to reveal the combination to the safe, burglars kill him. The chief criminal, it turns out, is George. Edward Mills's family is left penniless; George is sentenced to be hanged. Widows, orphans, and "tearful young girls" plea for a reprieve, but "for once" the governor will not yield. George is executed. Mourners place flowers by his headstone, which reads, "He has fought the good fight." Edward's unkempt grave bears this epitaph: "Be pure, honest, sober, industrious, considerate, and you will never—." People puzzle over the incomplete inscription and pity Edward's widow. She receives no pension or aid, but "a lot of appreciative people . . . have collected forty-two thousand dollars—and built a Memorial Church with it" (*CTS* I, 752).

"Edward Mills and George Benton" registers unmistakably Twain's disgust with sentimental reformers who lavish money and attention on the profligate and unworthy while the modest and virtuous must fend for themselves. He had already written the episode about Judge Thatcher's failed attempts to reform Pap in chapter 5 of *Huckleberry Finn* and was once again ridiculing a misplaced sympathy that served no social purpose other than to advertise the reformer's self-satisfied Christian charity. Clearly, Twain was looking back to a simpler form of justice and retribution he had seen in Ned Blakely and had dramatized in "A Trial." He expressed the same desire for simplicity and his impatience with complicated bureaucratic process in "The Man Who Put Up at Gadsby's." In that tale, Twain recalls a conversation he had one wintry night in Washington with his "odd friend" Riley. They are interrupted by Mr. Lykins, who has traveled from California in order to secure the San Francisco postmastership. Lykins wants Riley to help him push the appointment through Congress right away, for as Lykins says, "I ain't the talking kind, I'm the *doing* kind" (*TA*, 264). Riley is amused by the man's spunk and decides to tell him the story of a man from Tennessee who, in 1834, came up to Washington to collect on a minor claim against the government.

This Tennessee man also wanted to conduct business promptly and get back home, but perceiving that there would be some delay, he put up at local hotel, Gadsby's. In a matter of months, he had sold all he owned for the sake of that small claim; 30 years later, the man is still in Washington and still anxious to settle and get back to Tennessee. Lykins fails to perceive the relevance of this tale and finds it rather long and pointless to be told on a snowy street corner. Riley slyly brings the sum and substance of his little parable home: "O, there isn't any particular point to it. Only, if you are not in *too* much of a hurry to rush off to San Francisco with that post-office appointment, Mr. Lykins, I'd advise you to '*put up at Gadsby's*' for a spell, and take it easy" (*TA*, 270–71). Lykins never gets Riley's parable, but then, he never gets the post office appointment either.

"The Man Who Put Up at Gadsby's" bears a resemblance in theme and tone to "The Facts in the Case of the Great Beef Contract" and "The Facts in the Great Landslide Case"; indeed, an earlier version of the sketch was written about the same time as those stories, in 1868, and published in the *Territorial Enterprise*. Twain rewrote and expanded this piece and interpolated it into *A Tramp Abroad*, a book about his travels in Switzerland, Germany, and Italy. In the context of that book, the immediate appropriateness of the sketch is the narrator's amused observation of Swiss fishermen lining the banks of a lake in front of his hotel. After waiting a good while to see a fish caught, the narrator concludes "that the man who proposes to tarry till he sees somebody hook one of those well-fed and experienced fishes will find it wisdom to 'put up at Gadsby's' and take it easy' " (*TA*, 271). However, this reworked story participates in the same sort of emotional state that seems to have prompted the creation of another tale interpolated into *A Tramp Abroad* and widely regarded as one of Twain's finest stories, "Jim Baker's Blue Jay Yarn."

In order to fully appreciate both stories, we must back up a bit. Riley is a cagey storyteller, but Twain regards his friend as a bit "odd," and Lykins is too self-absorbed and obtuse to see the point of the story at all. As a storyteller, Riley is profoundly misunderstood, but then Twain himself had been in a similar position when he delivered his notorious "Whittier Birthday Speech" on December 17, 1877. Howells had arranged for Clemens to make an after-dinner speech on the occasion of John Greenleaf Whittier's 70th birthday, in the presence of Boston's literary elite. This speech, about Twain trying out the virtue of his nom de plume on a lonely California miner, was an amusing and gracious way of affirming the humorist's pleasure, and his right, to be in the presence of New England's literary worthies.

The miner is unimpressed by Twain's credentials, for he is the fourth literary fellow to visit the miner in 24 hours. The night before, three men on their way to Yosemite and claiming to be Emerson, Longfellow, and Oliver Wendell Holmes had imposed upon the man's hospitality. Emerson was a "seedy little bit of a chap," the miner recalled, Longfellow was built like a "prizefighter," and Holmes was "fat as a balloon." The men had been drinking and were disposed to quote (or misquote) lines of verse. They ate the miner's food, drank his whiskey, and in the end, stole his boots. The miner confesses that he "ain't suited to a littery atmosphere" and means to move away from there. Twain assures the man that those three intruders were imposters; the miner eyes him and replies, "Ah—imposters, were they?—are *you?*" (*CTS* I, 699). The comedy of this exquisite little speech, as Twain and Howells somewhat inaccurately remembered it, was largely lost on the dinner guests, who remained quizzically and courteously silent.[37]

Howells thought the speech a "hideous mistake," a "fatality," an offense that might eventually be repaired but carrying with it a shame that could not be outlived. Critical newspaper notices seemed to confirm Howells's perception. Twain was humiliated by the event and, at Howells's urging, wrote notes of apology to Longfellow, Emerson, and Holmes, protesting the innocence of his intent and at the same time describing himself as a heedless "savage." No mossy dwarf of conscience could have shamed Twain as much that unfortunate occasion. On December 23, Twain wrote to Howells, "My sense of disgrace does not abate. It grows. I see that it is going to add itself to my list of permanencies—a list of humiliations that extends back to when I was seven years old, & which keep on persecuting me regardless of my repentancies" (*MTHL* I, 212). Twain even offered to withdraw his story of the telephone romance between Alonzo Fitz Clarence and Rosannah Ethelton, scheduled for publication in the *Atlantic Monthly*, and concluded that it "will be best that I retire from before the public at present." In fact, Twain did retire from the scene. Though he had planned the trip beforehand, when he took his family to Germany the next April, the journey had the quality of guilty escape.

Quite apart from any exaggerated sense of impropriety, however, the "Whittier Birthday Speech" must have contributed to Twain's sense of confusion about literary respectability and his proper audience. Since the publication of "A True Story," he had published 16 pieces in the prestigious *Atlantic Monthly*. In 1876, he had also written *[Date 1601] Conversation, As It Was by the Social Fireside, in the Time of the Tudors* in the form of a letter to his friend and Hartford pastor, Joseph Twichell. Twain knew well enough that this ribald story of profanity and flatulence in Queen Elizabeth's court was vulgar; in his "Autobiography," he recalled that he put into the mouths of these august figures "grossnesses not to be found outside Rabelais."[38] Twain never sought to publish *1601*, but it was read and circulated privately, and he knew that the piece was a hit among respectable New England gentlemen.

The next year, again indulging the coarser side of his fancy, Twain wrote up a little tale that Twichell had told him when they traveled to Bermuda. This piece was meant for publication but would not see print until five years later. Twain had published in the *Atlantic* "Some Rambling Notes of an Idle Excursion" in a four-part series beginning in October 1877, but Howells had advised that Twain exclude "The Invalid's Story" from this contribution because it was indelicate. Later, Howells recommended that he remove it from *A Tramp Abroad*. Twain continued to like the piece, however, and he included it in his collection *The Stolen White Elephant, Etc.* (1882). It is true that this tale of a man accompanying what he takes to be a casket containing a dead friend (actually, due to a mix-up at the train station, he is tending a crate of guns) is crude. The crate has been placed beside a carton of Limburger cheese, and the narrator and the baggage man mistake the ripeness of the cheese for the putrefaction of his friend. Twain gets some good scatological fun out of the mistake, and the tale is notable for the vigorous slang of the baggage man.

The mountain of genteel respectability had not come to Mark Twain, so Mark Twain had gone to the mountain. He had tried to adjust to life in New England and to the requirements of his literary fame, but he seemed to be getting mixed signals. He may well have had a rather contradictory sense of what would play in the parlor for mixed company, as opposed to in the smoking room. He knew that a reader's expectations in Virginia City differed from those in Hartford or Boston, but the difference was hard to define. He knew as well that his popularity seemed to rest on his western point of view, while his reputation as a serious writer depended on other, and presumably higher, considerations. That a Connecticut pastor who had an earthy sense of humor might tell him a story unsuitable for the *Atlantic* was surely perplexing. Henry Nash Smith admirably summarizes the author's predicament: "The confusion of tastes and attitudes in nineteenth-century American culture made it impossible for Mark Twain to arrive at a workable idea of his vocation. If he hoped to be accepted as a serious writer, he was apparently obliged to conform to the priestly role of the man of letters. If he devoted himself to humor he must be content with the humble function of providing comic relief from higher concerns. The program of the Whittier dinner was virtually a pageant translating his problem into quasi-dramatic terms."[39]

The failure of the Whittier speech only exacerbated Twain's sense of confusion and frustration. He may have rightly concluded that if a man wants his due from a coterie of Boston Brahmins, he may as well " 'put up at Gadsby's' and take it easy." But it was difficult for a proud and self-conscious man to take it easy. His performance that December night seemed to haunt him with uncertainty; many years later, in 1906, he inspected the speech once again and concluded that it "hasn't a defect in it. . . . It is smart; it is saturated with humor. There isn't a suggestion of coarseness or vulgarity in it anywhere." But a few days later, he reversed himself: "I find it gross, coarse . . . I didn't like any part of it, from the beginning to the end." A few days after that unequivocal judgment, he reversed his opinion yet again.[40]

Whether we locate this confusion of taste and attitude in nineteenth-century culture or in Twain himself hardly matters, but as we will see in the final chapter, the literary persona that in the early days had allowed him to speak with an original and authentic voice had itself become the problem, not the solution. Quite apart from the vocational difficulty Twain faced, Clemens's dignity had been compromised, or so he thought, and he indulged in a muted form of revenge when he came to write "Jim Baker's Blue Jay Yarn."

Twain prepares the reader of *A Tramp Abroad* for the blue jay yarn with marvelous grace and facility. He recalls that he had been reading deeply in German legends and fairy tales, and when he got lost in the Neckar forest outside of Heidelburg, he "fell into a train of dreamy thought about animals which talk" and other "legendary stuff" (*TA*, 31). Through vagrant thoughts and imaginings, he adopts the "right mood to enjoy the supernatural" (*TA*, 32), and at that moment, a raven appears and seems to be inspecting him. Twain's meditative mood suddenly turns to humiliation and anger: "I felt something of the same sense of humiliation and injury which one feels when he finds that a human stranger has been clandestinely inspecting him in his privacy and mentally commenting upon him" (*TA*, 32). Soon, another raven joins in the scrutiny, and the narrator becomes more and more embarrassed. They seem to rain insults down on him—"What a hat!" "O, pull down your vest!"—and that sort of thing "hurts you and humiliates you, and there is no getting around it with fine reasoning and pretty arguments" (*TA*, 35).

The ostensible purpose of these introductory paragraphs is to serve as a transition into the blue jay story. Twain's experience in the forest reminds him that animals do indeed talk and that the only man he ever knew who could understand them was Jim Baker. This bridging device is simple and effective. However, in the course of those few pages, Twain has also recapitulated the sort of shame he felt in the aftermath of the Whittier birthday speech.

Unlike the roles he had his persona sometimes play, the Mark Twain who is insulted and humiliated here is truly innocent. He has committed no crimes, domestic or civil; he has made no thoughtless blunders. Instead, his embarrassment is the result of being too minutely inspected, as though by naturalists who have discovered a new kind of bug. He has merely wandered into alien territory and been found to be a curiosity by a few pesky ravens who ridicule his hat and vest and ask, "Well, what do *you* want here?" (*TA*, 32).

The story that follows is one of Twain's finest tall tales, and Walter Blair rightly describes it, with *Huckleberry Finn*, as the author's "other masterpiece."[41] The story is remarkable, at any rate, for the apparent ease with which Twain returned to the idiom and a freedom of view he had practiced 15 years earlier, and the story is in fact among those he had heard Jim Gillis tell in Calaveras County. Like Simon Wheeler and Jim Blaine and other of Twain's vernacular narrators, Jim Baker is a "simple-hearted" fellow, but he is neither abstracted nor tipsy, and he does not speak in a monotone. Instead, he knows blue jays, and he has passionate convictions about them: "whatever a blue-jay feels, he can put into language. And no mere commonplace language, either, but rattling, out-and-out book-talk—and bristling with metaphor, too—just bristling!" (*TA*, 36). Cats use good grammar, it is true, but they are excitable creatures and in a fight use grammar that would give a person "lockjaw." When blue jays use bad grammar, they are ashamed of themselves. Cats can swear, of course, but not like a blue jay. A jay can swear and scold and laugh and cry and gossip and reason and plan. What is more, a blue jay has a sense of humor: "a jay knows when he is an ass just as well as you do—maybe better. If a jay ain't human, he better take in his sign, that's all" (*TA*, 37).

This brag on behalf of blue jays requires some proof, and Jim Baker immediately begins to tell "a true fact" about some blue jays. The story is simple enough: A blue jay finds a hole in the roof of an abandoned cabin next to the miner's. He tries to fill up the hole with acorns and gets mighty mad in the process. A fellow jay comes along to see what all the cussing is about, and then another, and another. A last the mystery is discovered, and every jay in the neighborhood falls to laughing over the fact that the first jay had tried to fill up a whole house with acorns. But the manner of Jim Baker's telling is a masterful blend of awe and insistent conviction.

That animals can talk is not to be doubted; that is the incontrovertible premise of the beast fable. Baker's story is as eloquent as a jay's, and just bristling with metaphor: When the blue jay spies the hole, he shuts one eye and peers into it "like a 'possum looking down a jug," he gives a "wink or two" with his wings, his smile fades away "like breath off'n a razor," he works so hard at filling the hole that he is "sweating like an ice-pitcher," and so many blue jays come around to see what the trouble is that "the whole region 'peared to have a blue flush about it" (*TA*, 38–41). As Howells observed of Twain, as a writer, he was a slave to the concrete detail. These metaphors are not merely bristling, they are a brilliant fusion of minute observation and fantastic conception, and their accuracy lends an air of credibility to the absurd tale he tells.

In only a few pages, Twain gives us the luxurious feeling of relaxed recollection, but the tale itself is neither aimless nor wandering and is remarkable for its compactness. The yarn is meant to corroborate Baker's steadfast beliefs about animals in general, and blue jays in particular. Blue jays can reason, he insists, and Baker's jay does just that. After scrutinizing the hole, the jay arrives at a syllogism: "It looks like a hole, it's located like a hole,—blamed if I don't believe it *is* a hole" (*TA*, 38). Blue jays can ponder and plan: "must be a mighty long hole; however, I ain't got no time to fool around here, I got to 'tend to business; I reckon it's all right—chance it, anyway." A blue jay can curse: "Then he began to get mad. . . . his feelings got the upper hand of him presently, and he broke loose and cussed himself black in the face" (*TA*, 39). We know that a blue jay can gossip because it isn't long before every bird in the United States knows of that first jay's struggle with that hole. Perhaps most important, blue jays have a sense of humor, and each one takes a turn looking into the cabin floor strewn with acorns and nearly suffocates with laughter.

There are elements in the blue jay yarn that are reminiscent of the Whittier speech and the humiliation Twain felt afterward. In what amounts to a prologue to the tale, Twain records his undeserved feelings of injury occasioned by scoffing ravens, and we are left to imagine the embarrassment the blue jay feels at the hands of his fellow creatures. There are other parallels as well. Both take place near a lonely miner's cabin in California; both, though in rather different ways, dramatize the comedy of misjudgment and of being imposed upon; and both make telling references to visiting a natural wonder of the West. In the birthday speech, the three impostors are on their way to Yosemite and stop at the miner's cabin along the way. In the blue jay yarn, another visitor from the East stops by to see the legendary hole. Every bird in the country could see the point of the story of the jay and the hole "except an owl that come from Nova Scotia to visit the Yo Semite, and he took this thing in on his way back. He said he couldn't see anything funny in it. But then he was a good deal disappointed about Yo Semite, too" (*TA*, 42). A humorless owl from the East, equally unresponsive to the natural grandeur of Yosemite and local folklore and humor, is far more pathetic than an overeager jay who tries to fill a bottomless hole with acorns.

Comedians are perpetually vulnerable to those who will not or cannot see the point of their good-natured, if excessive, humor, but they typically have a ready rejoinder—"To hell with them if they can't take a joke." Twain managed to get something of that quality into his blue jay yarn, but it would be a mistake to see the story exclusively as disguised but bitter remonstrance. After all, at about the same time that he wrote this story, he confessed in a letter to Howells that he was having difficulty managing the satire he meant to get into *A Tramp Abroad*: "Of course a man can't write successful satire except he be in a calm judicial good-humor . . . in truth I don't ever seem to be in a good enough humor with ANYthing to *satirize* it" (*MTHL* I, 248–49). "Jim Baker's Blue Jay Yarn" is not exactly satire, but the story does show that the author was in good enough humor with the subject of the tale to draw upon his richest resources as a humorist.

And the story is masterful. In a brief space, Twain manages to move his beast fable from a mood of evocative enchantment to firm and eager conviction to full-fledged tall-tale humor. From the opening description of the German forest as possessing a certain twilight melancholy, one is led to expect something on the order of "Rip Van Winkle" or "The Legend of Sleepy Hollow." But Twain effortlessly shifts his scene and his tone from the comic Gothicism of an Irving to the straightforward and insistent claims of a lonely California miner. The question for Jim Baker is not whether under the magical influence of a forest reverie one might almost believe that animals can talk—"Animals talk to each other, of course. There can be no question about that" (*TA*, 36). Instead, the question is which sort of animal is the best talker, and this is the sort of question that may be resolved according to accepted rational criteria. Which animal is never at a loss for words? has the largest vocabulary? can take profanity to a new level of expression? uses the best grammar? has the most fluent delivery? The blue jay, of course. What is more, a blue jay has a full range of concerns and is subject to vacillations of thought and feeling that make his gifts not merely articulate but eloquent. However frustrated Twain might have been with writing *A Tramp Abroad*, he must have taken an exquisite pleasure in writing this story, and the reader who fails to respond to the infectious joy of the blue jay yarn ought to pass up Yosemite as well.

In addition to "The Man Who Put Up at Gadsby's" and "Jim Baker's Blue Jay Yarn," Twain originally intended to include in *A Tramp Abroad* "The Stolen White Elephant," but he changed his mind, and it appeared as the title story in a collection of sketches published in 1882. Twain was always tempted by burlesque, and this was one of the reasons he could never quite shake the reputation of funny fellow. This rollicking treatment of the incompetence of detectives was inspired by a recent and unusual kidnapping. The body of a wealthy New York merchant was stolen from a cemetery vault, and the robbers demanded $50,000 ransom. Newspapers avidly covered the case, reporting in sensational detail the failed efforts of police and detectives to recover the body.

The humor of Twain's tale, told by a Siamese gentleman, is largely topical and, though it retains much of its hilarity, seems somewhat dated now. The idea that the gift of a white elephant, bound from Siam to England as a means of "propitiating an enemy" (*CTS* I, 804), should be lost in Jersey City is amusing enough. So are the ridiculous efforts of Inspector Blunt and his crew of detectives to locate the beast. Perhaps of most lasting interest is Twain's shrewd understanding of the nature of public reputation. Blunt is a thinly disguised version of Alan Pinkerton, who established his national detective agency in 1850 and promoted its reputation through several detective novels based on the work of his operatives. Blunt is unflappable despite the comic misadventures of his investigators. He knows that incompetence is no obstacle to greatness;

one may be famous for being famous. He tells his client, the desperate Siamese gentleman, "As to the newspapers, we *must* keep in with them. Fame, reputation, constant public mention—these are the detective's bread and butter. . . . We must constantly show the public what we are doing, or they will believe we are doing nothing" (*CTS* I, 812). Due to Blunt's expensive strategies to retrieve the elephant, the Siamese gentleman loses his reputation and his fortune, but his continuing admiration for Blunt amounts to a form of idolatry. Since Twain himself had only recently decided to retire from the public eye for a while, this story of self-promotion has a certain poignancy about it.

Another story, "The Professor's Yarn," was also meant for *A Tramp Abroad* but was removed and would eventually appear in chapter 36 of *Life on the Mississippi* (1883). An early version of Karl Ritter's revenge story, usually reprinted as "A Dying Man's Confession," was probably composed at about the same time and may have been intended for inclusion in *A Tramp Abroad* as well; it would appear as chapters 31 and 32 of *Life on the Mississippi*. However, as Horst H. Kruse has shown, the Ritter story was so altered to fit into the narrative plan of the Mississippi book that to take the Ritter tale as a freestanding short story may be unwise.[42] "The Burning Brand" was certainly prepared for *Life on the Mississippi*, though it may have been written solely for the purpose of padding the book in order to meet the requirements of an agreement Twain had with his publisher; it appeared as chapter 52 of the volume.

None of these stories merit special commentary, nor does the story "A Curious Experience," which Twain published in the November 1881 issue of *Century Magazine*. It should be pointed out, however, that all of them deal, in greater or lesser degree, with mistaken identity. When one recalls that Twain's longer works during this period—*A Tramp Abroad*, *Life on the Mississippi*, *The Prince and the Pauper*, and, of course, *Huckleberry Finn*—also often deal in masquerade, deception, and misplaced sympathy, it becomes clear that mistaken identity was a preoccupation with Samuel Clemens, a.k.a. Mark Twain. As Everett Emerson has persuasively argued, Clemens wanted above all else to be "authentic," even if his authenticity appeared in the person of his nom de plume. However, at this time, the literary persona seemed to be fracturing; at least it seems to play no vital role in the short fiction that appeared below his name. During this period, there is often a distancing of the Twain persona who begins the tale from the story to be told. Sometimes, as in "A Dying Man's Confession" or in "The Professor's Yarn," the tale is told by a casual acquaintance, who may recur to an experience several decades old. Sometimes the stories, such as "A Curious Experience" or "The Burning Brand," are twice-told tales, more or less faithful accounts derived from earlier documents or published materials, and leave little room for the author's exuberant improvisations. In either case, Mark Twain as literary persona is not much of a player in the fiction, nor a vital part of the dramatic scene of its telling.

He had more than compensated for any loss of imaginative power invested in his literary persona, however, by cultivating in his longer works the art of ventriloquism. In *A Connecticut Yankee in King Arthur's Court* (1889), Mark Twain plays only a small role, preparing the stage for Hank Morgan's weird adventures in time travel. And in *Adventures of Huckleberry Finn* (1885), a novel the author had been working on since 1876, Twain is obliterated altogether. Evidently the author felt that his young hero required no testimonials from him about Huck's simple heart and no apologies for his untutored gifts as a storyteller. Huck simply declares in the opening paragraph that "Mr. Mark Twain" told some "stretchers" in *Tom Sawyer* and then launches into the narrative without further delay.

When Clemens decided to allow Huck Finn to tell his own story, Mark Twain humbly retreated into the background. For any number of reasons, Twain's identification with Huck was a strong one. Although Twain had little in common with this unwashed and illiterate boy, the author obviously envied Huck's innocent freedom and admired his self-sufficiency. He knew that Huck had a story to tell and that only Huck could tell it. When the novel was at last completed, however, Clemens made sure that his readers knew unmistakably that it was Mark Twain, not Huckleberry Finn, who wrote this novel—he inserted a heliotype of the Karl Gerhardt bust of himself as a frontispiece and provided both a "Notice" and an "Explanatory" by "The Author" that called attention to Twain as a deliberate artist and as the creator of the work. Mark Twain wished to preside over this novel without being particularly implicated in it; this is not a criticism (part of the genius of the novel derives from the author's invisibility), but it does say something about what Everett Emerson calls "the disappearance of Mark Twain."[43]

Eight years elapsed between the appearance of the three relatively uninspired stories in *Life on the Mississippi* and the publication of the story "Luck" in the August 1891 issue of *Harper's Magazine*. But we should not leave this period in Twain's career without mentioning a piece that, while not strictly speaking a work of fiction, benefited from his craft as a storyteller at the same time that it seemed to reinvent his literary persona. In May 1885, Robert Underwood Johnson, an editor for *Century Magazine*, requested that Twain contribute a piece to his "Battles and Leaders of the Civil War" series. The result was "The Private History of a Campaign That Failed," published in the *Century* the following December. Though this autobiographical reminiscence looks back to a period before Samuel Clemens adopted his nom de plume, it is signed "Mark Twain." There is even some reason to suppose that Clemens thought of his "war-paper" as a short story, for he later included it in his collection of short fiction, *Merry Tales* (1892).

Whether one considers it autobiography or fiction, "The Private History of a Campaign That Failed" is an exquisite piece of writing. Moreover, there are several departures from perpendicular fact (whether these are the result of a faulty memory, minor wish fulfillment, or conscious dramatic invention does not matter), and the whole bears the unmistakable impress of a shaping creative intelligence. This piece has a discernible resemblance to the recently published *Huckleberry Finn* in several different ways: Twain's record of his adventures in 1861 in the outfit of Confederate irregulars known as the Marion Rangers is spoken from the point of view of a social pariah, a deserter. Perhaps he and the countless other deserters like him who set out to do something but did not "ought not to be allowed much space among better people," but there must be some value to an account that may "explain the process by which they didn't do anything" (*CTS* I, 863).

That process is largely a mixture of moral and political confusion coupled with a boyish inclination to play the part of warriors only when it is convenient and appeals to their fancy. The action of the piece, as John Gerber observed, "is precisely the pattern which recurs repeatedly in *Huckleberry Finn.* . . . Huck gets into a series of scrapes of increasing complexity and annoyance until finally when matters reach a climax he can't stand any longer, he 'lights out.' "[44] Most of these soldiers conform to military observances only when they don't interfere with swimming, smoking, or fishing; and they are full of Tom Sawyeresque romantic pretension; one fellow goes so far as to change his name from the ordinary Peterson Dunlap to the majestic "Pierre d'Unlap."

They move in and around Marion County, retreating mostly, and face no greater danger to their "holiday" than an encounter with a few dogs. Much of "The Private History" is sheer burlesque, but Twain introduced an episode that was surely an invention but gave his story a moral center. The soldiers are nervous from hearing rumors that enemy troops are in the vicinity, and one night, a stranger rides close to their encampment in a barn. They fire upon the man, only to discover that he is unarmed and not in uniform. They watch him gasp out his dying breath. For Twain, at least, their campaign was "spoiled." The author's expressed feelings of guilt and remorse are vivid, but because in all likelihood there was no stranger and no killing, they are a powerful fiction posing as an autobiographical fact: "The thought of him got to preying upon me every night; I could not get rid of it. I could not drive it away, the taking of that unoffending life seemed such a wanton thing. And it seemed an epitome of war" (*CTS* I, 880).

The feeling of moral revulsion Twain describes here is precisely the sort he had dramatized several times in Huck Finn—in his witnessing the Boggs shooting, or the death of his friend Buck Grangerford, even the tarring of the king and the duke. In the character of Huckleberry Finn, Twain had created a boy who had "a sound heart and a deformed conscience," as he said. In "The Private History," Twain presented himself as the possessor of that heart and that conscience. As Huck had done so many times in the novel, Twain displays no overt contempt for a cruel and wicked world but criticizes himself for his failure to understand and function in that world: "My campaign was spoiled. It seemed to me that I was not rightly equipped for this awful business; that war was intended for men, and I for a child's nurse. I resolved to retire from this avocation of sham soldiership while I could save some remnant of my self-respect" (*CTS* I, 880). In this "war-paper," Twain was rewriting his own life according to the experience of another Missouri boy, Huck Finn, who did not seem to fit in.

Part of Twain's motive for writing "The Private History of a Campaign That Failed," however, had to do with criticisms made about his recent association with Ulysses S. Grant. Twain's newly formed publishing house had an agreement to publish the *Personal Memoirs of U. S. Grant.* In "The Private Campaign," Twain says that his outfit came within a few hours of encountering Grant at a time "when he was as unknown as I was myself" (*CTS* I, 882), but this was another fiction. Twain and Grant actually came within a few weeks of meeting each other, but no closer. By 1885, both men were not at all unknown, of course, and in a curious way, Twain is asserting his right to share with Grant a nation's esteem. Grant was a soldier, and his reputation rested upon his demonstrated military heroism. Twain was a humorist, but he wanted to be known as Howells knew him, as one with "an indignant sense of right and wrong" and an "ardent hate of meanness and injustice."[45] His war-paper was an attempt to justify himself on individual moral grounds at the same time that it recorded his avoidance of military duty.

After his brief experience as a soldier, Clemens, like Huck Finn, lighted out for the territory; it was in Nevada that Samuel Clemens became Mark Twain. By reinventing his own history in 1885 and presenting himself as someone who, in 1861, went West to avoid any further contamination of his virtue and to preserve his self-respect instead of to improve his own opportunities, Twain was reaffirming his identity as a serious writer who also happened to be funny. By defining his moral nature in terms that better applied to Huck Finn than Sam Clemens, and by locating this dramatic representation of himself at a point in his life just before he became a professional writer, Twain was somehow coloring the whole of his whole literary career.

After publishing "The Private History," Twain turned to other projects. He was overseeing his publishing house; he was also attempting to continue the adventures of Huck Finn and Tom Sawyer in another novel, but that project stalled. Twain the short fiction writer would return soon enough, however, and when he did, there would often be a sombreness, even a bitterness, in his fables that no one would mistake for the antics of a mere humorist. But there would be imaginative vitality, too, and, despite recurring creative faltering and hesitation, genuine literary achievement. That is the subject of the final chapter.

The Late Years, 1891–1910:
False Starts and Flights of Fancy

Late in his life, Twain published in the *North American Review* chapters from his ongoing and never to be completed autobiography. In one of those chapters, he recalled his frustration with a burglar alarm, an experience that contributed to one of the McWilliams sketches, but he attributed his impatience to his fundamental temperament: "Complexities annoy me; they irritate me; then this progressive feeling presently warms into anger."[46] The age was complex in ways far more serious than those represented by the intricate vagaries of a burglar alarm, and Twain was not alone in his sense of confusion and frustration. Since the Civil War, as everyone knew, the rules had changed, but no one seemed to know what code or set of protocols had replaced them. This sort of uncertainty is reflected in the novels of manners by Henry James and William Dean Howells, by Kate Chopin and Edith Wharton, in Harold Frederic's *The Damnation of Theron Ware*, Abraham Cahan's *The Rise of David Levinsky*, or James Weldon Johnson's *The Autobiography of an Ex-Colored Man*.

Twain tended to take the ethos of the era personally, however, and his annoyance sooner or later warmed into full-fledged anger. One of the complexities that annoyed him surely had to do with his own case of mistaken identity, and many of his short stories betray his concern with presenting himself to the public in a way that did not injure his self-respect or his purse. Simplicity, directness, and authenticity were both luxuries and values for Clemens, and he was likely to be angered by a game that had rules he couldn't quite follow. Samuel Clemens knew that he earned a living by being Mark Twain, but he was uneasy being what Mark Twain had become. Howells had years before detected a growing seriousness in the man, but in the popular mind, Mark Twain remained an inept but genial fool, a man who could make light of almost anything and be both amused and amusing at will.

That such uneasiness was very much with him in the 1890s is evident in a sketch he published in the *London Illustrated News* in December

1891 and in the San Francisco *Examiner* the next month. "Playing Courier" records Twain's comic inability to play the role of courier and to make the necessary travel arrangements for an expedition of tourists bound from Geneva to Bayreuth. Despite his "systematic" efforts, nearly everything that could go wrong does go wrong—he fails to get money for the trip and reservations for the hotel, he loses the trunks, he forgets his umbrella and his cigars, and he manages to irritate everyone in his party. Twain buys railway tickets to Bayreuth at a cigar shop, but at the station, he discovers that they are actually tickets for a lottery drawn two years earlier. His fellow travelers are disgruntled, but Twain must pretend to be amused by the incident, for what else is he to do? He keeps his distress a secret from the expedition, but he defines his private emotional state accurately for the reader:

> One of the hardest situations in life, I think, is to be full of grief and a sense of defeat and shabbiness that way, and yet have to put on an outside of archness and gaiety, while all the time you know that your own expedition, the treasures of your heart, and whose love and reverence you are by the custom of our civilization entitled to, are being consumed with humiliation before strangers to see you earning and getting a compassion which is a stigma, a brand—a brand which certifies you to be—oh, anything and everything which is fatal to human respect. (*CTS* II, 27)

This outbreak of unmistakable seriousness in an otherwise droll story suggests that the mask of Mark Twain has slipped momentarily and Clemens is speaking for himself instead of recording in comic detail the blunders of his literary persona. The passage also suggests the humiliation that his loved ones feel before strangers, whose pity for him they must endure. The public celebrity of that humorous fellow, Mark Twain, had intruded upon the privacy and dignity of the Clemens family.

Twain records elsewhere in his autobiography a telling anecdote that is frequently cited as evidence of his wife's effort to reform him, to tone down his lavish and unruly imagination and to make it proper and acceptable to Victorian sensibilities:

> The children always helped their mother to edit my books in manuscript. She would sit on the porch at the farm and read aloud, with her pencil in her hand, and the children would keep an alert and suspicious eye upon her right along, for the belief was well grounded in them that

whenever she came across a particularly satisfactory passage, she would strike it out. The passages that were so satisfactory to them always had an element of strength in them which sorely needed modification or expurgation, and were always sure to get it at their mother's hand.[47]

Whatever significance this anecdote might have in helping us to determine how Twain had become tamed and domesticated, what is most striking about this glimpse into the Clemens household is that the young girls were allowed to listen to the "unexpurgated" Twain. And their father sometimes salted his manuscripts with strong stuff, knowing full well that Olivia would excise the offending passages, or that if she did not, he would do it himself later. This anecdote indicates that his wife was not so refined and genteel as some have supposed; instead, Sam's good nature was ample warrant for his frequent excesses, and the children needed no protection from his grotesque humor or his strong language. Instead, what was at stake was his professional reputation. How might the public, which did not know him as his friends and family did, interpret his apparent irreverence and vulgarity?

In his autobiography, Twain occasionally quotes passages from his daughter Susy's biography of him, without improving upon the young girl's grammar or spelling. Susy expressed the heartfelt wish of the whole family when she wrote how "enuyed" she was that "so few people know papa, I mean realy know him, they think of Mark Twain as a humorist joking at everything."[48] For Susy, *The Prince and the Pauper* revealed more of her father's "kind and sympathetic nature" than the humor of his "old style." From the time of the Whittier birthday speech, if not earlier, Clemens's sense of his audience and of himself as author had begun to stratify—those who delighted in his humor tended to see nothing but fun in the man, while those who failed to get the jokes were embarrassed for him. Either way, he was a curiosity. Mark Twain, as a literary persona, had become an unstable compound, and at times the author abandoned his nom de plume altogether or radically redefined his audience. Clemens sometimes opted to publish works anonymously, fearing that the reader of a work bearing the Twain label would automatically expect a joke that might not be forthcoming. Late in his career, he insisted that certain of his writings not be published until long after his death; in those instances, he imaginatively spoke from beyond the grave in order that he might speak honestly to a world yet to be born. These are only two of the methods he devised as solutions to a long-standing problem.

In 1891, when Twain returned to publishing short fiction after a several-year break, he contributed to the August issue of *Harper's Magazine* another mistaken-identity story and called it simply "Luck." The story had actually been written several years earlier, shortly after Joseph Twichell had told Twain about a blunderer who had succeeded in the world. But financial problems were forcing Twain back into the literary marketplace. In 1889, he had announced his permanent retirement from literature (*MTHL* II, 610–11), believing that he could live comfortably off the profits from a typesetting machine devised by James W. Paige. Twain had invested $3,000 a month for 44 consecutive months in the project, but by 1891, he had stopped those payments altogether and was in serious debt. His own recent experience had been anything but lucky, and things were going to get worse. In any event, his story made it clear that circumstances might conspire in the favor of a fool; the author did not have to say that they seemed to have conspired against him.

"Luck" begins with Twain falling into conversation with an unnamed clergyman at a banquet honoring a man whom Twain refers to as Scoresby. The clergyman confides to an astonished Twain that Scoresby is a complete fool and an ass, and then recounts the tale of this genial and good-natured simpleton who rises in the world. The clergyman's sympathy for the fellow led him to try to help him. When Scoresby was a student, the clergyman wanted to spare the boy the pain and embarrassment of exposure. He drilled into the boy certain facts of history and principles of mathematics. The clergyman merely wanted to break the young man's fall, but the examiners asked for the very information the clergyman had so assiduously crammed into Scoresby's head and no more. The student took first prize in the examination.

Shortly thereafter, when the Crimean War breaks out, better men are passed over, and Scoresby is made a captain. The clergyman feels the responsibility of a Dr. Frankenstein who has unwittingly created a monster, and he buys a cornetcy so that he might follow Scoresby to the Crimea and prevent a military disaster. In one military encounter, Scoresby, because he does not know his right hand from his left, leads his regiment over a hill where he discovers the Russian army gathering forces. The Russians cannot believe that a single regiment would attack them, and they scatter. Scoresby's stupidity transforms certain defeat into glorious victory.

The clergyman explains the reasons for Scoresby's success and his own exasperation: "Blunders?—why, he never did anything *but* blunder.

But, you see, nobody was in the fellow's secret. Everybody had him
focused wrong, and necessarily misinterpreted his performance every
time. Consequently they took his idiotic blunders for inspirations of
genius" (*CSS*, 252). Twain himself suffered the opposite plight—the
public often took his serious literary inspirations for comic blunders—
but he must have felt that he and Scoresby had one thing in common:
everyone had both of them focused wrong and misinterpreted their performances. This sketch is unexceptional, although as with many of
Twain's minor pieces, it had the potential for extended and rich cultural
satire. Slight in itself, "Luck" prefigures such narratives of a fool's
progress as James Branch Cabell's *Figures of the Earth*, Jerzy Kosinski's
Being There, and Winston Groom's *Forrest Gump*.

By the time "Luck" was published, the Clemens family was already in
Europe. They had closed down their house in Hartford, sold their
horses, and placed their servants; their absence from their home and the
peace and security it represented would be a long one. Samuel
Clemens's immediate concern was for his wife's health, and he hoped
that the prescribed medicinal baths would cure a developing heart problem. Perhaps they would also relieve the rheumatic pain in his arm, a
condition that made writing difficult. Concerns about health and money
complicated Clemens's life a great deal; at the same time, as severe circumstances tend to do, they made him contemplate in imaginative
terms life's ironies and liabilities alongside its elemental and fundamental blessings. The five stories he published in 1893 were prepared
in haste, and they show it. But nothing Twain ever wrote is wholly without interest, and the tales do dramatize in remarkably different ways an
alert understanding of his circumstance and his appreciation of what
was most valuable to him.

"The Californian's Tale" was written in 1892 but was first published
in Arthur Stedman's collection *The First Book of the Authors Club, Liber
Scriptorum* (1893). "The £1,000,000 Bank-Note" appeared in the January 1893 issue of the *Century*. "Extracts from Adam's Diary" was
intended for periodical publication but was revised so that it might be
included in a collection put together by Irving Underhill, who wanted to
use his *Niagara Book* to publicize Niagara Falls as a tourist attraction. To
accommodate the purposes of the volume, Twain transported the Garden of Eden to Niagara and made other minor adjustments in the
text.[49] During this period, also, Twain signed an agreement with *Cosmopolitan* to supply 12 pieces for $5,000; "Is He Living or Is He Dead?"

and "The Esquimau Maiden's Romance" were probably intended to be two of those contributions. The first was published in the September 1893 issue of *Cosmopolitan* and the second in November.

"The Californian's Tale" is often dismissed for its cloying sentimentality. The conclusion of the story is sentimental, but one would not predict that quality from the cheerless beginning of the tale. Twain recalls the desperation of all those pioneers who had gone west with hopes of improving their lot, acquired a fortune and then lost it, and in their "humiliation" chose "to sever all communication" with their relatives and to live "thenceforth as one dead" (*CSS*, 267). In the story, Twain comes across a cabin and a man that seem to be an exception to the rule. Henry, the miner, invites him into a well-kept and cozy home that miraculously displays all those "little unclassifiable tricks and touches that a woman's hand distributes about a home" (*CSS*, 268) and tells him that his wife is gone now but will be back in a few days.

The miner encourages Twain to stay so that he might meet the woman responsible for the miner's home and his joy, and Twain agrees. Several miners stop by to ask after the wife, and on Saturday evening they bring their musical instruments in preparation for her return. Henry is worried because it is late and his wife has not yet arrived, but his friends encourage him to have another drink. At length they waltz him off to bed in a drunken stupor. In one of those O. Henry–style surprise endings Twain was overly fond of, it is at last revealed that Henry's wife has been dead for 19 years, and on the anniversary of the day she failed to return home, Henry's friends come around and pretend to share in his anxious happiness. They get him drunk and put him to bed, knowing that he will be able to muddle through another year until his madness surfaces once again.

Twain's imagination was often retrospective and immediate at the same time. Present circumstances prompted certain memories of days gone by, sometimes serving as tonic relief from his own harried and frustrating life, sometimes providing a clarifying and proportioned sense of his present difficulties. "The Californian's Tale" seems to be something of a "what if" tale. Shortly before he wrote this story, Clemens had learned that his wife's heart problem was not as serious as the doctors had thought. Olivia's health had always been frail, but this recent concern for her was more troubling than usual, and Twain may have received the news of her promised recovery with the feeling that he had had a close call. In any event, Twain dramatizes in "The Californian's Tale" his own potential reaction to his wife's death. Had Olivia died,

91

how would Sam respond? Would he, like Henry, become something of a madman? He knew already that he missed terribly the house they had left in Hartford, its furnishings and arrangements subtly reflecting a woman's touch that he found both gratifying and mysterious. Would Twain become one of those "living dead men" he had seen on the Western slope, whose "secret thoughts were made all of regrets and longings—regrets for their wasted lives, and longings to be out of the struggle and done with it all?" (*CSS*, 267).

Clemens's relief about his wife's health allowed him to turn to pressing financial obligations with a will and a purpose; he knew that he had to write himself out of his difficulty. That summer, in addition to writing "The Californian's Tale," he began *Tom Sawyer Abroad* (1894) and *Pudd'nhead Wilson* (1894) and wrote nine essays and four other stories, among them "The £1,000,000 Bank-Note" and "Extracts from Adam's Diary." These two stories are first-person narratives; Clemens's literary persona does not appear in either of them. The first story is told by Henry Adams, who at a dinner party claims precedence in seating because his name indicates that he is the "direct posterity" (*CTS* II, 72) of the father of us all, while the Duke of Shoreditch belongs to a "collateral branch" of the great family tree. The second story is told by the original first person, Adam himself.

The premise of "The £1,000,000 Bank-Note" is preposterous enough to make for rollicking comedy, but the story is not particularly funny, merely droll. A San Francisco clerk sails too far out in the bay one day and is picked up by an English brig. Against his wishes, he is taken to London and, a penniless man, dropped in the middle of the great city. Two brothers have been arguing about whether a man who had a £1,000,000 banknote, which as a matter of course could not be cashed, could survive for a month. They spy Henry Adams through the window and make him the subject of an experiment to settle the wager by presenting him with just such a banknote. Through the haphazardly plotted tale of his adventures in simultaneous poverty and extraordinary wealth, Adams not only survives the month but also meets his true love. In the process, through the adroit management of influence based on his reputation as a rich man, he makes £200,000 for himself.

Perhaps Clemens's own circumstances were too absurd for him to exploit the latent comedy in this dramatic situation, but the situation itself provided the opportunity for a telling critique of capitalist culture. G. B. McCutcheon's best-selling novel *Brewster's Millions* (1902), for example, bears an analogous, if inverted, relation to Twain's tale.

McCutcheon's story of a man who must spend a million dollars in one month in order to collect a substantial inheritance became a popular play and was seven times adapted to film. "The £1,000,000 Bank-Note" comments more immediately and more interestingly on Twain's recent experience than on the state of the republic, however. At the same time that he was deep in debt and forced to seek loans to sustain his investments and his publishing company, Clemens had a private dinner with Kaiser William II and met Edward, Prince of Wales. The irony of an impoverished celebrity dining with the Kaiser could not have been lost on him. Twain has Henry Adams describe his own paradoxical situation, but it was one that the creator shared with his character: "and so, pauper as I was, I had money to spend, and was living like the rich and the great. I judged that there was going to be a crash by and by, but I was in, now, and must swim across or drown. You see there was just that element of impending disaster to give a serious side, a sober side, yes, a tragic side, to a state of things which would otherwise have been purely ridiculous" (*CTS* II, 68). Adams's reputation, not his banknote, is his currency, and he knows that he has acquired the "enduring gold of fame" when the British magazine *Punch* caricatures him. (A caricature of Twain would appear on the cover of *Punch* in June 1907, by the way.)

Folded into this story of a pauper's experiment in luxury is the love story between Adams and Portia Langham. Henry takes Portia into his confidence and tells her that he is not a rich man. She instantly loves him nonetheless, and they plan to marry after his impersonation is concluded. In another O. Henry–like twist, Portia is revealed to be the stepdaughter of one of the rich brothers who contracted the bet. Adams is welcomed into the family as a prospective son-in-law on the basis of his honesty and intelligence. The love plot is extraneous to the story and might be judged a sentimental defect were it not for the fact that it contributes to the emotional coherence of the tale. Portia Langham's name and circumstances are close enough to Olivia Langdon Clemens's to suggest that the author was making a sincere comment on his own experience. Aware of the "tragic side" of his financial situation, and clearly hoping for, but not really counting on, the sort of windfall Henry Adams receives, Twain identifies his love for his wife as one of those simple yet invaluable blessings that outweighs catastrophe. He would return to this theme from a very different and far more original perspective in "Extracts from Adam's Diary."

Twain's interest in biblical subjects was long-standing, spanning a period from his work on the unpublished and now lost "Noah's Ark book" in the 1860s to "Etiquette for the Afterlife: Advice to Paine," written only a few weeks before Twain's death in 1910. There is wonderful comic audacity in Twain's several attempts to rewrite or to supplement biblical accounts of the Creation, the Fall, and the Flood, but there is a serious quality about them too. By casting his eye backward to the Creation, the author was giving the broadest possible field for his humor. In this setting, Twain might frame earnest philosophical and theological questions without particularly sacrificing his gifts as a humorist; he could measure the immensity of the universe against pitiful human self-absorption or question the divinity of a Creator who gave his creatures a moral sense but punished them for their intuitive sympathies; he could dramatize in familiar, not to say heretical, terms his own deterministic philosophy and with satirical efficiency contrast it to holy acts of Providence; or he could test, if only in the imagination, his thoughts about the here and hereafter.

By taking the point of view of Adam, Twain adopted the perspective of a true innocent while at the same time introducing ordinary adult annoyance and concern in ways that guaranteed affective comedy. "Extracts from Adam's Diary" begins on a Monday with Adam complaining in his diary that the "new creature" is always hanging around and talking. "It" (Eve later tells him that she is a "she," not an "it") uses unfamiliar words such as "we," and the new creature appears intent on improving paradise. Eve puts up signs everywhere and is always tidying up things. She worries about Adam going over the falls in a barrel, and she cannot understand why fanged creatures and buzzards are forced to live on grass instead of flesh. She informs Adam that Sunday is a day of rest, whereas Adam thought all seven days were. From the moment of that revelation, Adam observes of every Sunday thereafter that he "pulled through." These are some of the "unaccountable things" (*CTS* II, 99) Eve introduces into Adam's life. He looks upon the ordinary with childlike innocence, but also with adult consternation and irritation. Twain gets great fun out of a domestic farce conducted in the Garden of Eden, but he also registers in a sardonic key a certain skepticism about the wisdom of the Creator and his injunctions.

When Adam sees that caution and complaint have no influence upon Eve, he emigrates. But she follows him. When Abel is born, Adam does not know what sort of creature it is. Adam tries an experiment to settle the matter. He throws the hairless and toothless creature into the water on the theory that it might be a fish. Eve retrieves the animal and holds it to her breast, and Adam cannot understand why she seems to favor this animal over the others in the garden. With inductive zeal, Adam studies the new creature and rejects in turn several hypotheses: It is not a frog, a bird, or a snake, because it does not hop, fly, or crawl. He decides that it is "either an enigma or some kind of bug" (*CTS* II, 104), but he cannot rest easy in that explanation and becomes so certain that the creature is a kangaroo that he gives it a name, "*Kangaroorum Adamiensis*" (*CTS* II, 105). Eve said that she found it in the forest, so Adam sets traps baited with milk for others that must be waddling about. At the age of three months, the creature exhibits characteristics that disqualify it as a kangaroo, and Adam suspects that it may be an "unclassifiable zoological freak" (*CTS* II, 105), either that or a tailless bear. What most exasperates Adam, however, is that while he has worn himself out hunting for a second specimen of this drooling, goo-gooing creature, Eve has caught another one: "I never saw such luck. I might have hunted these woods a hundred years, I never would have run across that thing" (*CTS* II, 107). Eve names the creature Cain.

For reasons that are not entirely clear, when Twain revised his story to make it conform to the purposes of Underhill's *Niagara Book*, he shifted the blame for the Fall from Eve to Adam. Actually, "blame" is too pejorative a term. Eve's decision to taste the apple has little or nothing to do with a desire to partake of the tree of knowledge. Instead, when Adam points out that violating God's prohibition will bring death into the world, she realizes that the forlorn lions and tigers might at last have something substantial to eat. In this earlier version, Eve's compassion for living creatures motivates her actions, and thus Twain was able to dramatize his angry conviction that God had implanted in men and women an intuitive moral sense at the same time that he meant to punish his creation for acting on that sense. In the Niagara version, Eve blames Adam for the Fall. The serpent has told her that the forbidden fruit is not apples but chestnuts, and "that 'chestnut' was a figurative term meaning an aged and mouldy joke" (*CTS* II, 103). Because Adam has been guilty of telling himself a joke in order to pass the time, and because he did not know it was old but thought it original with him, he is full of remorse: "Alas, I am indeed to blame. Would that I were not witty; oh, would that I had never had that radiant thought" (*CTS* II, 103).

In the end, Twain brings his comedy of first things around to the same sort of conclusion he had in "The £1,000,000 Bank-Note." In the final paragraph, Adam's diary jumps forward 10 years. Long before, Adam realized that the small, toothless creatures were his sons, and he recognizes that his fall from paradise was a fortunate one, but not because he feels some mighty, transcendent destiny within him. His reasons are more simple than that:

> After all these years, I see that I was mistaken about Eve in the begin-
> ning; it is better to live outside the Garden with her than inside it
> without her. At first I thought she talked too much; but now I should
> be sorry to have that voice fall silent and pass out of my life. Blessed be
> the chestnut that brought us near together and taught me to know the
> goodness of her heart and the sweetness of her spirit! (*CTS* II, 107–8)

"The Esquimau Maiden's Romance" is a snarled and tangled affair, but it does share with "The Californian's Tale," "The £1,000,000 Bank-Note," and "Extracts from Adam's Diary" a preoccupation with financial distress, domestic security, and simple human affection. In all these tales, Twain ponders the "unaccountable things" that make life satisfying alongside the distress of "impending disaster" that gave the ridiculous a serious and tragic side. In "The Esquimau Maiden's Romance" both these themes are present, but they vie for the reader's attention, and Twain makes little effort to coordinate them, even with something so improbable and rickety as the sort of plot he manufactured in "The £1,000,000 Bank-Note."

Lasca, the Eskimo maiden, is the daughter of the most important man in her tribe, and she gleefully tells Twain of her magnificent opulence and sadly of her thwarted love affair. She lives in a great mansion of snow blocks with two slop tubs in the parlor and ample furs on the sleeping benches. Her father's unimaginable wealth consists of 22 iron fishhooks, and she is admired by all around her. One of the most attractive features of this story is the way Clemens manages his literary persona, a man supremely mindful of Lasca's pride yet charmed by her innocence. When Lasca discloses the extent of her father's wealth, 22 fishhooks, Twain pretends to be dumbfounded:

> Mr. Twain, every word of it is true—every word. . . . *Say* you believe
> me—*do* say you believe me.
> "I—well, yes, I do—I am *trying* to. But it was all so *sudden*. So sud-
> den and prostrating. You shouldn't do such a thing in that sudden
> way. . . ."
> But oh, dear, I ought certainly to have *known* better. Why—
> "You see, Lasca, if you had said five or six hooks to start with, and
> then gradually—"

> Oh, I see, I see—then gradually added one, and then two, and then—ah, why couldn't I have thought of that!
> "Never mind, child, it's all right—I am better now—I shall be over it in a little while. *But*—to spring the whole twenty-two on a person unprepared and not very strong anyway—." (*CTS* II, 124)

This is the voice of Twain from earlier and more good-natured days. Even in times of financial worry and emotional distress, however, Twain refuses to condescend to his created characters. His feelings about wealth and the wealthy were clearly not so gracious as his treatment of Lasca would suggest. He had been trying with little success to secure loans from people who had the Wall Street equivalent of 22 fishhooks. In *Pudd'nhead Wilson*, a book he had been working on at this time, a rather more sardonic quality surfaces in one of his maxims: "The holy passion of Friendship is of so sweet and steady and loyal and enduring a nature that it will last through a whole lifetime, if not asked to lend money." The same bitter point is made in a more charitable way when he speaks to Lasca, however. He asks the maiden where her father keeps his treasure, and when she turns suspicious, Twain says, "Oh, come, don't you be afraid about me. At home we have seventy millions of people, and although I say it myself that shouldn't, there is not one person among them all but would trust me with untold fish-hooks" (*CTS* II, 125).

Lasca is delighted by the impression she is making on Mr. Twain, but Lasca is not happy, for she was "born for love," and her riches have been an impediment. She has had many suitors, but each proved to love not her but her money. Lasca curses all "millionaires," saying, "Our tribe was once plain, simple folk, and content with the bone fish-hooks of their fathers; now they are eaten up with avarice and would sacrifice every sentiment of honor and honesty to possess the debasing iron fish-hooks of the foreigner" (*CTS* II, 127). This is a sentiment that Twain would put to the test in his masterful "The Man That Corrupted Hadleyburg," but here the author's observation is merely an attitude, not yet a story.

Lasca does meet a young man who knows nothing of her wealth and loves her for herself, but he is accused of stealing a fishhook from her father. He faces "trial by water." He is thrown into the sea; if he drowns, he is innocent; if he swims, he is guilty. He swims to a nearby iceberg and floats away, still declaring his undying love for the Eskimo maiden, but Lasca is saddened and angered by her lover's apparent guilt. Nine months later, she combs her hair and the fishhook falls out. Lasca's only chance for real love has passed, and her father will never smile again. Twain draws a moral from this tale of unrequited love, but not one the reader is quite prepared for: "since a hundred million dollars in New York and twenty-two fish-hooks on the border of the Arctic Circle represent the same financial supremacy, a man in straitened circumstances is a fool to stay in New York, when he can buy ten cents' worth of fish-hooks and emigrate" (*CTS* II, 133).

I have been emphasizing the originality in Twain's short fiction, even when the stories are not particularly good. Twain's comparison of the so-called primitive Eskimo culture to New York millionaires is crude and comes more out of personal animus than a fully articulated social vision. However, it should perhaps be pointed out that Thorstein Veblen was the first economist to analyze the customs of the very wealthy in anthropological terms by vivid and telling comparisons of New York millionaires with the customs and beliefs of "primitive" cultures. Edith Wharton, who had read Veblen, would get some of the same quality into her satire of wealthy New Yorkers in *The House of Mirth*. Veblen's *The Theory of the Leisure Class* was published in 1899; *The House of Mirth* was published in 1905. If only in conception, Twain got there ahead of the rest.

"Is He Living or Is He Dead?" is also original and prophetic in its way, for it casts in dramatic fictional terms what the historian Daniel Boorstin calls a "pseudo-event." Boorstin saw one cause for twentieth-century America's debilitating sense of confusion of purpose and direction to be the popular preference for the image of reality to life as it really is. We need not accept Boorstin's thesis to appreciate the appropriateness of the term to Twain's tale of another sort of manufactured reality. Pseudo-events, according to Boorstin, possess four defining characteristics: they are not spontaneous, but planned and planted; they are planted for the immediate purpose of being reported and circulated; their relation to the underlying reality of the situation is ambiguous; and they are usually intended as self-fulfilling prophecies.[50] A comparison of a twentieth-century historian's social analysis to a nineteenth-century yarn spinner's fable may seem strained, but in this instance, the analogy helps to distinguish "Is He Living or Is He Dead?" from the sort of hoax tale we found in "The Capitoline Venus."

The story is a simple one. In a hotel in Mentone, on the French Riviera, Twain falls into conversation with a man he calls Smith. Smith points out to Twain a man he identifies as a rich silk merchant from Lyons. Despite the merchant's affluence, "he always looks sad and dreamy, and doesn't talk with anybody. His name is Theophile Magnan" (*CTS* II, 109). Later that evening, Smith tells Twain a story of four struggling artists—himself, Claude Frère, Carl Boulanger, and François Millet. Twain is astonished that Smith knew the great Millet, but Twain is told that Millet was not always great but once so poor he lived on turnips. The four artists are talented but desperate until Boulanger concocts a scheme that will relieve them of their poverty. He bases his idea on a law of history—"the merit of many a great artist has never been acknowledged until after he was starved and dead" (*CTS* II, 113)—and announces that one of the four must die, and they will draw lots to decide which one.

Millet is chosen. He will not really die, of course, but his "notorious funeral" must be elaborately prepared. They will enlarge his stock of paintings and sketches, each containing "some peculiarity or mannerism easily detectable as his" (*CTS* II, 113). When the funeral is announced, they will have a "ton" of Millets ready at hand. But before that fatal day, they must embark on a campaign to invent and enlarge the unknown Millet's reputation. They travel about "starting items" in the local newspapers, "not an item announcing that a new painter had been discovered, but an item which let on that everybody knew François Millet; not an item praising him in any way but merely a word concerning the present condition of the 'master'—sometimes hopeful, sometimes despondent, but always tinged with fears for the worst" (*CTS* II, 115). The fatal day arrives; a magnificent funeral is conducted in Paris, and the four once impoverished artists, including Millet himself, are pallbearers of a coffin containing a wax figure.

In a surprise ending that, for once, actually works, Smith at last returns to the rich silk merchant he had pointed out earlier in the day. That man was François Millet, he announces. This revelation in the closing paragraphs colors and transforms the story that has preceded it. The public had been hoodwinked into appreciating and paying substantial prices for Millet's work, but the secret of the fraud is never revealed and does not really function as a hoax that exposes human gullibility. Moreover, Twain never suggests that the paintings are not worth the attention or the money. The ostensible moral of the tale is announced, or rather half-remembered, by Smith at the beginning of the story as he tries to recall the Hans Christian Andersen story of the boy who loved but neglected his caged bird. The bird dies, and in his remorse, the boy spends time and effort on the bird's funeral that otherwise might have kept it alive and singing. But there is more to Twain's story.

This elaborately planned pseudo-event seems at first glance a happy alternative to Andersen's parable, but it has its serious side, too. The ambiguous relation of Millet's funeral to Theophile Magnan's prosperous new life is announced in the story's title; he joins that host of living dead men Twain had described in "The Californian's Tale," and Magnan's fate is registered in his sad and dreamy look. Twain makes it an even question whether Millet is alive or dead, but this story comments on the author's situation as well. Like Millet, he had been hastily producing a "ton" of original Twains—often, like the Millets, these works were merely "skeleton sketches, studies, parts of studies, fragments of studies" (*CTS* II, 113). Many were never to be finished, but all bore some peculiarity that marked them as distinctly his. In 1893, Twain's distress about his indebtedness, his concern about the management of his public persona, and his fear of losing those closest to him were intertwined in his imagination as they were, or soon would be, in his life. Given his financial situation, he must have wondered whether he would have to die to get any value out of his work or, perhaps worse, outlive his desperation and prosper, in a sad and dreamy way, but at the expense of his self-respect and his craft. For better or for worse, he would find out soon enough.

The cluster of tales published in 1893 share an emotional coherence, in the author, that is rather uniform, even monotonous, but the remarkable variety of form and expression that characterize them amply demonstrates an imaginative vitality coexisting with, and to some extent correcting, Twain's bitterness and distress. In the short fiction from the early days, Twain had absorbed the folklore, legend, and tales he had heard, and he had used his persona as a means to introduce and make vivid the stories of other people's lives. In many of these later stories, however, the imaginative process worked all the other way round. Twain projected a part of himself into imagined characters inhabiting other circumstances and living in other lands. For that reason, perhaps, many of his late short stories seem almost arbitrarily located, divested of his customary attachment to region and local speech. (He could move the Garden of Eden to Niagara easily enough, and Hadleyburg could be almost any village in America.) The result of this shift meant that he relied more heavily on plot than dramatic occasion, and plotting was not Twain's strongest talent. Still, his imagination served him well, for through these creative transformations, he relieved the pressures of a world that was too much with him, and sometimes he produced powerful and memorable fictions.

After the 1893 tales, Twain would not publish any short fiction for another four years. During that interval, things went from bad to worse for the Clemens family. In 1894, Clemens gave the Standard Oil executive Henry Huttleston Rogers power of attorney over all his business affairs. Rogers, in turn, assigned Clemens's property, including his copyrights, to Olivia. Later that year, Clemens declared bankruptcy. Rogers superintended Twain's financial affairs with a shrewdness and efficiency that eventually pulled the author out of debt, but he did so, in part, through the artful management of the public's perception of Clemens's literary persona. In other words, Rogers rehabilitated the author's borrowed good name by using corporate lawyers, overseas employees, and publicity agents to record, publish, and to a degree manufacture Twain's reinvigorated character.[51] Samuel Clemens might well have wondered about his longtime companion, Mark Twain, "Is he living, or is he dead?" In any event, for a time at least, Mark Twain was something of a pseudo-event himself.

But there were other more serious reasons why he might ask the same question of Samuel Clemens. He had been troubled by ill health and was bedridden in 1894 and again in 1895. He and Olivia embarked on an exhausting around-the-world lecture tour in 1895, not because he enjoyed lecturing but because it was a way to pay his creditors. He was out of the country when, on August 18, 1896, the news of the death of their daughter Susy reached him. Olivia was already on a boat bound for America, and Clemens had planned to join the rest of the family shortly thereafter. A heavy sadness settled into the Clemens household, as if to stay. More for the relief from depression than anything else, Clemens threw himself into his work on *Following the Equator*. He described his emotional condition to Howells in a letter dated February 23, 1897: "I don't mean that I am miserable; no—worse than that, indifferent. Indifferent to nearly everything but work. I like that; I enjoy it, & stick to it. I do it without purpose & without ambition; merely for the love of it." He went on to say that he and his wife were "dead people" who go through the motions of life. "Indeed I am a mud image, & it puzzles me to know what it is in me that writes, & that has comedy-fancies & finds pleasure in phrasing them. . . . the thing in me forgets the presence of the mud image & goes its own way wholly unconscious of it & apparently of no kinship with it" (*MTHL* II, 664).

Following the Equator appeared in 1897, and Twain interpolated into this travel book three stories—"Cecil Rhodes and the Shark," "The Joke That Made Ed's Fortune," and "A Story without End." He apparently did not think much of them as stories; at least he did not choose to publish them separately. Only the first story had much, if anything, to do with the purposes and subject matter of his book, for it expressed his contempt for the real Cecil Rhodes, whose involvement in the Boer War Twain saw as callous opportunism. "The Joke That Made Ed's Fortune" tells of pranksters supplying Ed Jackson with a fraudulent letter of introduction to Cornelius Vanderbilt; Vanderbilt takes the letter to be real, and Jackson prospers from the joke instead of being humiliated by it. "A Story without End" resembles "A Medieval Romance" in that it offers a plot so full of complexities and irreconcilable developments that it cannot come to a satisfactory conclusion. Unlike the earlier tale, however, this irresolution is not a hoax so much as it is a conundrum.

Thematically, at least, "Cecil Rhodes and the Shark" and "The Joke That Made Ed's Fortune" belong with other stories that dramatize an unexpected reversal of fortunes and may indicate that Clemens still harbored hopes for some sudden change in his own financial circumstance. "A Story without End," if only by mere suggestion, may refer to the several incomplete manuscripts Twain had on hand. What is more interesting, however, is that all three stories deal with messages that have misfired—a German's diary entry recording his intent to do his patriotic duty and go to war is written in London but winds up in the hands of Cecil Rhodes in Australia and serves the crass purposes of financial speculation; a phony letter written with the purpose of embarrassing Ed Jackson instead launches him on a new and more prosperous career and puts the jokers in his employment; and a once complete story meant for entertainment becomes, many years later, all the more interesting as a fragment and a riddle. Whatever the purposes of their respective authors, these texts serve ends that run against the grain of deliberate intention. Just this sort of irony had recently been brought home to Clemens when he visited a group of prisoners in South Africa and made a joke about their treatment; the witticism was wrongly understood to mean he thought they were being treated too leniently. Their imprisonment was made harsher, and Clemens had to see government officials and explain the joke. The prisoners were released shortly thereafter.

One could hardly predict from the stories he included in *Following the Equator* that Twain's next short story would attain the high quality of literary achievement critics have typically accorded "The Man That Corrupted Hadleyburg." He wrote this story in Vienna in 1898; it was published in the December 1899 issue of *Harper's Monthly*. Since that time, the story has been the subject of extensive and diverse critical debate. Various towns and villages have been nominated as the original for the author's depiction of Hadleyburg. Such literary influences as Chaucer, Milton, Dante, Poe, and others have been identified; and Carl Dolmetsch has suggested the interesting possibility that Twain took some of his inspiration for the tale from a cartoon of him as the "American Diogenes" in a Viennese humor magazine.[52] The mysterious stranger who corrupts the town has been identified as the Deity and as Satan, and the story itself has been variously characterized as a satire, a fable, an allegory, and a quasi-philosophical essay masquerading as a short story. At all events, "The Man That Corrupted Hadleyburg" is rich in interpretive possibility, even if no single interpretive explanation seems sufficient to it.

This story of the temptation and corruption of an American town is too familiar to require summary. The author's evident firmness of tone and narrative control over his material suggest a corresponding firmness of purpose as well, but the range of interpretive opinion makes it clear that that purpose may be indecipherable. Is "The Man That Corrupted Hadleyburg" a story of revenge or of redemption? Has the untested virtue of the community been exposed as nothing more than sanctimonious and irremediable self-delusion, or has the temptation imparted to the town a degree of understanding that, in turn, will make it a chastened but wiser village? Is the story a naturalistic tale dealing with the inexorable effects of training, and in that sense the fictive accompaniment to Twain's deterministic philosophical dialogue *What Is Man?* (1906), which he was working on at the same time? Or is the story a moral fable that presupposes human freedom, a story about human fallibility that ultimately encourages one to make moral choices uninfluenced by social opinion?

Perhaps "Hadleyburg" is an absurdist's nihilistic parable, full of misfired messages, dramatizing the impossibility of accurate understanding and communication. Even the injured stranger who concocts the temptation and corruption is deceived, believing as he does that Mary and Edward Richards are blameless. Edward Richards's deathbed confession is a sincere act of atonement, but it is prompted by a quality of sarcasm he mistakenly detects in Burgess's note to him. Richards performs yet another injustice to Burgess, though Richards intends something else altogether. Halliday, the gadfly and cynic, having lost his sense of self-respect long before, revels in the town's misery, but even he does not know the real depth of Hadleyburg's corruption and cannot even guess at it.

These and other matters of interpretation are best left to the judgment of individual readers. Leaving interpretive questions aside, however, we see in this tale a remarkable narrative detachment mysteriously working in concert with a tone that registers the author's fascination with his material. The author's rendering of his created characters is almost clinical, and his analysis of their motives and moral failings is minutely dispassionate, but the seemingly endless ways that moral corruption works its way through the town are engrossing. The dramatic situation itself seems contrived, but in deliberate ways that make the story something of a laboratory experiment. We know, for example, that the stranger has suffered an injury in Hadleyburg and is a bitter and vengeful man, but we do not know what that injury is or how a whole town could have committed it, for he means to punish the entire community, not individuals within it. We know that Burgess is innocent of some unidentified offense sufficiently outrageous for the citizens to want to ride him out of town on a rail, but we do **not** know the nature of the crime or the guilty party. What is remarkable about these gaps in the narrative is not that they go unanswered but that the narrator so manages events and drives his tale relentlessly forward that we are not particularly curious about them.

"The Man That Corrupted Hadleyburg" is written in a style that very rarely calls attention to itself. The prose is wonderfully cadenced, but it is stripped for action and running headlong toward some undisclosed end. Twain seldom pauses to indulge in the sort of lavish humorous metaphors that characterize his earlier work. There are exceptions, of course. When the townspeople gather at the town hall to learn who will be the recipient of the bag of gold, for example, the room is noisy with conversation. But when Reverend Burgess lays his hand on the sack, the place becomes so quiet "he could hear his microbes gnaw" (*CTS* II, 412). It is not that Twain actively resists outlandish figures and high comedy, however, but that his creative energies have found other outlets.

At the time Twain wrote this story, he was engaged in at least four other projects. He had begun to write two of the three manuscript versions of *The Mysterious Stranger*—early chapters of "The Chronicle of Young Satan" and the "Schoolhouse Hill" version; these and a third attempt, "No. 44, The Mysterious Stranger" were left incomplete at the time of his death.[53] Twain was also "up to his ears" in drama, as he told Henry Huttleston Rogers—translating German plays into English, dramatizing "Is He Living or Is He Dead?" and collaborating with an Austrian dramatist.[54] Twain had also begun to write his philosophical debate, *What Is Man?* and to embody in dialogue form his deterministic philosophy. Last, he had returned to writing portions of his autobiography, most notably the masterful "Early Days" chapter. Each work required a different creative strategy, but the real beneficiary of Twain's involvement in these various projects seems to have been his story of the corruption of a village, for he had approached the Hadleyburg story sometimes with the instincts of a dramatist and sometimes with the calculated intellectual interests of a philosopher, and throughout with the spontaneous trust that the tale would tell itself just as his autobiography seemed to be doing.

The third section of "Hadleyburg" might be put on stage with very little alteration. In conception and execution, Twain draws upon dramaturgical devices he had been recently experimenting with and effortlessly weaves them into his narrative. The "stage directions" Twain so admired in Howells are present here in undisguised and rather bareboned but effective fashion, as is evident in this specimen passage:

Several voices cried out:
   "Read it! read it! What is it!"
So he began in a dazed and sleep-walker fashion:
   " 'The remark which I made to the unhappy stranger was this: "You are far from being a bad man. [The house gazed at him, marvelling.] Go and reform." ' [Murmurs: "Amazing! what can this mean?"] This one," said the Chair, "is signed Thurlow G. Wilson." (CTS II, 415)

The imaginative extravagance here and elsewhere lies in the boldness of conception and the freedom of view Twain adopted to explore his theme, not in verbal expression. Section three is pure dramatic comedy, full of hypocritical speeches, whispered asides, and catcalling crowd scenes. Part of its biting humor derives from musical comedy. Twain has the crowd literally sing out its delighted contempt—at moments adapting lines from Gilbert and Sullivan's operetta *The Mikado* to their purpose; at others chanting "You are f-a-r from being a b-a-a-a-d man" in the rhythms of a familiar church hymn; and sometimes giving three cheers and a tiger for "Hadleyburg purity."

The dramatic quality of this story also permitted the author to express himself on philosophical matters without being particularly responsible to intellectual consistency or logical rigor. In *What Is Man?* and the *Mysterious Stranger* manuscripts, he attempted to embody ideas in fictional or semifictional form. In "Hadleyburg," Twain speaks at odd moments through his created characters, though he does not identify himself or his point of view exclusively with any one of them. Mary Richards, for example, might speak her own version of determinism, though what Twain would call a materialistic determinism she names the "designs of Providence": "Ordered! Oh, everything's *ordered*, when a person has to find some way out when he has been stupid. Just the same, it was *ordered* that the money should come to us in this special way" (*CTS* II, 400). And Edward Richards also speaks for Twain when he comments on the town's "training" in virtue: "we have been trained all our lives long, like the whole village, till it is absolutely second nature to us to stop not a single moment to think when there's an honest thing to be done" (*CTS* II, 400). However, both of these intellectual positions are undercut by the irony of the narrative. Although the ideas may be Twain's, the characters have, at best, a partial understanding of their situation, and much of the comedy of the tale derives from the fact that they bend their righteousness to the exigency of the moment and that their acts contradict their statements.

The subject matter of Mark Twain's autobiographical writing during this period has little to do with the purposes of this story, but the manner of its composing probably does. Twain once confessed that his best work came out of a certain spontaneity of inspiration combined with an instinctual feel for the proper shape a story should take; he also observed that "the minute the book tried to shift to *my* head the labor of contriving its situations, inventing its adventures and conducting its conversations, I put it away."[55] Part of the problem he had with the *Mysterious Stranger* stories originated in this shift from an unconscious project of the imagination to a matter for the head, but his interest in "The Man That Corrupted Hadleyburg" did not flag.

Twain found that the creative strategies he devised for work on his autobiography benefited from the uncalculated, spontaneous manner of writing. The fluency of "The Man That Corrupted Hadleyburg" (filled as it is with inconsistencies of the head, though not of the nerves) suggests that the author submitted himself to the dramatic situation without preconcerted efforts to make it conform to any single idea. Perhaps Twain was playing the role of an American Diogenes, searching in every nook and cranny of his imagined village for some shred of honesty, and all in vain. For some readers, however, the flexibility of the narrator's approach to his theme may prove disappointing. Gladys Bellamy was probably right when she wrote of this tale that "there is no continuity of motivation, no steadiness of emotional effect, no philosophical unity to the story."[56] But even Bellamy admits that the tale has great "power," and that power stems, in part, from the author's fascination with his material.

The dramatic situation of a mysterious stranger tempting and corrupting an American village is, in itself, interesting, and Twain seems to luxuriate in the way a third-person narrative allows him to inspect it from so many angles. He moves easily from individual circumstance to social condition. Twain dramatizes the household argument of the Richardses, but he notes that the spat is a "plagiarism" of the one the Coxes were having at the same time and for the same reason. Similarly, the 19 recipients of the letter from Stephenson worry over the same issues, contrive in the imagination unlikely memories of noble acts, and engage in the same sort of rationalizations that Edwards does. The wives of these 19 dream and plan how they will spend their anticipated wealth. The spite and envy of neighboring towns show Hadleyburg in a very different light, and the perspective broadens when the news gets out. All of America has its eyes trained on Hadleyburg, and the town has instantly become a national emblem of virtue.

Twain is alternately psychological and sociological at will—his representation of the rationalizations, duplicity, and general erosion of virtue in the Richardses is detailed and exact, but so is his enactment of the crowd's envious admiration, followed swiftly by its gleeful contempt. Hadleyburg, as an American village, is both representative and anomalous. Its vanity and self-satisfaction derive from placing itself above other towns, but Hadleyburg relies upon other towns and on strangers to corroborate its inflated sense of self-regard. On the other hand, the indefinite location of Hadleyburg, its endorsement of public and widely held virtues, and its easy temptation make it representative as well.

Twain suggests the representative and symbolic quality of his fable when he has the town sing out to a tune from *The Mikado* that "Corruptibles far from Hadleyburg are—But the Symbols are here, you bet!" (*CTS* II, 421–22). The symbolic, almost allegorical, representation of venality and hypocrisy in this tale is strangely out of keeping with Twain's customary allegiance to the specific features of region and place, but in some instances, he was prepared to make all-encompassing judgments. In 1895, Twain published the essay "What Paul Bourget Thinks of Us," and what he says there has a certain bearing on "Hadleyburg." The essay is an indignant and largely patriotic response to the French novelist's *Outre-Mer: Impressions of America* (1895). Twain is particularly contemptuous of Bourget's tendency to make large generalizations about the American people. Unlike Bourget, Twain writes, American novelists are content to lay "plainly before you the ways and speech and life of a few people grouped in a certain place." Together, many such novelists give us pictures of "the life of a group in a New England village; in a New York village; in a Texan village; in an Oregon village . . . a hundred patches of life and groups of people in a dozen widely separated cities" (*CTS* II, 167). This is the predictable reaction of a regionalist writer, but later in the essay, he identifies a qualified exception to his rule: "The world seems to think that the love of money is 'American'; and that the mad desire to get suddenly rich is 'American.' I believe that both of these things are merely and broadly human, not American monopolies at all" (*CTS* II, 173).

We have already seen in several stories that Twain found the theme of the desire for a sudden reversal of fortunes transportable from the Arctic Circle to southern France, from Australia to London; he had his Eskimo maiden observe that her people seemed willing to sacrifice every sentiment of honor and honesty for a few iron fishhooks. Twain had shown that same willingness in the citizens of Hadleyburg, a town that could be any American village, and his recent financial indebtedness had perhaps revealed similar motives in himself. In any event, Hadleyburg joins that stretch of towns, real and imagined, from Sleepy Hollow in the Hudson valley to Winesburg, Ohio. "The Man That Corrupted Hadleyburg" belongs to a large class of narratives depicting the American village, a subject that has interested writers ranging from Washington Irving, Edgar Watson Howe, William Dean Howells, and Charles Chesnutt to Willa Cather, Sinclair Lewis, Sherwood Anderson, Thornton Wilder, and Larry McMurtry. Twain's masterful treatment of the subject in "Hadleyburg" may make his story the most representative of them all. Whatever else might be said about this mysteriously powerful story, certainly it is among the most devasting comments on the desire for riches to be found in American literature.

Twain did not object to wealth as such; rather, it was the desire for sudden and unearned prosperity that he condemned. That desire was a family curse he had inherited. In 1847, Clemens's father had acquired 70,000 acres of Tennessee land; John Clemens believed, and cultivated the belief in his family, that that land would one day make them all rich. Twain recalls this questionable legacy in his autobiography: "It put our energies to sleep and made visionaries of us—dreamers and indolent . . . It is good to begin life poor; it is good to begin life rich—these are wholesome; but to begin it *prospectively* rich! The man who has not experienced it cannot imagine the curse of it."[57] Twain returned to the themes he had developed in "Hadleyburg" a few years later in his story "The $30,000 Bequest," but there was a personal element in this later story that prevented it from attaining the mastery of "The Man That Corrupted Hadleyburg."

"The $30,000 Bequest" was published in *Harper's Weekly* on December 10, 1904. The story tells of a happy and hardworking couple, Saladin and Electra Foster, who receive word from a distant relative named Tilbury that they will receive $30,000 upon his death so long as they do not speak of the gift, ask after the relative's health, or attend the funeral. This unexplained and rather preposterous premise for the story allows Twain to blend dream and reality and to measure one against the other. The legacy, we learn, is a gift of spite; Tilbury Foster says money has caused him nothing but trouble, and he hopes that the money will continue to do its "malignant work" (*CTS* II, 599) with Saladin and Electra. And it does. Almost instantly, the couple, constitutionally romantic anyway, begins to live in an imagined life of profitable investment and ever-increasing wealth. The acquistive wife dreams of turning the $30,000 into several hundred millions; the self-indulgent husband is forbidden from dipping into the principal, but within the limits his wife allows him, he nevertheless dreams of wild and lavish purchases.

The Fosters neglect their business and real interests in preference to imagined luxury, and along the way, they forfeit their happiness. For several years, they wait for the news of Tilbury's death and of their inheritance; meantime they live in an invented "Dream-life" and rather mechanically and absentedmindedly attend to their "Fact-life." They imagine marrying their daughters to ever more respectable and wealthy husbands; they mentally build and rebuild their cottage into a mansion; their Baptist faith does not use enough candles, so they will become Roman Catholics; the wife fancifully endows universities and sponsors missionaries, and the husband buys a yacht and drinks champagne; one becomes profligate, and the other philanthropic. Perhaps worst of all, they break the Sabbath.

The moral deterioration of the Fosters is as clear and as unremitting as that of the Richardses in Hadleyburg. However, it remains a private fantasy that poses no social danger, but neither does it offer redemptive understanding or arrive at any coherent and instructive end. Eventually, the Fosters learn that Tilbury Foster had died five years earlier and, besides, had no money to bequeath. For the next two years, they live in "mental night, always brooding, steeped in vague regrets and melancholy dreams," and then at last they die on the same day (*CTS* II, 625). Saladin Foster's dying words demonstrate that they have learned nothing from their experience: Tilbury "left us but thirty thousand, knowing we would try to increase it, and ruin our life and break our hearts. Without added expense he could have left us far above desire of increase, far above the temptation to speculate" (*CTS* II, 626).

There is a great deal of bitterness in "The $30,000 Bequest," but there is humor, too. Twain has firm control over his material here, and he manages to intermingle dream and reality in wonderfully adroit and comic ways. But the bitterness seems directed inwardly, and the moral contempt is more cautionary than corrective. This is due, I think, to the personal quality of the tale. It has been observed before that the Foster household, including the two daughters, resembles the Clemens household. We know that Twain's financial investments were sometimes disastrous and nearly always wrongheaded, and we also know that his indebtedness required drastic solutions. Henry H. Rogers acquired Twain's power of attorney, and his copyrights were assigned to Olivia. It seems hardly accidental that Saladin Foster should be called "Sally," and Electra "Aleck." Sally's name, the narrator tells us, was a "curious and unsexing one," and he readily defers to his wife's judgments about money matters because he knows he is better at spending than investing. Twain probably felt "unsexed" himself and by events that were largely his own doing. At any rate, the tone of this story lacks the angry sympathy of "The Man That Corrupted Hadleyburg"; it is more often mocking and contemptuous than compassionate, and Twain reserved the majority of that contempt for himself. However, Twain had a surplus of cantankerousness and indignant anger, enough, in fact, to offer large helpings to the world at large.

Mark Twain greeted the twentieth century tersely in a single paragraph printed in the New York *Herald* on December 31, 1900. He handed over to the new century a "stately matron named Christendom," "bedraggled, besmirched, and dishonored" with the foul experience of imperialism, "her soul full of meanness, her pocket full of boodle, and her mouth full of pious hypocrisies" (*CTS* II, 456). These were not the words of a man whose moral seriousness was in question.

Some of Twain's best writing during the last years of his life appeared not in his fiction but in polemical essays such as "The United States of Lyncherdom," "To the Person Sitting in Darkness," or "King Leopold's Soliloquy." The countervailing weight to Twain's outraged invective and spleen was, in the estimate of many critics, a maudlin, even cloying, sentimentality. James Wilson observes that during this period, Twain's "mood vacillated from bitterness and rage over personal, social, and cosmic injustices to sentimental effusions of tender emotion, usually connected with childhood innocence and courageous virtue." James Cox divides Twain's work in the last years of his life into two categories, the ironic and the sentimental, the latter consisting mostly of "more or less nauseating" short fiction.[58]

There is no point in disputing this judgment. Much of Twain's short fiction in his last years is unquestionably sentimental, though it might be added that he could manufacture the sentimental at will and wield it as a club in the service of moral purposes that even the most tough-minded critics could approve. Sometimes Twain did this on request. "A Dog's Tale," for example, was written from the point of view of a dog who saves her master's child and later watches her pup undergo vivisection at the hands of the same man. This story, written largely to satisfy his daughter Jean's opposition to such cruelty, was published in *Harper's Magazine* in 1903 and later issued as a pamphlet by the British National Anti-Vivisection Society. "A Horse's Tale" was also written upon request to serve a similar end; it was published in the August and September 1906 issues of *Harper's Monthly*. The actress Minnie Madden Fiske asked Twain for a story that might help combat the brutality of bull-fighting. Once again, Twain adopted an animal's point of view (the story is told, in part, by Buffalo Bill's horse, Soldier Boy) and communicates in a tone more bewildered than outraged the peculiar barbarity of human creatures. The point here is not whether these tales willfully pull at the reader's heartstrings; they do. However, it is not always easy to determine when Twain is being sentimental or merely shrewd.

Howells gives us a more measured assessment of Twain during his so-called "bad mood" period. He describes how total Twain's despair was after his wife's death in 1904 but also notes a certain resiliency and vitality in him: Mark Twain "said that he never saw a dead man whom he did not envy for having had it over and being done with it. Life had always amused him, and in the resurgence of its interests after his sorrow had ebbed away he was again deeply interested in the world and in the human race, which, though damned, abound in subjects of curious inquiry."[59]

It is an angry but engrossed curiosity that lends power to "The Man That Corrupted Hadleyburg"—how many fascinating ways the human race proves itself damned, Twain seems to be saying. But in the closing pages of the story, Twain had also demonstrated a quality of sympathy for the Richardses, who for all intents and purposes die of heartbreak. That sympathy, mostly detectable at the level of tone, has little to do with the characters as compromised and fallible individuals; instead, Twain's pity (and his anger, too) stemmed from what he believed to be the injustice of the human condition.

In 1901 and 1902, Twain published six stories. "Two Little Tales" appeared in the *Century* for November 1901; "The Death Disk" was published in the December issue of *Harper's Monthly* the same year. "A Double-Barreled Detective Story" was published in two installments, in the January and February issues of *Harper's Monthly*. "The Five Boons of Life" was published in *Harper's Weekly* for July 5, 1902, and "The Belated Russian Passport" on December 6, 1902, also in *Harper's Weekly*. "Was It Heaven? Or Hell?" appeared in *Harper's Monthly* in December 1902. Except for "A Double-Barreled Detective Story," an antic and funny (if somewhat rambling) burlesque of Arthur Conan Doyle's detective fiction, all these tales have the force, if not the form, of parable. That is to say, the author might suggest, without fully articulating, the morals of his stories.

The least interesting of this group of stories, to my mind, are "Two Little Tales" and "The Five Boons of Life." The first of the two "little tales" recites a man's difficulty getting word of a new kind of military boot to the War Office. The friend who hears this story counters with his own, a story about "How the Chimney-Sweep Got the Ear of the Emperor." The chimney sweep knows that everyone has a friend slightly above him on the social ladder and that news can be forwarded far more efficiency through the route of friendship and trust than through bureaucratic channels. In "The Five Boons of Life," a fairy offers a young man the choice between Fame, Love, Riches, Pleasure, and Death, noting that only one is really valuable. Four times the man chooses wrongly. When he has grown old and at last recognizes that Death is the most valuable possession, the fairy tells the man that he is too late. She has given the gift to a young child who was wise enough to have the fairy choose for her. In both instances, a child's innocent wisdom is preferable to adult desires and methods.

"The Belated Russian Passport" is another satire of bureaucracy. Alfred Parrish, a homesick American student, is in Berlin and is persuaded by an aggressively friendly stranger named Jackson to visit St. Petersburg before returning home. The timid young man is suspicious but cannot resist the importuning of Major Jackson, who claims that he has influence and will pave the way for the trip. Through a series of missteps, Parrish finds himself in Russia without a passport and faces a 10-year sentence in Siberia if he cannot produce one in 24 hours. Major Jackson's influence has failed him, and the girlish Parrish swoons at his prospects. In desperation, they try the American embassy, but the young man has no proof of his identity and therefore is ineligible for a passport. At the last minute, through casual conversation, it becomes clear that the embassy secretary had once roomed in the Parrish household many years ago, and when Parrish describes a painting the secretary had done, he is issued a passport at the last minute. "The Belated Russian Passport," like the second of the "Two Little Tales," pits the simplicity of friendship and fond associations against the complex—and in this instance, dangerous—rules of institutions. This story had possibilities, for Twain suggested early in the tale that a mysterious friend might cause as much mischief as a vengeful stranger. But that narrative strain is never developed, and the author fell back on a surprise ending to conclude the piece.

Inspiration for "The Death Disk" came from a passage Twain had read in Thomas Carlyle's *The Letters and Speeches of Oliver Cromwell*. In one of his autobiographical dictations, Twain reports that he had struggled to find the proper form of the tale for many years until one day when it essentially told itself in a few hours. In the story, Cromwell, the iron-willed Puritan, requires the death penalty of one of three of his colonels who, although victorious, exceeded their authority in battle. He decides that a child passing by will choose which man will die. Cromwell is quite taken by the girl's vivacity and innocence, and she believes that he is playing some amusing game when he gives her three disks, two white and one red, and asks her to give one to each man. Cromwell does not know it at the time, but the girl is actually the daughter of one of the accused. Because she believes the red disk to be the prettiest, she naturally gives it to her father. When the girl realizes what she has done, she recurs to a pledge she had extracted from the Lord Protector and asks him to pardon the prisoner. Cromwell, greatly relieved, does so with the following words: "God be thanked for the saving accident of that unthinking promise. . . . The prisoner is pardoned; set him free" (*CSS*, 401).

Though admired in its day, "The Death Disk" is now typically discounted for its obvious sentimentality. However, one cannot help wondering whether Twain was not rather managing that effect to his private satisfaction. When the Lord Protector hits upon his scheme for deciding who will die, he praises the Lord: "Of a surety that good thought came to me in my perplexity from Him who is an ever-present help to them that are in doubt and seek His aid. . . . Another would err, but He cannot err. Wonderful are His ways, and wise—blessed be His holy Name!" (*CSS*, 400). These are words of praise for an unfailing Providence, but when the girl countermands his decision, Cromwell again praises God, this time for a "saving accident" and an "unthinking promise." The spontaneous promptings of his heart, not his righteous submission to God's will, led him to make and to keep that promise to the little girl.

For Twain, it seems, Cromwell's act was attributable to a moral sense that stood in opposition to righteousness. In a little sketch called "A Fable," published in 1909, Twain made the moral of his animal fable explicit: "You can find in a text whatever you bring, if you will stand between it and the mirror of your imagination. You may not see your ears, but they will be there" (*CTS* II, 879). Twain had so managed the narrative that if readers of "The Death Disk" responded to its calculated emotional sentiment, their benign feelings, like Cromwell's, were morally proper but religiously suspect. Whether his readers knew it or not, their ears were showing. Twain's private quarrel with the Maker had to do with his conviction that human beings had been equipped with an intuitive moral sense that seemed strangely to contradict Providential design. By playing on the predictable sentiments of his readers, Twain was perpetrating an unusual sort of literary hoax—he might air his own grievances and verify his own personal suspicions in a way that did not openly challenge religious orthodoxy. In other words, the predictable emotional response of his readers enabled Twain to entangle them in an ethical position unsupported by, and perhaps insupportable to, religious doctrine. Nowhere is this strategy more evident than in "Was It Heaven? Or Hell?"

In the summer of 1902, Howells told Twain a story about two women who protected their dying niece by not telling her that her own daughter was also dying of the same illness. This was the germ for "Was It Heaven? Or Hell?" In his story, Twain made the two elderly women severely religious and opposed to any form of lie, and he introduced a stern and impatient doctor who scolds them for not lying to the niece for the sake of her health. At length, the aunts relent and comfort the dying woman with stories of her daughter's health and happiness, though the daughter is dangerously ill in a room downstairs. The niece dies, but her daughter recovers. At midnight, an angel appears before the two old women, who believe they are condemned by their lies. The angel demands that the women repent of their sins, but they cannot: "we are poor creatures who have learned our human weakness, and we know that if we were in those hard straits again our hearts would fail again, and we should sin as before" (*CTS* II, 546). The angel leaves to report to the "chancery of heaven" and returns with its final decree. The angel whispers the verdict to the women, but Twain leaves his readers in doubt—"Was it Heaven? Or Hell?" In this story, Twain condemns what he called elsewhere an "immoral piety," but the sentimental quality of the tale also forces upon his readers a sympathy that implies an emotional loyalty to one's own kind over and above any declared allegiance to divine decree.

That same loyalty is present in "Eve's Diary." It was written a year after Olivia died and published in the Christmas 1905 issue of *Harper's Monthly*. Though composed more than a decade after "Extracts from Adam's Diary," the tale was meant to be a companion piece to the earlier work. Eve is drawn with such affective simplicity in this "diary" that one can easily understand why Adam might prefer living outside the Garden with her to living inside the Garden without her. But she is a good deal more than a lovely presence in paradise; she is altogether superior to her companion in Eden. It is Eve, not Adam, who names the animals in the Garden; before Adam can get a word out, Eve gives them the proper names because she simply "knows" the right name. It is also Eve who discovers fire and gives it a name. Eve reasons upon her experience and observations, and she coins wise maxims. She loves the Garden and the creatures within it, but Adam has "low tastes, and is not kind" (*CTS* II, 698). All he seems to want to do is to stay out of the rain and to "thump" the melons and finger the fruits "to see how those properties are coming along" (*CTS* II, 702).

Eve regards herself as an "experiment." She describes her own behavior and curiosity with a quizzical, slightly amazed interest, for she is unsure why she was made. She knows that she loves beauty. She grieves when the moon seems to have slipped from its perch, and she tries to "clod" stars from the sky so that she might put some in her hair. She is strangely attracted to the other "experiment," a creature she takes to be a reptile but eventually concludes is a man. Eve follows him and tries to talk to him, and she fears for his safety. She does not know why she finds the creature attractive; he is moody and not as smart or as comely as she is, and when he deigns to talk at all, he uses strong, expressive words that she does not understand. At last she concludes that love is "not a product of reasoning and statistics" (*CTS* II, 707) and knows only that she loves the creature because he is "masculine" and he is "mine." Eve knows instinctively that she is "the first wife; and in the last wife I shall be repeated." But Twain has carefully prepared for Adam, not Eve, to have the last word in this diary and to speak his own love for the wife he has lost. Forty years after the Fall, Adam stands at Eve's grave. His words are simple: "Wheresoever she was, *there* was Eden" (*CTS* II, 709).

It is fitting that we should conclude this study of Twain's short fiction with a consideration of "Extract of Captain Stormfield's Visit to Heaven," for in a very real sense, the story had grown up alongside its author. The genesis of this story was a long and complicated one. Early in 1868, as Twain later recalled in his autobiography, Captain Ned Wakeman told Twain about a dream vision Wakeman had had of a visit to heaven. Twain made some notes for a possible story based on Wakeman's account and within a couple of months, as he remembered it, had a narrative of some 40,000 words. At some point, though surely not as early as Twain recalled, the story had become a burlesque of Elizabeth Stuart Phelps's novel *The Gates Ajar* (1868), but he was not satisfied with it. Twain unfairly characterized Phelps's imagining of heaven as a "mean little ten-cent heaven about the size of Rhode Island—a heaven large enough to accommodate about a tenth of one percent of the Christian billions who had died in the past nineteen centuries. I raised the limit."[60] Phelps herself had by no means described such an exclusionary heaven; she had certainly left the pearly gates ajar and open to more souls than narrow Christian piety might allow. Nevertheless, if Phelps upped the ante, Twain did raise the limit considerably. Twain's depiction of heaven is the ultimate tall tale, and the story of Captain Stormfield is one of his most expansive and generous flights of fancy.

Twain continued to work on this story throughout the 1880s and 1890s, sometimes with an eye toward publishing it, sometimes, as he told Howells, "merely for the love of it" (*MTHL* I, 376), and frequently read portions of the manuscript at social gatherings. He made notes, interpolated episodes, and made some revisions during these years, but in 1905 or early 1906, he returned to the manuscript with a certain determination to finish it.[61] He thought that much he had written would be too shocking to readers and might damage his reputation, but he submitted slightly altered versions of chapters 3 and 4 to *Harper's Monthly*. They were published in two installments as "Extract from Captain Stormfield's Visit to Heaven" in the December 1907 and January 1908 issues. Later in 1908, Harper's issued a somewhat modified version of the tale under a separate cover; this slender volume was the last book Twain published in his lifetime.

The printed tale begins with Stormfield telling an unidentified man named Peters that he had been dead for 30 years and ever since had been sailing in space as "straight as a dart for the Hereafter" (*CTS* II, 826). Stormfield did not yet know that he was bound for heaven (in fact, he suspected that his destination was the "Everlasting Tropics"), but he did know that he was lonesome in the vast and dark expanse. The wind was in his favor, he recalls, and he was making good speed, about a million miles a minute. He passed a few ordinary comets traveling 200,000 miles a minute, but there was no contest—"It was as if the comet was a gravel-train and I was a telegraph despatch." Then he spied a real, honest-to-goodness comet, and as he gained on it, he felt "like a gnat closing up on the continent of America." But the gnat was up to the challenge, and he decided that a race was in order. Soon enough, the Captain realized, "I'd woke up a pretty ugly customer" (*CTS* II, 827).

The race is close until Stormfield thumbs his nose at the competition. The disheveled captain of the comet has just awakened and is in no mood for insults. It turns out his craft is carrying souls to Satan, and he commands the crew to lighten the load. They dump overboard "Eighteen hundred thousand billion quintillions of kazarks" of the damned; a "kazark," we are told, is "exactly the bulk of *a hundred and sixty nine worlds like ours*" (*CST* II, 829). The comet zooms out of sight, and Stormfield is left in its wake humiliated. His embarrassment is temporary, however, for his attention is soon directed to the horizon and what he takes be the fiery furnaces of hell. He is mistaken. He arrives at the gates of heaven, but he has entered at the wrong port.

This episode serves well as a prologue to the captain's visit to heaven, for it casts in comic terms Stormfield's distinctive qualities. In an introductory note that Twain chose not to publish in *Harper's*, he defined clearly the moral nature of his created character: "He was a rugged, weather-tanned sailor, with a picked-up education, a sterling good heart, an iron will, abundant pluck, unshakable beliefs and convictions, and a confidence in himself which had no discoverable limits."[62] Stormfield, in other words, is a man equal to any situation, and, in Twain's estimation at least, fully worthy of paradise. However, experience has not prepared Stormfield for the situation he now finds himself in, and much of the affecting comedy of the piece has to do with the seasoned innocence he brings to heaven. Although he confronts uncanny circumstance with pluck and goodwill, many of the beliefs and expectations that have been bred into him will be as roundly defeated as he was in his race with the comet; it soon becomes apparent to him that he will have to pick up an education in the ways of the Hereafter. Stormfield is struck by the magnitude of space and eternity, but he is neither paralyzed nor dumbfounded by his situation, and part of the charm of this tale resides in his slangy intimacy with imponderables and his awkward and muscle-bound willingness to try his hand at immortality.

Stormfield's race with the comet put him off course a point. He arrives at one of the billion gates of heaven and finds himself in the company of blue people, each with one leg and seven heads. When asked where he is from, he proudly announces "San Francisco," but soon finds that the gatekeepers have not heard of San Francisco, California, America, or even "the world." At last, one angel searches a vast map of the universe with a magnifying glass and finds Earth, or "the Wart," as it is locally known. They direct the captain to his appropriate district in heaven, where he is greeted by a familiar voice, that of a "Pi Ute Injun I used to know in Tulare County" (*CTS* II, 835), and is promptly issued standard angel gear—a halo (size 13), a hymn book, a harp, a palm branch, and a pair of wings. The captain then sets out in search of the nearest cloud bank.

Twain's divine comedy is compounded of several amusing episodes of social and physical awkwardness, vernacular dialogue characterized by a rough-and-ready commonsense realism that throws absurd earthly expectations of the afterlife into dramatic relief, and an affecting search for a cozy and comfortable place in the vastness of paradise. Stormfield dutifully begins to play what he assumes is his appointed role by strumming on his harp and playing the only tune he knows. A bashful neighbor on the same cloud ventures a complaint:

> "Don't you know any tune but the one you've been pegging at all day?'
> "Not another blessed one," says I.
> "Don't you reckon you could learn another one?" says he.

"Never," says I; "I've tried to, but I couldn't manage it."
"It's a long time to hang to the one—eternity, you know."
(*CTS* II, 837)

Stormfield sighs at the prospect, and the two agree that this is not the idea of bliss they had in mind. Moments such as these are scattered throughout the tale, and they simultaneously demonstrate Stormfield's earnestness and goodwill and the preposterous ideas and yearnings mortals have of immeasurable happiness.

Stormfield resolves to learn how to use his wings, but he has only limited success. At one point, he makes a mad dash with them, but he is unlucky: "First off, I flew thirty yards, and then fouled an Irishman and brought him down. . . . Next I had a collision with a Bishop—and bowled him down, of course. We had some sharp words" (*CTS* II, 843). At another point, he invites his friend Sandy McWilliams over for some "manna and quails," and Sandy sets him straight on the way things work in heaven. "You see, on earth we jump to such foolish conclusions as to things up here," says Sandy (*CTS* II, 862). We are brought up to believe that everything is level in heaven, but it is a monarchy, not a republic. Some folks come to heaven expecting to hug and weep over Abraham, Isaac, and Jacob, but it doesn't stand to reason that these biblical patriarchs have nothing better to do than welcome 60,000 people a day. Besides, says Sandy, if they did consent to get hugged and wept over all the time, "They would be tired out and as wet as muskrats" (*CTS* II, 847).

This story is wonderful satire, of course, but it is more than that. The "main charm" of heaven is that it admits all kinds and provides many avenues to happiness. "When the Deity builds a heaven," Sandy says, "it is built right and on a liberal plan." He recalls a reception to welcome Charles Peace, "the Bannercross Murderer," when all sorts of folks turned out: "I saw Esquimaux there, and Tartars, negroes, Chinamen—people from everywhere" (*CTS* II, 848). Each segment of the vast populations of the earth brings along with it customs, traditions, and languages, and each individual has a collection of personal habits and desires that must find satisfaction in heaven. The idea of paradise as a bunch of "warbling ignoramuses" (*CTS* II, 838), always young and spry and fatuous and with time on their hands, was not Twain's idea of heaven.

In a "sane" heaven, people would have something to do and a place to smoke and to talk. Because happiness is only "a *contrast* with something

119

that ain't pleasant," there is "plenty of pain and suffering in heaven—consequently there's plenty of contrasts, and just no end of happiness" (*CTS* II, 839). This much of Twain's picture of heaven seems to have derived from the utilitarian and deterministic philosophy he had been espousing for some 20 years. As early as 1883, he had told the Monday Evening Club that human beings are merely trained "machines" incapable of originality or self sacrifice, but he had never completely convinced himself that this was the case.[63] In any event, the most radical part of Twain's vision of heaven has to do not with training or a desire for public approval but with intrinsic merit and absolute moral justice.

Much of the second half of this "extract" concerns the high drama of angels attending a reception for a barkeeper from Jersey City who found religion not long before he died. This is merely a literary device and mostly serves as an occasion for Sandy to describe the "heavenly justice" of a true meritocracy. Good people often suffered unjustly in life, he says; they "warn't rewarded according to their deserts, on earth, but here they get their rightful rank" (*CTS* II, 852). Unlike Scoresby in the story "Luck," everyone in heaven is "focused" right at last. Thus, a sausage maker from Hoboken, who on earth quietly gave spare meat to the deserving poor but had the public reputation of being a mean man, in heaven becomes Sir Richard Duffer, Baronet. Charles the Second, in the English section, is fast becoming a first-rate comedian. Caesar and Napoleon must walk behind a horse doctor from Afghanistan, a knife grinder from ancient Egypt, and a bricklayer from Boston who, though they never saw combat, had a superior military greatness in them.

The most remarkable person in heaven, however, is Edward Billings. The biblical prophets must walk behind Shakespeare and Homer, but the greatest poet who ever lived was a tailor from Tennessee. He wrote poetry "Homer and Shakespeare couldn't begin to come up to; but nobody would print it, nobody read it but his neighbors, an ignorant lot, and they laughed at it" (*CTS* II, 852). The villagers crowned the sick and starving Billings with cabbage leaves and mocked him and rode him around the town on a rail. He died the next morning. Sandy McWilliams recalls that his reception in heaven was very different. Even the three great poets from other galaxies, Saa, Bo, and Soof, showed up to welcome Billings. No one outside our solar system has ever heard of Moses or Adam, but Billings's name "will be carried pretty far, and it will make our system talked about, and maybe our world too, and raise us in the respect of the general public in heaven. Why, look here—Shakespeare walked backwards before that tailor from Tennessee, and scattered flowers for him to walk on, and Homer stood behind his chair and waited on him at the banquet" (*CTS* II, 855).

There is plenty of cantankerousness and even bitter humor in this tale, and Twain's satire is pointed enough to name names and to specify occasions. But the author is merely claiming his rights. When Sandy McWilliams asks, "Would heaven be heaven if you couldn't slander folks?" (*CTS* II, 843), we can guess at Twain's answer. Nevertheless, the prevailing mood of the piece is not scorn or contempt but generous and charitable complaint. Twain ridicules absurd earthbound notions of our final reward, but more important is his expressed belief in unacknowledged goodness. Virtue and courage, talent and decency, are not lacking in the world, but they are often despised or rendered ineffectual by their obscurity. How much has the world lost by its neglect of a tailor from Tennessee or its indifference to a knife grinder from ancient Egypt?

In his last years, Twain had more often than not discerned in the damned human race envy, venality, hypocrisy, and hatred. But this "extract" from Captain Stormfield's visit reaffirmed an earlier faith he had never entirely abandoned. For nearly 50 years, Twain had populated his short fiction with obscure but worthy figures of the imagination. They came from the Mississippi valley, Virginia City, the Pacific slope, or western New York. They had names like Dick Baker, Scotty Briggs, Aunt Rachel, Simon Wheeler, Sarah Wilkerson, and Captain Eli Stormfield. They were rather ordinary. Some of them were proud and bullheaded, some were sly, and some were absentminded. Many of them had greatness in them; most of them were denied their opportunities; all of them had stories to tell.

Six months after "Extract from Captain Stormfield's Visit to Heaven" was published, Twain visited for the first time the house he was having built in Redding, Connecticut. He loved the house and moved in shortly thereafter. Twain decided to give it a name reminiscent of his first successful book—"Innocents at Home." His daughter Clara convinced him to change the name to "Stormfield," however.

Stormfield was to be Twain's final port. His daughter Clara was married in the house in October 1909 and then moved with her husband to Europe. Twain's other daughter, Jean, died in the house the day before Christmas 1909. Shortly after Jean's funeral, Twain traveled to Bermuda, but he was suffering from chest pains and decided to return home. Along the way, he noticed that Halley's comet was visible in the night sky; perhaps Twain was reminded of his sea captain, who on his last voyage out had had the audacity to race a comet. Samuel Clemens died at Stormfield on April 21, 1910. On April 24, he was buried in Elmira, New York, beside his wife and his three deceased children, Langdon, Susy, and Jean.

Notes to Part 1

1. Twain should not be given too much credit for this anthology, even though the title bears his name. Charles H. Clark and William Dean Howells did most of the work on it, though Clemens had final authority over what went into the collection and the final, somewhat haphazard arrangement of the pieces. Nevertheless, it is clear that Clemens was widely read in American humorists and seems to have had rather definite opinions about most of them.

2. William Dean Howells, *My Mark Twain: Reminiscences and Criticisms* (New York: Harper and Brothers, 1910), 17.

3. Justin Kaplan, introduction to *Mark Twain's Short Stories*, by Mark Twain (New York: Signet, 1985), xiv.

4. Mark Twain, *Mark Twain in Eruption: Hitherto Unpublished Pages about Men and Events*, ed. Bernard DeVoto (New York: Harper and Brothers, 1940), 199.

5. See Walter Blair, "Mark Twain and the Mind's Ear," in *The American Self: Myth, Ideology, and Popular Culture*, ed. Sam B. Girgus (Albuquerque: University of New Mexico Press, 1981), 231–39.

6. One should not confuse Twain's statements on the indwelling form of a tale with Henry James's notion of the "germ" for a narrative. Both are organic conceptions, but Twain's statement, if it was to be mangled into a "theory" of the short story, would likely come closer to Aristotle's idea of an *entelechy*, as the essential principle that discloses the essence of a form. This is not a distinction without a difference. For James "the real thing" was a composite of the thing itself plus the imagination; for Twain, the world existed in its own right, and the imagination (or his at least) functioned as a midwife to the realization of a form that had its own qualities.

7. Quoted in editorial note in *RI*, 685–86.

8. Howells, *My Mark Twain*, 120.

9. Quoted in Henry Wonham, *Mark Twain and the Art of the Tall Tale* (New York: Oxford University Press, 1993), 35.

10. I am speaking here of the conditions that make the fiction "work" for a multitude of readers. As such, the moral perspective detectable in Twain's short fiction functions as a technique, regardless of whether it is sound philosophy or valid anthropology. Indeed, in *Following the Equator* (1897) and elsewhere, Twain expresses some doubts in an overarching, humanistic moral position as anything more than an excuse and disguise for Western imperialism. For an extended study of Twain's interest in a universalizable moral perspective, par-

ticularly as it was elaborated in the Scottish Common Sense philosophers, see Gregg Camfield, *Sentimental Twain: Samuel Clemens in the Maze of Moral Philosophy* (Philadelphia: University of Pennsylvania Press, 1994).

11. Louis J. Budd, *Mark Twain: The Ecstasy of Humor, Quarry Farm Papers* 6 (Elmira, N.Y.: Elmira College Center for Mark Twain Studies, 1995): 8.

12. Twain, *Mark Twain in Eruption*, 202.

13. Bret Harte, *The Lectures of Bret Harte*, comp. Charles Meeker Kozlay (New York: Charles Meeker Kozlay, 1909), 25.

14. Harte, *Lectures of Bret Harte*, 27–28.

15. See Albert Bigelow Paine, *Mark Twain: A Biography*, vol. 1 (New York: Harper and Brothers, 1912), 272.

16. See *ETS* II, 262–72.

17. See John C. Gerber, "Mark Twain's Use of the Comic Pose," *PMLA* 77 (June 1962): 297–304.

18. Mark Twain, *Mark Twain's Letters Volume 1: 1853–1866*, ed. Robert Pack Browning, Michael B. Frank, and Kenneth M. Sanderson (Berkeley and Los Angeles: University of California Press, 1988), 324.

19. Flannery O'Connor, *Wise Blood*, in *3 by Flannery O'Connor* (New York: Signet, 1964), 67.

20. See Edgar M. Branch, "Mark Twain: Newspaper Reading and the Writer's Creativity," *Nineteenth-Century Fiction* 37 (March 1983): 576–603.

21. See David E. E. Sloane, *Mark Twain as a Literary Comedian* (Baton Rouge: Lousiana State University Press, 1979), 84–103.

22. See Jeffrey Steinbrink, *Getting to Be Mark Twain* (Berkeley and Los Angeles: University of California Press, 1991), esp. 188–92.

23. Twain was well aware of the preconceived notions about him as a writer and sometimes published pieces anonymously (such as "The Curious Republic of Gondour") because he thought his readers might suspect a hoax or a joke and therefore misread him.

24. See Henry Nash Smith, *Mark Twain: The Development of a Writer* (Cambridge: Harvard University Press, 1962), 52–70.

25. Camfield, *Sentimental Twain: Samuel Clemens in the Maze of Moral Philosophy*, x.

26. Steinbrink, *Getting to Be Mark Twain*, 137–38.

27. Twain, *Mark Twain's Letters* 1, 324.

28. For example, in 1877, when John Lewis, a black servant for the Cranes, performed a remarkable feat of heroism by stopping a runaway cart with Olivia's sister-in-law aboard, Clemens's reaction was telling. He interceded in what was largely a family matter and claimed that because he had grown up among blacks and therefore knew what they would most appreciate, he would advise the family on the proper way to reward Lewis. See Arthur G. Pettit, *Mark Twain and the South* (Lexington: University of Kentucky Press, 1974), 96.

29. Twain may have altered the details of the recognition scene between Rachel and her son. In "A True Story," Aunt Rachel uses a phrase she had picked up from her mother: "I wa'nt bawn in de mash to be fool' by trash! I's one o' de ole Blue Hen's Chickens, I is!" The expression appropriately emphasizes Aunt Rachel's pride and her righteous indignation and is distinctive enough to confirm Henry's suspicions that she is his mother. However, the story, as it was told among Mary Cord's descendants, notes that Henry recognized his mother by the ring he had given her when he was a child. See Herbert A. Wisbey Jr., "The True Story of Auntie Cord," *Mark Twain Society Bulletin* 4, no. 2 (June 1981): 1, 3–5.

30. Philip Foner, *Mark Twain: Social Critic* (New York: International Publishers, 1958), 204.

31. Kaplan, introduction to *Mark Twain's Short Stories*, xii.

32. Howells, *My Mark Twain*, 121.

33. Howells, *My Mark Twain*, 122.

34. Quoted in Gladys Bellamy, *Mark Twain as a Literary Artist* (Norman: University of Oklahoma Press, 1950), 135.

35. Howard Baetzhold, *Mark Twain and John Bull: The British Connection* (Bloomington: Indiana University Press, 1970), 57–58.

36. Howells, *My Mark Twain*, 141.

37. For a discussion of this speech and its cultural significance for Twain, Howells, and others, see Harold K. Bush Jr., "The Mythic Struggle between East and West: Mark Twain's Speech at Whittier's 70th Birthday Celebration and W. D. Howells' *A Chance Acquaintance*," *American Literary Realism* 27, no. 2 (Winter 1995): 53–73.

38. Mark Twain, *The Autobiography of Mark Twain*, ed. Charles Neider (New York: Harper & Row, 1959), 293.

39. Smith, *Mark Twain: The Development of a Writer*, 110.

40. Quoted in Smith, *Mark Twain: The Development of a Writer*, 112.

41. Walter Blair, "Mark Twain's Other Masterpiece: 'Jim Baker's Blue-Jay Yarn,' " *Studies in American Humor* 1, no. 3 (January 1975): 132–47.

42. See Horst H. Kruse, *Mark Twain and "Life on the Mississippi"* (Amherst: University of Massachusetts Press, 1981), 22–30.

43. See Everett Emerson, *The Authentic Mark Twain: A Literary Biography* (Philadelphia: University of Pennsylvania Press, 1984), 100–126.

44. John Gerber, "Mark Twain's 'Private Campaign,' " *Civil War History* 1 (March 1955): 37–60.

45. Howells, *My Mark Twain*, 141.

46. Mark Twain, *Mark Twain's Own Autobiography: The Chapters from the North American Review*, ed. Michael J. Kiskis (Madison: University of Wisconsin Press, 1990), 40.

47. Twain, *Mark Twain's Own Autobiography*, 49.

48. Twain, *Mark Twain's Own Autobiography*, 48–49.

49. Late in his life, Twain revised the tale once again, ridding it of allusions to Niagara Falls. This final version has now been published in *The Bible According to Mark Twain*, ed. Howard G. Baetzhold and Joseph B. McCullough (Athens: University of Georgia Press, 1995), 8–16. My citations are to the first printed version, as it was published in *Niagara Book* and reprinted in Budd. For an instructive history of this text, see Joseph McCullough, "Mark Twain's First Chestnut: Revisions in 'Extracts from Adam's Diary,' " *Essays in Arts and Sciences* (October 1994): 49–58.

50. Daniel Boorstin, *The Image: A Guide to Pseudo-Events in America* (New York: Atheneum, 1978), 11–12.

51. See Greg Zacharias, "Henry Rogers, Public Relations, and the Recovery of Mark Twain's 'Character,' " *Mark Twain Journal* 31, no. 1 (1993): 2–17.

52. Carl Dolmetsch, *"Our Famous Guest": Mark Twain in Vienna* (Athens: University of Georgia Press, 1992), 232.

53. In 1916, *The Mysterious Stranger* was published as a single, self-sufficient text. In 1963, however, John S. Tuckey revealed that this text was actually a hoax perpetrated by Twain's official biographer, Albert Bigelow Paine, and Frederick A. Duneka, an editor at Harper's. The 1916 version of *The Mysterious Stranger* is a composite text patched together from Twain's work on the several manuscripts and does not represent the intentions of the author.

54. Mark Twain, *Correspondence with Henry Huttleston Rogers*, ed. Lewis Leary (Berkeley and Los Angeles: University of California Press, 1969), 316.

55. Twain, *Mark Twain in Eruption*, 196.

56. Bellamy, *Mark Twain as a Literary Artist*, 309.

57. Twain, *Mark Twain's Own Autobiography*, 111.

58. See James Wilson, *A Reader's Guide to the Short Stories of Mark Twain* (Boston: G. K. Hall, 1987), 46, and James Cox, *Mark Twain: The Fate of Humor* (Princeton: Princeton University Press, 1966), 265.

59. Howells, *My Mark Twain*, 91.

60. Twain, *The Autobiography of Mark Twain*, 302.

61. The most complete account of the genesis of this story is by Baetzhold and McCullough in *The Bible According to Mark Twain*, 129–38. The fullest version of the story is also to be found in this book (139–88); however, my references are to the first magazine publication, published in Budd, *CTS* II, 826–63.

62. Twain, *The Bible According to Mark Twain*, 139.

63. See Walter Blair, *Mark Twain and Huck Finn* (Berkeley and Los Angeles: University of California Press, 1960), 337.

Part 2

THE WRITER

Introduction

Mark Twain was not a literary theorist, nor in any familiar sense was he a literary critic. In the early days, he did write a bit of drama criticism, and he occasionally wrote book reviews, but as a rule, he did not feel inclined, nor particularly qualified, to play the role of critic. When he did adopt that role, as Sydney J. Krause points out, Twain avoided the burdens of being merely an analyst and typically adopted the persona of a "muggins" or a "grumbler."[1] Twain had his likes and dislikes, to be sure, but by temperament and training, he was more often drawn to burlesque as the most congenial form of criticism. He could burlesque virtually any literary form—the romance, the political speech, the sentimental poem, the dramatic soliloquy, the detective novel—and most any literary artist—Arthur Conan Doyle, Elizabeth Stuart Phelps, James Fenimore Cooper, William Shakespeare, even the "sweet singer of Michigan," Julia A. Moore. Nevertheless, Twain did have a set of working principles that enabled him to measure his own artistic achievement as well as to appreciate the work of others.

The essays gathered together here enunciate those principles well enough, in both negative and positive terms. In 1870, Twain and a friend named David Gray were asked to judge an annual literary competition, and Twain predicted that their choices would likely be at variance with popular opinion and conventional expectation. In his "Report to the Buffalo Female Academy," Twain defended his selections, noting that the prize-winning essays were "instinct with *naturalness*," while observing that as a rule, school readers included "unspeakably execrable models which young people are defrauded into accepting as fine literary compositions" and thereby encouraged in adopting overblown sentiments and artificial eloquence. In 1895, he would make the same points and many others in a rollicking and antic way when he enumerated "Fenimore Cooper's Literary Offences."

These two essays, fault finding and grumbling though they are, are useful in assessing Twain's own practice, but the author sometimes spoke plainly about his own methods and appreciatively of writers he admired. In "Reply to the Editor of 'The Art of Authorship,' " Twain compared his acquisition of a distinctive style to culling through a myriad of model sentences (or "bricks") and systematically, though unconsciously, selecting those that might eventually serve to erect the "edifice" one calls style. That style is to be put in the service of the author's craft, of course, but must also be appropriate to the subject matter. For Twain, the selection of precisely the right "brick" was crucial to the realist's art—it meant the difference between "the lightning bug and the lightning."

"How to Tell a Story" is the most famous of Twain's literary statements. In this essay, he identifies the requirements for practicing the "high and delicate art" of telling a humorous story, a comic form he believed to be distinctively American. The humorous storyteller must be able to utter incongruities and absurdities casually and without apparent purpose and, all the while, appear unaware that there is anything funny in the tale. Add the ability to drop an occasional "studied remark" and to "slur the point" along with a perfect mastery of the pause, and one has the storyteller par excellence. "How to Tell a Story" is an important index to Twain's peculiar genius, and his allegiance to an oral tradition should not be underestimated. However, this essay concerns how to "tell" a story, not how to write one. At least as important for him was the writer's capacity to create the illusion of immediacy and spontaneous talk, and achieving this effect is more a matter of the dramatic management of the tale. For that reason, I have also included Twain's essay "William Dean Howells."

In this essay, Twain identifies features of Howells's artistry that, at his best, were Twain's as well. He praises the clearness and compression of Howells's prose, his "verbal exactness," and his unconscious naturalness of phrasing. These are qualities that make Howells's pictures of life "photographs with feeling in them . . . photographs taken in a dream, one might say." But Twain also discerns in Howells a gift for what he calls " 'stage directions'—those artifices that authors employ to throw a kind of human naturalness around a scene and a conversation, and help the reader to see the one and get at meanings in the other which might not be perceived if intrusted unexplained to the bare words of the talk." Twain was devoted to the "bare words" of talk, but he knew instinctively that those words would not become vivid without the inconspicuous assistance of proper stage directions.

Note

1. See parts 1 and 2 of Sydney J. Krause, *Mark Twain as Critic* (Baltimore: Johns Hopkins University Press, 1966).

Report to the Buffalo Female Academy

I beg leave to offer the report of the committee appointed to sit in judgment upon the compositions of the graduating and collegiate classes. We have done our work carefully and conscientiously; we have determined the degrees of literary excellence displayed, with pitiless honesty; we have experienced no sort of difficulty in selecting and agreeing upon the two first-prize compositions—and yet, after all, we feel that it is necessary to say a word or two in vindication of our verdict.

Because, we have misgivings that our choice might not be the choice of the Academy, if the choice were left to them—nor of this assemblage— nor of a vote of the general public. Let this comfort those fair competitors whom our verdict has wronged. But we have judged these compositions by the strict rules of literary criticism, and let *this* reassure those whom our verdict has exalted.

We have chosen as the two prize essays the least showy of the eighteen submitted, perhaps, but they are the least artificial, the least labored, the clearest and shapeliest, and the best carried out. The paper we have chosen for the first prize of the graduates is very much the best literary effort in the whole collection, and yet it is almost the least ambitious among them. It relates a very simple little incident, in unpretentious language, and then achieves the difficult feat of pointing it with one of those dismal atrocities called a Moral, without devoting double the space to it which it ought to occupy and outraging every canon of good taste, relevance and modesty. It is a composition which possesses, also, the very rare merit of *stopping when it is finished.* It shows a freedom from adjectives and superlatives which is attractive, not to say seductive—and let us remark instructively, in passing, that one can seldom run his pen through an adjective without improving his manuscript. We can say further, in praise of this first-prize composition, that there is a singular aptness of language noticeable in it—denoting a

"Report to the Buffalo Female Academy" first appeared as part of a longer article in the Buffalo *Express* on June 24, 1870, the source of this text.

shrewd faculty of selecting just the right word for the service needed, as a general thing. It is a high gift. It is the talent which gives accuracy, grace and vividness in descriptive writing.

The other first prize—the collegiate—is so simple and unpretending that it seems a daring thing to prefer it before certain of its fellows which we could name, but still we of the committee rigidly decree that it is perceptibly superior to the best of them. It is nothing in the world but just a bright and fresh little bit of fancy, told with a breezy dash, and with nothing grand or overpowering about it. Attached to it is the inevitable Moral, but it is compressed into a single sentence, and is delivered with a snap that is exhilarating and an unexpectedness that is captivating. And we are furthermore able to say, in justification of this Moral, that the composition would not be symmetrical, keenly and cleanly pointed and complete, without it. An application, or a "nub," or a moral that *fits*, is a jewel of price. It is only the awkward, irrelevant and pinchbeck moral that this committee snubs.

Now, if you have observed, we have decided that the graduates' first-prize possesses the several merits of unpretentiousness, simplicity of language and subject, and marked aptness and accuracy of wording—and that the collegiate first-prize has the merits of modesty and freshness of subject and grace and excellence of treatment. But both of these possess one other merit, or cluster of merits, which strongly attracted us. They were instinct with *naturalness*—a most noble and excellent feature in composition, and one which is customarily lacking in productions written for state occasions, from the Friday composition in a village school all the way up to the President's message—and you may verify my words by critically examining any written speech that ever *was* written—except this one I am reading. The two prize essays possess naturalness, and likewise a happy freshness that marks them as the expression of the original thoughts and fancies of the minds that wrought them, and not stale and venerable platitudes and commonplaces absorbed from good but stupid books and drowsy sermons, and delivered at secondhand in the same unvarying and monotonous sequence—a sequence which they have grown so familiar with since Adam and each of his descendants in turn used them in his appointed season, that now one needs only write down the first of them and the rest fall into line without a murmur or ever a missing veteran.

We consider it a plain duty to observe that while the disposition in all school compositions to contemplate all subjects from high moral and religious altitudes would be matter for sincere praise and gratulation, if such disposition came from a strong spontaneous impulse on the part of the student, it is not matter for praise or gratulation either when that disposition is strained or forced. Nearly all the compositions submitted to us would have been right creditable specimens of literary handiwork, if the sermons had been left out of them. But, while some of these latter were the expression of a genuine impulse, the great majority of them were so manifestly dragged in and hitched on to the essay (out of pure force of habit and therefore unconsciously, we are willing to believe, but still plainly dragged in), that they sadly marred some of the compositions and entirely spoiled one or two. Religion is the highest and holiest thing on earth, and a strained or compulsory expression of it is not gracious, or commendable, or befitting its dignity.

However, we have the hardihood to say, in this place, that considering the "Standard School Readers" and the other popular and unspeakably execrable models which young people are defrauded into accepting as fine literary composition, the real wonder is, not that pupils attempt subjects which they would be afraid of at forty, and then write floridly instead of simply, and start without premises and wind up without tangible result, but that they write at all without bringing upon themselves suspicions of imbecility.

The dead weight of custom and tradition have clogged school method and discipline from a past date which we cannot name, until the present time. They have worn these dead weights so long that they unconsciously continue to wear them in these free, progressive latter days. For lingering ages, seemingly, the seminary pupil has been expected to present, at stated intervals, a composition constructed upon one and the same old heart-rending plan. It is not necessary to detail this plan—it is familiar to all. This ancient model is so ingrained in the method of the schools, and has so long been allowed to pass unchallenged as being the correct idea, that it will require a considerable time to eradicate it. To the high credit of the principal and teachers of this academy, however, it can be said that they are faithfully doing what they can to destroy it and its influence and occupy their place with something new and better. But when we of the committee take into consideration that much of this atmosphere of old custom and tradition necessarily still lingers around this unquestionably excellent Female Academy, we feel that we are more than complimentary when we say that the compositions we have been examining average well indeed. When the old sapless composition model is finally cast entirely aside and the pupil learns to write straight from his heart, he will apply his own language and his own ideas to his subjects and then the question with committees will not be which composition to select for first prize, but which one they dare reject.

Reply to the Editor of
"The Art of Authorship"

Your inquiry has set me thinking, but, so far, my thought fails to materialise. I mean that, upon consideration, I am not sure that I have methods in composition. I do suppose I have—I suppose I must have—but they somehow refuse to take shape in my mind; their details refuse to separate and submit to classification and description; they remain a jumble—visible, like the fragments of glass when you look in at the wrong end of a kaleidoscope, but still a jumble. If I could turn the whole thing around and look in at the other end, why then the figures would flash into form out of the chaos, and I shouldn't have any more trouble. But my head isn't right for that to-day, apparently. It might have been, maybe, if I had slept last night.

However, let us try guessing. Let us guess that whenever we read a sentence and like it, we unconsciously store it away in our model-chamber; and it goes with the myriad of its fellows to the building, brick by brick, of the eventual edifice which we call our style. And let us guess that whenever we run across other forms—bricks—whose colour, or some other defect, offends us, we unconsciously reject these, and so one never finds them in our edifice. If I have subjected myself to any training processes, and no doubt I have, it must have been in this unconscious or half-conscious fashion. I think it unlikely that deliberate and consciously methodical training is usual with the craft. I think it likely that the training most in use is of this unconscious sort, and is guided and governed and made by-and-by unconsciously systematic, by an automatically-working taste—a taste which selects and rejects without asking you for any help, and patiently and steadily improves itself without troubling you to approve or applaud. Yes, and likely enough when the structure is at last pretty well up, and attracts attention, *you* feel

"Reply to the Editor of 'The Art of Authorship' " was first published in the collection *The Art of Authorship*, ed. George Bainton (New York: D. Appleton, 1890), 85–88, which is the source of this text.

136

complimented, whereas you didn't build it, and didn't even consciously superintend. Yes; one notices, for instance, that long, involved sentences confuse him, and that he is obliged to re-read them to get the sense. Unconsciously, then, he rejects that brick. Unconsciously he accustoms himself to writing short sentences as a rule. At times he may indulge himself with a long one, but he will make sure that there are no folds in it, no vaguenesses, no parenthetical interruptions of its view as a whole; when he is done with it, it won't be a sea-serpent, with half of its arches under the water, it will be a torchlight procession.

Well, also he will notice in the course of time, as his reading goes on, that the difference between the *almost right* word and the *right* word is really a large matter—'tis the difference between the lightning-bug and the lightning. After that, of course, that exceedingly important brick, the *exact* word—however, this is running into an essay, and I beg pardon. So I seem to have arrived at this: doubtless I have methods, but they begot themselves, in which case I am only their proprietor, not their father.

Fenimore Cooper's Literary Offences

The Pathfinder and *The Deerslayer* stand at the head of Cooper's novels as artistic creations. There are others of his works which contain parts as perfect as are to be found in these, and scenes even more thrilling. Not one can be compared with either of them as a finished whole.

The defects in both of these tales are comparatively slight. They were pure works of art.

—Prof. Lounsbury

The five tales reveal an extraordinary fulness of invention.

. . . One of the very greatest characters in fiction, "Natty Bumppo." . . .

The craft of the woodsman, the tricks of the trapper, all the delicate art of the forest, were familiar to Cooper from his youth up.

—Prof. Brander Matthews

Cooper is the greatest artist in the domain of romantic fiction yet produced by America.

—Wilkie Collins

It seems to me that it was far from right for the Professor of English Literature in Yale, the Professor of English Literature in Columbia, and Wilkie Collins, to deliver opinions on Cooper's literature without having read some of it. It would have been much more decorous to keep silent and let persons talk who have read Cooper.

Cooper's art has some defects. In one place in *Deerslayer,* and in the restricted space of two-thirds of a page, Cooper has scored 114 offences against literary art out of a possible 115. It breaks the record.

There are nineteen rules governing literary art in the domain of romantic fiction—some say twenty-two. In *Deerslayer* Cooper violated eighteen of them. These eighteen require:

"Fenimore Cooper's Literary Offences" was first published in the *North American Review* (July 1895): 1–12, which is the source of this text.

1. That a tale shall accomplish something and arrive somewhere. But the *Deerslayer* tale accomplishes nothing and arrives in the air.

2. They require that the episodes of a tale shall be necessary parts of the tale, and shall help to develop it. But as the *Deerslayer* tale is not a tale, and accomplishes nothing and arrives nowhere, the episodes have no rightful place in the work, since there was nothing for them to develop.

3. They require that the personages in a tale shall be alive, except in the case of corpses, and that always the reader shall be able to tell the corpses from the others. But this detail has often been overlooked in the *Deerslayer* tale.

4. They require that the personages in a tale, both dead and alive, shall exhibit a sufficient excuse for being there. But this detail also has been overlooked in the *Deerslayer* tale.

5. They require that when the personages of a tale deal in conversation, the talk shall sound like human talk, and be talk such as human beings would be likely to talk in the given circumstances, and have a discoverable meaning, also a discoverable purpose, and a show of relevancy, and remain in the neighborhood of the subject in hand, and be interesting to the reader, and help out the tale, and stop when the people cannot think of anything more to say. But this requirement has been ignored from the beginning of the *Deerslayer* tale to the end of it.

6. They require that when the author describes the character of a personage in his tale, the conduct and conversation of that personage shall justify said description. But this law gets little or no attention in the *Deerslayer* tale, as "Natty Bumppo's" case will amply prove.

7. They require that when a personage talks like an illustrated, gilt-edged, tree-calf, hand-tooled, seven-dollar Friendship's Offering in the beginning of a paragraph, he shall not talk like a negro minstrel in the end of it. But this rule is flung down and danced upon in the *Deerslayer* tale.

8. They require that crass stupidities shall not be played upon the reader as "the craft of the woodsman, the delicate art of the forest," by either the author or the people in the tale. But this rule is persistently violated in the *Deerslayer* tale.

9. They require that the personages of a tale shall confine themselves to possibilities and let miracles alone; or, if they venture a miracle, the author must so plausibly set it forth as to make it look possible and reasonable. But these rules are not respected in the *Deerslayer* tale.

10. They require that the author shall make the reader feel a deep interest in the personages of his tale and in their fate; and that he shall make the reader love the good people in the tale and hate the bad ones. But the readers of the *Deerslayer* tale dislikes the good people in it, is indifferent to the others, and wishes they would all get drowned together.

11. They require that the characters in a tale shall be so clearly defined that the reader can tell beforehand what each will do in a given emergency. But in the *Deerslayer* tale this rule is vacated.

In addition to these large rules there are some little ones. These require that the author shall

12. *Say* what he is proposing to say, not merely come near it.

13. Use the right word, not its second cousin.

14. Eschew surplusage.

15. Not omit necessary details.

16. Avoid slovenliness of form.

17. Use good grammar.

18. Employ a simple and straightforward style.

Even these seven are coldly and persistently violated in the *Deerslayer* tale.

Cooper's gift in the way of invention was not a rich endowment; but such as it was he liked to work it, he was pleased with the effects, and indeed he did some quite sweet things with it. In his little box of stage properties he kept six or eight cunning devices, tricks, artifices for his savages and woodsmen to deceive and circumvent each other with, and he was never so happy as when he was working these innocent things and seeing them go. A favorite one was to make a moccasined person tread in the tracks of the moccasined enemy, and thus hid his own trail. Cooper wore out barrels and barrels of moccasins in working that trick. Another stage-property that he pulled out of his box pretty frequently was his broken twig. He prized his broken twig above all the rest of his effects, and worked it the hardest. It is a restful chapter in any book of his when somebody doesn't step on a dry twig and alarm all the reds and whites for two hundred yards around. Every time a Cooper person is in peril, and absolute silence is worth four dollars a minute, he is sure to step on a dry twig. There may be a hundred handier things to step on, but that wouldn't satisfy Cooper. Cooper requires him to turn out and find a dry twig; and if he can't do it, go and borrow one. In fact the Leather Stocking Series ought to have been called the Broken Twig Series.

I am sorry there is not room to put in a few dozen instances of the delicate art of the forest, as practiced by Natty Bumppo and some of the other Cooperian experts. Perhaps we may venture two or three samples. Cooper was a sailor—a naval officer; yet he gravely tells us how a vessel, driving toward a lee shore in a gale, is steered for a particular spot by her skipper because he knows of an *undertow* there which will hold her back against the gale and save her. For just pure woodcraft, or sailorcraft, or whatever it is, isn't that neat? For several years Cooper was daily in the society of artillery, and he ought to have noticed that when a cannon ball strikes the ground it either buries itself or skips a hundred feet or so; skips again a hundred feet or so—and so on, till it finally gets tired and rolls. Now in one place he loses some "females"—as he always calls women—in the edge of a wood near a plain at night in a fog, on purpose to give Bumppo a chance to show off the delicate art of the forest before the reader. These mislaid people are hunting for a fort. They hear a cannon-blast, and a cannon-ball presently comes rolling into the wood and stops at their feet. To the females this suggests nothing. The case is very different with the admirable Bumppo. I wish I may never know peace again if he doesn't strike out promptly and *follow the track* of that cannon-ball across the plain through the dense fog and find the fort. Isn't it a daisy? If Cooper had any real knowledge of Nature's ways of doing things, he had a most delicate art in concealing the fact. For instance: one of his acute Indian experts, Chingachgook (pronounced Chicago, I think), has lost the trail of a person he is tracking through the forest. Apparently that trail is hopelessly lost. Neither you nor I could ever have guessed out the way to find it. It was very different with Chicago. Chicago was not stumped for long. He turned a running stream out of its course, and there, in the slush in its old bed, were that person's moccasin-tracks. The current did not wash them away, as it would have done in all other like cases—no, even the eternal laws of Nature have to vacate when Cooper wants to put up a delicate job of woodcraft on the reader.

We must be a little wary when Brander Matthews tells us that Cooper's books "reveal an extraordinary fulness of invention." As a rule, I am quite willing to accept Brander Matthews's literary judgments and applaud his lucid and graceful phrasing of them; but that particular statement needs to be taken with a few tons of salt. Bless your heart, Cooper hadn't any more invention than a horse; and I don't mean a high-class horse, either; I mean a clothes-horse. It would be very difficult to find a really clever "situation" in Cooper's books; and still more difficult to find one of any kind which he has failed to render absurd by his handling of it. Look at the episodes of "the caves;" and at the celebrated scuffle between Magua and those others on the table-land a few days later; and at Hurry Harry's queer water-transit from the castle to the ark; and at Deerslayer's half hour with his first corpse; and at the quarrel between Hurry Harry and Deerslayer later; and at—but choose for yourself; you can't go amiss.

If Cooper had been an observer, his inventive faculty would have worked better, not more interestingly, but more rationally, more plausibly. Cooper's proudest creations in the way of "situations" suffer noticeably from the absence of the observer's protecting gift. Cooper's eye was splendidly inaccurate. Cooper seldom saw anything correctly. He saw nearly all things as through a glass eye, darkly. Of course a man who cannot see the commonest little everyday matters accurately is working at a disadvantage when he is constructing a "situation." In the *Deerslayer* tale Cooper has a stream which is fifty feet wide, where it flows out of a lake; it presently narrows to twenty as it meanders along for no given reason, and yet, when a steam acts like that it ought to be required to explain itself. Fourteen pages later the width of the brook's outlet from the lake has suddenly shrunk thirty feet, and become "the narrowest part of the stream." This shrinkage is not accounted for. The stream has bends in it, a sure indication that it has alluvial banks, and cuts them; yet these bends are only thirty and fifty feet long. If Cooper had been a nice and punctilious observer he would have noticed that the bends were oftener nine hundred feet long than short of it.

Cooper made the exit of that stream fifty feet wide in the first place, for no particular reason; in the second place, he narrowed it to less than twenty to accommodate some Indians. He bends a "sapling" to the form of an arch over this narrow passage, and conceals six Indians in its foliage. They are "laying" for a settler's scow or ark which is coming up the stream on its way to the lake; it is being hauled against the stiff current by a rope whose stationary end is anchored in the lake; its rate of progress cannot be more than a mile an hour. Cooper describes the ark, but pretty obscurely. In the matter of dimensions "it was little more than a modern canal boat." Let us guess, then, that it was about 140 feet long. It was of "greater breadth than common." Let us guess, then, that it was about sixteen feet wide. This leviathan had been prowling down bends which were but a third as long as itself, and scraping between banks where it had only two feet of space to spare on each side. We cannot too much admire this miracle. A low-roofed log dwelling occupies "two-thirds of the ark's length"—a dwelling ninety feet long and sixteen feet wide, let us say—a kind of vestibule train. The dwelling has two rooms—each forty-five feet long and sixteen feet wide, let us guess. One of them is the bed-room of the Hutter girls, Judith and Hetty; the other is the parlor, in the day time, at night it is papa's bed chamber. The ark is arriving at the stream's exit, now, whose width has been reduced to less than twenty feet to accommodate the Indians—say to eighteen. There is a foot to spare on each side of the boat. Did the Indians notice that there was going to be a tight squeeze there? Did they notice that they could make money by climbing down out of that arched sapling and just stepping aboard when the ark scraped by? No; other Indians would have noticed these things, but Cooper's Indians never notice anything. Cooper thinks they are marvelous creatures for noticing, but he was almost always in error about his Indians. There was seldom a sane one among them.

The ark is 140 feet long; the dwelling is 90 feet long. The idea of the Indians is to drop softly and secretly from the arched sapling to the dwelling as the ark creeps along under it at the rate of a mile an hour, and butcher the family. It will take the ark a minute and a half to pass under. It will take the 90-foot dwelling a minute to pass under. Now, then, what did the six Indians do? It would take you thirty years to guess, and even then you would have to give it up, I believe. Therefore, I will tell you what the Indians did. Their chief, a person of quite extra-ordinary intellect for a Cooper Indian, warily watched the canal boat as it squeezed along under him, and when he had got his calculations fined down to the exactly the right shade, as he judged, he let go and dropped. And *missed the house!* That is actually what he did. He missed the house, and landed in the stern of the scow. It was not much of a fall, yet it knocked him silly. He lay there unconscious. If the house had been 97 feet long, he would have made the trip. The fault was Cooper's, not his. The error lay in the construction of the house. Cooper was no architect.

There still remained in the roost five Indians. The boat has passed under and is now out of their reach. Let me explain what the five did—you would not be able to reason it out for yourself. No. 1 jumped for the boat, but fell in the water astern of it. Then No. 2 jumped for the boat, but fell in the water still further astern of it. Then No. 3 jumped for the boat, and fell a good way astern of it. Then No. 4 jumped for the boat, and fell in the water *away* astern. Then even No. 5 made a jump for the boat—for he was a Cooper Indian. In the matter of intellect, the difference between a Cooper Indian and the Indian that stands in front of the cigar shop is not spacious. The scow episode is really a sublime burst of invention; but it does not thrill, because the inaccuracy of the details throws a sort of air of fictitiousness and general improbability over it. This comes of Cooper's inadequacy as an observer.

The reader will find some examples of Cooper's high talent for inaccurate observation in the account of the shooting match in *The Pathfinder*: "A common wrought nail was driven lightly into the target, its head having been first touched with paint." The color of the paint is not stated—an important omission, but Cooper deals freely in important omissions. No, after all, it was not an important omission; for this nail head is *a hundred yards* from the marksman and could not be seen by them at that distance no matter what its color might be. How far can the best eyes see a common house fly? A hundred yards? It is quite impossible. Very well, eyes that cannot see a house fly that is a hundred yards away cannot see an ordinary nail head at that distance, for the size of the two objects is the same. It takes a keen eye to see a fly or a nail head at fifty yards—one hundred and fifty feet. Can the reader do it?

The nail was lightly driven, its head painted, and game called. Then the Cooper miracles began. The bullet of the first marksman chipped an edge of the nail head; the next man's bullet drove the nail a little way into the target—and removed all the paint. Haven't the miracles gone far enough now? Not to suit Cooper; for the purpose of this whole scheme is to show off his prodigy, Deerslayer-Hawkeye-Long-Rifle-Leather-Stocking-Pathfinder-Bumppo before the ladies.

> "Be all ready to clench it, boys!" cried out Pathfinder, stepping into his friend's tracks the instant they were vacant. "Never mind a new nail; I can see that, though the paint is gone, and what I can see, I can hit at a hundred yards, though it were only a mosquitoe's eyes. Be ready to clench!"
>
> The rifle cracked, the bullet sped its way and the head of the nail was buried in the wood, covered by the piece of flattened lead.

There, you see, is a man who could hunt flies with a rifle, and command a ducal salary in a Wild West show to-day, if we had him back with us.

The recorded feat is certainly surprising, just as it stands; but it is not surprising enough for Cooper. Cooper adds a touch. He has made Pathfinder do this miracle with another man's rifle, and not only that, but Pathfinder did not have even the advantage of loading it himself. He had everything against him, and yet he made that impossible shot, and not only made it, but did it with absolute confidence, saying, "Be ready to clench." Now a person like that would have undertaken that same feat with a brickbat, and with Cooper to help he would have achieved it, too.

Pathfinder showed off handsomely that day before the ladies. His very first feat was a thing which no Wild West show can touch. He was standing with the group of marksmen, observing—a hundred yards from the target, mind: one Jasper raised his rifle and drove the centre of the bull's-eye. Then the quartermaster fired. The target exhibited no result this time. There was a laugh. "It's a dead miss," said Major Lundie. Pathfinder waited an impressive moment or two, then said in that calm indifferent, know-it-all way of his, "No, Major—he has covered Jasper's bullet, as will be seen if any one will take the trouble to examine the target."

Wasn't it remarkable! How *could* he see that little pellet fly through the air and enter that distant bullet-hole? Yet that is what he did; for nothing is impossible to a Cooper person. Did any of those people have any deep-seated doubts about this thing? No; for that would imply sanity, and these were all Cooper people.

> The respect for Pathfinder's skill and for his *quickness and accuracy of sight* (the italics are mine) was so profound and general, that the instant he made this declaration the spectators began to distrust their own opinions, and a dozen rushed to the target in order to ascertain the fact. There, sure enough, it was found that the quartermaster's bullet had gone through the hole made by Jasper's, and that, too, so accurately as to require a minute examination to be certain of the circumstance, which, however, was soon clearly established by discovering one bullet over the other in the stump against which the target was placed.

They made a "minute" examination; but never mind, how could they know that there were two bullets in that hole without digging the latest one out? for neither probe nor eyesight could prove the presence of any more than one bullet. Did they dig? No; as we shall see. It is the Pathfinder's turn now; he steps out before the ladies, takes aim, and fires.

But alas! here is a disappointment; an incredible, an unimaginable disappointment—for the target's aspect is unchanged; there is nothing there but that same old bullet hole?

"If one dared to hint at such a thing," cried Major Duncan, "I should say that the Pathfinder has also missed the target."

As nobody had missed it yet, the "also" was not necessary; but never mind about that, for the Pathfinder is going to speak.

"No, no, Major," said he, confidently, "that *would* be a risky declaration. I didn't load the piece, and can't say what was in it, but if it was lead, you will find the bullet driving down those of the Quartermaster and Jasper, else is not my name Pathfinder."
A shout from the target announced the truth of this assertion.

Is the miracle sufficient as it stands? Not for Cooper. The Pathfinder speaks again, as he "now slowly advances towards the stage occupied by the females:"

"That's not all, boys, that's not all; if you find the target touched at all, I'll own to a miss. The Quartermaster cut the wood, but you'll find no wood cut by that last messenger."

The miracle is at last complete. He knew—doubtless *saw*—at the distance of a hundred yards—that his bullet had passed into the hole *without fraying the edges.* There were now three bullets in that one hole—three bullets imbedded processionally in the body of the stump back of the target. Everybody knew this—somehow or other—and yet nobody had dug any of them out to make sure. Cooper is not a close observer, but he is interesting. He is certainly always that, no matter what happens. And he is more interesting when he is not noticing what he is about than when he is. This is a considerable merit.

The conversations in the Cooper books have a curious sound in our modern ears. To believe that such talk really ever came out of people's mouths would be to believe that there was a time when time was of no value to a person who thought he had something to say; when it was the custom to spread a two-minute remark out to ten; when a man's mouth was a rolling-mill, and busied itself all day long in turning four-foot pigs of thought into thirty-foot bars of conversational railroad iron by attenuation; when subjects were seldom faithfully stuck to, but the talk wandered all around and arrived nowhere; when conversations consisted mainly of irrelevances, with here and there a relevancy, a relevancy with an embarrassed look, as not being able to explain how it got there.

Cooper was certainly not a master in the construction of dialogue. Inaccurate observation defeated him here as it defeated him in so many other enterprises of his. He even failed to notice that the man who talks corrupt English six days in the week must and will talk it on the seventh, and can't help himself. In the *Deerslayer* story he lets Deerslayer talk the showiest kind of book talk sometimes, and at other times the basest of base dialects. For instance, when some one asks him if he has a sweetheart, and if so, where she abides, this is his majestic answer:

> "She's in the forest—hanging from the boughs of the trees, in a soft rain—in the dew on the open grass—the clouds that float about in the blue heavens—the birds that sing in the woods—the sweet springs where I slake my thirst—and in all the other glorious gifts that come from God's Providence!"

And he preceded that, a little before, with this:

> "It consarns me as all things that touches a fri'nd consarns a fri'nd."

And this is another of his remarks:

> "If I was Injin born, now, I might tell of this, or carry in the scalp and boast of the expl'ite afore the whole tribe; or if my inimy had only been a bear"—and so on.

We cannot imagine such a thing as a veteran Scotch Commander-in-Chief comporting himself in the field like a windy melodramatic actor, but Cooper could. On one occasion Alice and Cora were being chased by the French through a fog in the neighborhood of their father's fort:

> "*Point de quartier aux coquins!*" cried an eager pursuer, who seemed to direct the operations of the enemy.
>
> "Stand firm and be ready, my gallant 60th!" suddenly exclaimed a voice above them; "wait to see the enemy; fire low, and sweep the glacis."
>
> "Father! father" exclaimed a piercing cry from out the mist; "it is I! Alice! thy own Elsie! spare, O! save your daughters!"
>
> "Hold!" shouted the former speaker in the awful tones of parental agony, the sound reaching even to the woods, and rolling back in solemn echo. " 'Tis she! God has restored me my children! Throw open the sally-port; to the field, 60ths, to the field; pull not a trigger, lest ye kill my lambs! Drive off these dogs of France with your steel."

Cooper's word-sense was singularly dull. When a person has a poor ear for music he will flat and sharp right along without knowing it. He keeps near the tune, but it is *not* the tune. When a person has a poor ear for words, the result is a literary flatting and sharping; you perceive what he is intending to say, but you also perceive that he doesn't *say* it. This is Cooper. He was not a word-musician. His ear was satisfied with the *approximate* word. I will furnish some circumstantial evidence in support of this charge. My instances are gathered from half a dozen pages of the tale called *Deerslayer.* He uses "verbal," for "oral"; "precision," for "facility"; "phenomena," for "marvels"; "necessary," for "predetermined"; "unsophisticated," for "primitive"; "preparation," for "expectancy"; "rebuked," for "subdued"; "dependent on," for "resulting from"; "fact," for "condition"; "fact," for "conjecture"; "precaution," for "caution"; "explain," for "determine"; "mortified," for "disappointed"; "meretricious," for "factitious"; "materially," for "considerably"; "decreasing," for "deepening"; "increasing," for "disappearing"; "embedded," for "enclosed"; "treacherous," for "hostile"; "stood," for "stooped"; "softened," for "replaced"; "rejoined," for "remarked"; "situation," for "condition"; "different," for "differing"; "insensible," for "unsentient"; "brevity," for "celerity"; "distrusted," for "suspicious"; "mental imbecility," for "imbecility"; "eyes," for "sight"; "counteracting," for "opposing"; "funeral obsequies," for "obsequies."

There have been daring people in the world who claimed that Cooper could write English, but they are all dead now—all dead but Lounsbury. I don't remember that Lounsbury makes the claim in so many words, still he makes it, for he says that *Deerslayer* is a "pure work of art." Pure, in that connection, means faultless—faultless in all details—and language is a detail. If Mr. Lounsbury had only compared Cooper's English with the English which he writes himself—but it is plain that he didn't; and so it is likely that he imagines until this day that Cooper's is as clean and compact as his own. Now I feel sure, deep down in my heart, that Cooper wrote about the poorest English that exists in our language, and that the English of *Deerslayer* is the very worst that even Cooper ever wrote.

I may be mistaken, but it does seem to me that *Deerslayer* is not a work of art in any sense; it does seem to me that it is destitute of every detail that goes to the making of a work of art; in truth, it seems to me that *Deerslayer* is just simply a literary *delirium tremens.*

A work of art? It has no invention; it has no order, system, sequence, or result; it has no lifelikeness, no thrill, no stir, no seeming of reality; its characters are confusedly drawn, and by their acts and words they prove that they are not the sort of people the author claims that they are; its humor is pathetic; its pathos is funny; its conversations are—oh! indescribable; its love-scenes odious; its English a crime against the language.

Counting these out, what is left is Art. I think we must all admit that.

How to Tell a Story

The Humorous Story an American Development.—Its Difference from Comic and Witty Stories.

I do not claim that I can tell a story as it ought to be told. I only claim to know how a story ought to be told, for I have been almost daily in the company of the most expert storytellers for many years.

There are several kinds of stories, but only one difficult kind —the humorous. I will talk mainly about that one. The humorous story is American, the comic story is English, the witty story is French. The humorous story depends for its effect upon the *manner* of the telling; the comic story and the witty story upon the *matter*.

The humorous story may be spun out to great length, and may wander around as much as it pleases, and arrive nowhere in particular; but the comic and witty stories must be brief and end with a point. The humorous story bubbles gently along, the others burst.

The humorous story is strictly a work of art,—high and delicate art,—and only an artist can tell it; but no art is necessary in telling the comic and the witty story; anybody can do it. The art of telling a humorous story—understand, I mean by word of mouth, not print—was created in America, and has remained at home.

The humorous story is told gravely; the teller does his best to conceal the fact that he even dimly suspects that there is anything funny about it; but the teller of the comic story tells you beforehand that it is one of the funniest things he has ever heard, then tells it with eager delight, and is the first person to laugh when he gets through. And sometimes, if he had had good success, he is so glad and happy that he will repeat the "nub" of it and glance around from face to face, collecting applause, and then repeat it again. It is a pathetic thing to see.

Very often, of course, the rambling and disjointed humorous story fin-

"How to Tell a Story" first appeared in *Youth's Companion* for October, 1895, the source of this text.

ishes with a nub, point, snapper, or whatever you like to call it. Then the listener must be alert, for in many cases the teller will divert attention from that nub by dropping it in a carefully casual and indifferent way, with the pretence that he does not know it is a nub.

Artemus Ward used that trick a good deal; then when the belated audience presently caught the joke he would look up with innocent surprise, as if wondering what they had found to laugh at. Dan Setchell used it before him, Nye and Riley and others use it to-day.

But the teller of the comic story does not slur the nub; he shouts it at you—every time. And when he prints it, in England, France, Germany and Italy, he italicises it, puts some whooping exclamation-points after it, and sometimes explains it in a parenthesis. All of which is very depressing, and makes one want to renounce joking and lead a better life.

Let me set down an instance of the comic method, using an anecdote which has been popular all over the world for twelve or fifteen hundred years. The teller tells it in this way:

The Wounded Soldier

In the course of a certain battle a soldier whose leg had been shot off appealed to another soldier who was hurrying by to carry him to the rear, informing him at the same time of the loss which he had sustained; whereupon the generous son of Mars, shouldering the unfortunate, proceeded to carry out his desire. The bullets and cannon-balls were flying in all directions, and presently one of the latter took the wounded man's head off—without, however, his deliverer being aware of it. In no long time he was hailed by an officer, who said:

"Where are you going with that carcass?"

"To the rear, sir—he's lost his leg!"

"His leg, forsooth?" responded the astonished officer; "you mean his head, you booby."

Whereupon the soldier dispossessed himself of his burden, and stood looking down upon it in great perplexity. At length he said:

"It is true, sir, just as you have said." Then after a pause he added, *"But he* TOLD *me* IT WAS HIS LEG!!!!!"

Here the narrator bursts into explosion after explosion of thunderous horse-laughter, repeating that nub from time to time through his gaspings and shriekings and suffocatings.

It takes only a minute and a half to tell that in its comic-story form;

and isn't worth the telling, after all. Put into the humorous-story form it takes ten minutes, and is about the funniest thing I have ever listened to—as James Whitcomb Riley tells it.

He tells it in the character of a dull-witted old farmer who has just heard it for the first time, thinks it is unspeakably funny, and is trying to repeat it to a neighbor. But he can't remember it; so he gets it all mixed up and wanders helplessly round and round, putting in tedious details that don't belong in the tale and only retard it; taking them out conscientiously and putting in others that are just as useless; making minor mistakes now and then and stopping to correct them and explain how he came to make them; remembering things which he forgot to put in in their proper place and going back to put them in there; stopping his narrative a good while in order to try to recall the name of the soldier that was hurt, and finally remembering that the soldier's name was not mentioned, and remarking placidly that the name is of no real importance, any way,—better, of course, if one knew it, but not essential, after all,—and so on, and so on, and so on.

The teller is innocent and happy and pleased with himself, and has to stop every little while to hold himself in and keep from laughing outright; and does hold in, but his body quakes in a jelly-like way with interior chuckles; and at the end of the ten minutes the audience have laughed until they are exhausted, and the tears are running down their faces.

The simplicity and innocence and sincerity and unconsciousness of the old farmer are perfectly simulated, and the result is a performance which is thoroughly charming and delicious. This is art—and fine and beautiful, and only a master can compass it; but a machine could tell the other story.

To string incongruities and absurdities together in a wandering and sometimes purposeless way, and seem innocently unaware that they are absurdities, is the basis of the American art, if my position is correct. Another feature is the slurring of the point. A third is the dropping of a studied remark apparently without knowing it, as if one were thinking aloud. The fourth and last is the pause.

Artemus Ward dealt in numbers three and four a good deal. He would begin to tell with great animation something which he seemed to think was wonderful; then lose confidence, and after an apparently absent-minded pause add an incongruous remark in a soliloquizing way; and that was the remark intended to explode the mine—and it did.

For instance, he would say eagerly, excitedly, "I once knew a man in New Zealand who hadn't a tooth in his head"—here his animation would die out; a silent, reflective pause would follow, then he would say dreamily, as if to himself, "and yet that man could beat a drum better than any man I ever saw."

The pause is an exceedingly important feature in any kind of story, and a frequently recurring feature, too. It is a dainty thing, and delicate, and also uncertain and treacherous; for it must be exactly the right length—no more and no less—or it fails of its purpose and makes trouble. If the pause is too short the impressive point is passed, and the audience have had time to divine that a surprise is intended—and then you can't surprise them, of course.

On the platform I used to tell a negro ghost story that had a pause in front of the snapper on the end, and that pause was the most important thing in the whole story. If I got it the right length precisely, I could spring the finishing ejaculation with effect enough to make some impressible girl deliver a startled little yelp and jump out of her seat—and that was what I was after. This story was called "The Golden Arm," and was told in this fashion. You can practise with it yourself—and mind you look out for the pause and get it right.

The Golden Arm

Once 'pon a time dey wuz a monsus mean man, en he live 'way out in de praire all 'lone by hisself, 'cep'n he had a wife. En bimeby she died, en he tuck en toted her way out dah in de prairie en buried her. Well, she had a golden arm—all solid gold, fum de shoulder down. He wuz pow'ful mean—pow'ful; en dat night he couldn't sleep, caze he want dat golden arm so bad.

When it come midnight he couldn't stan' it no mo'; so he git up, he did, en tuck his lantern en shoved out thoo de storm en dug her up en got de golden arm; en he bent his head down 'gin de win', en plowed en plowed en plowed thoo de snow. Den all on a sudden he stop (make a considerable pause here, and look startled, and take a listening attitude) en say: "My *lan'*, what's dat!"

En he listen—en listen—en de win' say (set your teeth together and imitate the wailing and wheezing singsong of the wind), "Bzzz-z-zzz"—en den, way back yonder whah de grave is, he hear a *voice!*—he hear a voice all mix' up in de win'—can't hardly tell 'em 'part—"Bzzz-zzz—W-h-o—g-o-t—m-y—g-o-l-d-e-n *arm?*—zzz—zzz—W-h-o g-o-t m-y g-o-l-d-e-n *arm?*" (You must begin to shiver violently now.)

En he begin to shiver en shake, en say, "Oh, my! *Oh,* my lan'!" en de win' blow de lantern out, en de snow en sleet blow in his face en mos' choke him, en he start a-plowin' knee-deep toward home mos' dead, he so sk'yerd—en pooty soon he hear de voice agin, en (pause) it 'us comin' *after* him! "Bzzz—zzz—zzz—W-h-o—g-o-t—m-y g-o-l-d-e-n—*arm?*"

When he git to de pasture he hear it agin—closter now, en a-*comin'!*— a-comin' back dah in de dark en de storm—(repeat the wind and the voice). When he git to de house he rush upstairs en jump in de bed en kiver up, head and years, en lay dah shiverin' en shakin'—en den way out dah he hear it *agin!*—en a-*comin'!* En bimeby he hear (pause—awed, listening attitude)—pat—pat—pat—*hit's a-comin' up-stairs!* Den he hear de latch, en he *know* it's in de room!

Den pooty soon he know it's a-*stannin' by de bed!* (Pause.) Den—he know it's a—*bendin' down over him*—en he cain't skasely git his breath! Den—den—he seem to feel someth'n *c-o-l-d,* right down 'most agin his head! (Pause.)

Den de voice say, *right at his year*—"W-h-o—g-o-t—m-y—g-o-l-d-e-n *arm?*" (You must wail it out very plaintively and accusingly; then you stare steadily and impressively into the face of the farthest-gone auditor,—a girl, preferably,—and let that awe-inspiring pause begin to build itself in the deep hush. When it has reached exactly the right length, jump suddenly at that girl and yell, *"You've* got it!")

If you've got the *pause* right, she'll fetch a dear little yelp and spring right out of her shoes. But you *must* get the pause right; and you will find it the most troublesome and aggravating and uncertain thing you ever undertook.)

William Dean Howells

Is it true that the sun of a man's mentality touches noon at forty and then begins to wane toward setting? Dr. Osler is charged with saying so. Maybe he said it, maybe he didn't; I don't know which it is. But if he said it, and if it is true, I can point him to a case which proves his rule. Proves it by being an exception to it. To this place I nominate Mr. Howells.

I read his *Venetian Days* about forty years ago. I compare it with his paper on Machiavelli in a late number of *Harper*, and I cannot find that his English has suffered any impairment. For forty years his English has been to me a continual delight and astonishment. In the sustained exhibition of certain great qualities—clearness, compression, verbal exactness, and unforced and seemingly unconscious felicity of phrasing—he is, in my belief, without his peer in the English-writing world. *Sustained.* I intrench myself behind that protecting word. There are others who exhibit those great qualities as greatly as does he, but only by intervalled distributions of rich moonlight, with stretches of veiled and dimmer landscape between; whereas Howell's moon sails cloudless skies all night and all the nights.

In the matter of verbal exactness Mr. Howells has no superior, I suppose. He seems to be almost always able to find that elusive and shifty grain of gold, the *right word*. Others have to put up with approximations, more or less frequently; he has better luck. To me, the others are miners working with the gold-pan—of necessity some of the gold washes over and escapes; whereas, in my fancy, he is quicksilver raiding down a riffle—no grain of the metal stands much chance of eluding him. A powerful agent is the right word: it lights the reader's way and makes it plain; a close approximation to it will answer, and much travelling is done in a well-enough fashion by its help, but we do not welcome it and applaud it and rejoice in it as we do when *the* right one blazes out on us. Whenever we come upon one of those intensely right words in a book or

"William Dean Howells" first appeared in *Harper's Monthly* (July 1906):221–25, which is the source for this text.

155

a newspaper the resulting effect is physical as well as spiritual, and elec-
tically prompt: it tingles exquisitely around through the walls of the
mouth and tastes as tart and crisp and good as the autumn-butter that
creams the sumac-berry. One has no time to examine the word and vote
upon its rank and standing, the automatic recognition of its supremacy
is so immediate. There is a plenty of acceptable literature which deals
largely in approximations, but it may be likened to a fine landscape seen
through the rain; the right word would dismiss the rain, then you would
see it better. It doesn't rain when Howells is at work.

And where does he get the easy and effortless flow of his speech? and
its cadenced and undulating rhythm? and its architectural felicities of
construction, its graces of expression, its pemmican quality of compression, and all that? Born to him, no doubt. All in shining good order in the
beginning, all extraordinary; and all just as shining, just as extraordinary
today, after forty years of diligent wear and tear and use. He passed his
fortieth year long and long ago; but I think his English of to-day—his
perfect English, I wish to say—can throw down the glove before his
English of that antique time and not be afraid.

I will go back to the paper on Machiavelli now, and ask the reader to
examine this passage from it which I append. I do not mean, examine it
in a bird's-eye way; I mean search it, study it. And, of course, read it
aloud. I may be wrong, still it is my conviction that one cannot get out
of finely wrought literature all that is in it by reading it mutely:

> Mr. Dyer is rather of the opinion, first luminously suggested by
> Macaulay, that Machiavelli was in earnest, but must not be judged as a
> political moralist of our time and race would be judged. He thinks that
> Machiavelli was in earnest, as none but an idealist can be, and he is the
> first to imagine him an idealist immersed in realities, who involuntar-
> ily transmutes the events under his eye into something like the vision-
> ary issues of reverie. The Machiavelli whom he depicts does not cease
> to be politically a republican and socially a just man because he holds
> up an atrocious despot like Cæsar Borgia as a mirror for rulers. What
> Machiavelli beheld round him in Italy was a civic disorder in which
> there was oppression without statecraft, and revolt without patriotism.
> When a miscreant like Borgia appeared upon the scene and reduced
> both tyrants and rebels to an apparent quiescence, he might very well
> seem to such a dreamer the savior of society whom a certain sort of
> dreamers are always looking for. Machiavelli was no less honest when
> he honored the diabolical force of Cæsar Borgia than Carlyle was when

at different times he extolled the strong man who destroys liberty in creating order. But Carlyle has only just ceased to be mistaken for a reformer, while it is still Machiavelli's hard fate to be so trammelled in his material that his name stands for whatever is most malevolent and perfidious in human nature.

You see how easy and flowing it is; how unvexed by ruggednesses, clumsinesses, broken metres; how simple and—so far as you or I can make out—unstudied; how clear, how limpid, how understandable, how unconfused by cross-currents, eddies, undertows; how seemingly unadorned, yet is all adornment, like the lily-of-the-valley; and how compressed, how compact, without a complacency-signal hung out anywhere to call attention to it.

There are twenty-one lines in the quoted passage. After reading it several times aloud, one perceives that a good deal of matter is crowded into that small space. I think it is a model of compactness. When I take its materials apart and work them over and put them together in my way I find I cannot crowd the result back into the same hole, there not being room enough. I find it a case of a woman packing a man's trunk: he can get the things out, but he can't ever get them back again.

The proferred paragraph is a just and fair sample; the rest of the article is as compact as it is; there are no waste words. The sample is just in other ways: limpid, fluent, graceful, and rhythmical as it is, it holds no superiority in these respects over the rest of the essay. Also, the choice phrasing noticeable in the sample is not lonely; there is a plenty of its kin distributed through the other paragraphs. This is claiming much when that kin must face the challenge of a phrase like the one in the middle sentence: "an idealist immersed in realities, who involuntarily transmutes the events under his eye into something like the visionary issues of reverie." With a hundred words to do it with, the literary artisan could catch that airy thought and tie it down and reduce it to a concrete condition, visible, substantial, understandable and all right, like a cabbage; but the artist does it with twenty, and the result is a flower.

The quoted phrase, like a thousand others that have come from the same source, has the quality of certain scraps of verse which take hold of us and stay in our memories, we do not understand why, at first: all the words being the right words, none of them is conspicuous, and so they all seem inconspicuous, therefore we wonder what it is about them that makes their message take hold.

> The mossy marbles rest
> On the lips that he has prest
>   In their bloom,
> And the names he loved to hear
> Have been carved for many a year
>   On the tomb.

It is like a dreamy strain of moving music, with no sharp notes in it. The words are all "right" words, and all the same size. We do not notice it at first. We get the effect, it goes straight home to us, but we do not know why. It is when the right words are conspicuous that they thunder—

> The glory that was Greece and the grandeur that was Rome!

When I go back from Howells old to Howells young I find him arranging and clustering English words well, but not any better than now. He is not more felicitous in concreting abstractions now than he was in translating, then, the visions of the eye of flesh into words that reproduced their forms and colors:

> In Venetian streets they give the fallen snow no rest. It is at once shovelled into the canals by hundreds of half-naked *facchini;* and now in St. Mark's Place the music of innumerable shovels smote upon my ear; and I saw the shivering legion of poverty as it engaged the elements in a struggle for the possession of the Piazza. But the snow continued to fall, and through the twilight of the descending flakes all this toil and encounter looked like that weary kind of effort in dreams, when the most determined industry seems only to renew the task. The lofty crest of the bell-tower was hidden in the folds of falling snow, and I could no longer see the golden angel upon its summit. But looked at across the Piazza, the beautiful outline of St. Mark's Church was perfectly pencilled in the air, and the shifting threads of the snowfall were woven into a spell of novel enchantment around the structure that always seemed to me too exquisite in its fantastic loveliness to be anything but the creation of magic. The tender snow had compassionated the beautiful edifice for all the wrongs of time, and so hid the stains and ugliness of decay that it looked as if just from the hand of the builder—or, better said, just from the brain of the architect. There was marvelous freshness in the colors of the mosaics in the great arches of the façade, and all that gracious harmony into which the temple rises, of marble scrolls and leafy exuberance airily supporting the statues of

the saints, was a hundred times etheralized by the purity and white-ness of the drifting flakes. The snow lay lightly on the golden globes that tremble like peacock-crests above the vast domes, and plumed them with softest white; it robed the saints in ermine; and it danced over all its work, as if exulting in its beauty—beauty which filled me with subtle, selfish yearning to keep such evanescent loveliness for the little-while-longer of my whole life, and with despair to think that even the poor lifeless shadow of it could never be fairly reflected in picture or poem.

Through the wandering snowfall, the Saint Theodore upon one of the granite pillars of the Piazzetta did not show so grim as his wont is, and the winged lion on the other might have been a winged lamb, so gentle and mild he looked by the tender light of the storm. The tow-ers of the island churches loomed faint and far away in the dimness; the sailors in the rigging of the ships that lay in the Basin wrought like phantoms among the shrouds; the gondolas stole in and out of the opaque distance more noiselessly and dreamily than ever; and a silence, almost palpable, lay upon the mutest city in the world.

The spirit of Venice is there: of a city where Age and Decay, fagged with distributing damage and repulsiveness among the other cities of the planet in accordance with the policy and business of their profes-sion, come for rest and play between seasons, and treat themselves to the luxury and relaxation of sinking the shop and inventing and squan-dering charms all about, instead of abolishing such as they find, as is their habit when not on vacation.

In the working season they do business in Boston sometimes, and a character in *The Undiscovered Country* takes accurate note of pathetic effects wrought by them upon the aspects of a street of once dignified and elegant homes whose occupants have moved away and left them a prey to neglect and gradual ruin and progressive degradation; a descent which reaches bottom at last, when the street becomes a roost for hum-ble professionals of the faith-cure and fortune-telling sort.

What a queer, melancholy house, what a queer, melancholy street! I don't think I was ever in a street before where quite so many profes-sional ladies, with English surnames, preferred Madam to Mrs. on their door-plates. And the poor old place has such a desperately conscious air of going to the deuce. Every house seems to wince as you go by, and button itself up to the chin for fear you should find out it had no shirt on,—so to speak. I don't know what's the reason, but these material tokens of a social decay afflict me terribly; a tipsy woman isn't dreadfuler than a haggard old house, that's once been a home, in a street like this.

Mr. Howells's pictures are not mere stiff, hard, accurate photographs; they are photographs with feeling in them, and sentiment, photographs taken in a dream, one might say.

As concerns his humor, I will not try to say anything, yet I would try if I had the words that might approximately reach up to its high place. I do not think any one else can play with humorous fancies so gracefully and delicately and deliciously as he does, nor has so many to play with, nor can come so near making them look as if they were doing the playing themselves and he was not aware that they were at it. For they are unobtrusive, and quiet in their ways, and well conducted. His is a humor which flows softly all around about and over and through the mesh of the page, pervasive, refreshing, health-giving, and makes no more show and no more noise than does the circulation of the blood.

There is another thing which is contentingly noticeable in Mr. Howells's books. That is his "stage directions"—those artifices which authors employ to throw a kind of human naturalness around a scene and a conversation, and help the reader to see the one and get at meanings in the other which might not be perceived if intrusted and unexplained to the bare words of the talk. Some authors overdo the stage directions, they elaborate them quite beyond necessity; they spend so much time and take up so much room in telling us how a person said a thing and how he looked and acted when he said it that we get tired and vexed and wish he hadn't said it at all. Other authors' directions are brief enough, but it is seldom that the brevity contains either wit or information. Writers of this school go in rags, in the matter of stage directions; the majority of them have nothing in stock but a cigar, a laugh, a blush, and a bursting into tears. In their poverty they work these sorry things to the bone. They say:

". . . replied Alfred, flipping the ash from his cigar." (This explains nothing; it only wastes space.)

". . . responded Richard, with a laugh." (There was nothing to laugh about; there never is. The writer puts it in from habit—automatically; he is paying no attention to his work, or he would see that there is nothing to laugh at; often, when a remark is unusually and poignantly flat and silly, he tries to deceive the reader by enlarging the stage direction and making Richard break into "frenzies of uncontrollable laughter." This makes the reader sad.)

". . . murmured Gladys, blushing." This poor old shop-worn blush is a tiresome thing. We get so we would rather Gladys would fall out of the book and break her neck than do it again. She is always doing it, and usually irrevelantly. Whenever it is her turn to murmur she hangs out her blush; it is the only thing she's got. In a little while we hate her, just as we do Richard.

". . . repeated Evelyn, bursting into tears." This kind keep a book damp all the time. They can't say a thing without crying. They cry so much about nothing that by and by when they have something to cry *about* they have gone dry; they sob, and fetch nothing; we are not moved. We are only glad.

They gravel me, these stale and overworked stage directions, these carbon films that got burnt out long ago and cannot now carry any faintest thread of light. It would be well if they could be relieved from duty and flung out in the literary back yard to rot and disappear along with the discarded and forgotten "steeds" and "halidomes" and similar stage-properties once so dear to our grandfathers. But I am friendly to Mr. Howells's stage directions; more friendly to them than to any one else's, I think. They are done with a competent and discriminating art, and are faithful to the requirements of a stage direction's proper and lawful office, which is to inform. Sometimes they convey a scene and its conditions so well that I believe I could see the scene and get the spirit and meaning of the accompanying dialogue if some one would read merely the stage directions to me and leave out the talk. For instance, a scene like this, from *The Undiscovered Country:*

". . . and she laid her arms with a beseeching gesture on her father's shoulder."

". . . she answered, following his gesture with a glance."

". . . she said, laughing nervously."

". . . she asked, turning swiftly upon him that strange, searching glance."

". . . she answered, vaguely."

". . . she reluctantly admitted."

". . . but her voice died wearily away, and she stood looking into his face with puzzled entreaty."

Mr. Howells does not repeat his forms, and does not need to; he can invent fresh ones without limit. It is mainly the repetition over and over again, by the third-rates, of worn and commonplace and juiceless forms that makes their novels such a weariness and vexation to us, I think. We do not mind one or two deliveries of their wares, but as we turn the pages over and keep on meeting them we presently get tired of them and wish they would do other things for a change:

"... replied Alfred, flipping the ash from his cigar."

"... responded Richard, with a laugh."

"... murmured Gladys, blushing."

"... repeated Evelyn, bursting into tears."

"... replied the Earl, flipping the ash from his cigar."

"... responded the undertaker, with a laugh."

"... murmured the chambermaid, blushing."

"... repeated the burglar, bursting into tears."

"... replied the conductor, flipping the ash from his cigar."

"... responded Arkwright, with a laugh."

"... murmured the chief of police, blushing."

"... repeated the housecat, bursting into tears."

And so on and so on; till at last it ceases to excite. I always notice stage directions, because they fret me and keep me trying to get out of their way, just as the automobiles do. At first; then by and by they become monotonous and I get run over.

Mr. Howells has done much work, and the spirit of it is as beautiful as the make of it. I have held him in admiration and affection so many years that I know by the number of those years that he is old now; but his heart isn't, nor his pen; and years do not count. Let him have plenty of them: there is profit in them for us.

Part 3

THE CRITICS

Introduction

Mark Twain has been lucky in his critics. There is an abundance of worthwhile Twain criticism, as I trust the selected bibliography makes clear. The selections included in this part are meant to be suggestive, not definitive. Moreover, I have included specimens of criticism that do not at every point corroborate what I have had to say in part 1. Instead, they are intended to augment, to challenge, and in some instances to contradict my analysis. This divergence of critical opinion is useful if for no other reason than it indicates the richness of Twain criticism and the nearly inexhaustible fascination he has had for readers for so long a time.

For all Twain's worry and complaint about being unappreciated or misunderstood, few professional writers have had so steadfast a friend and so astute and responsive a critic as Twain did in William Dean Howells. Howells's review of *Mark Twain's Sketches New and Old* (1875) identifies quite succinctly Twain's ample imaginative and artistic gifts as a humorist. But this review also insists upon the author's "growing seriousness of meaning," and Howells modestly but firmly corrects those reviewers who, somewhat miraculously as it may seem to us now, mistook "A True Story" for yet another humorous sketch. If Howells felt obliged to point out the serious side of his friend, he nevertheless predicted in another essay that there was an equal and opposite danger that future readers might overemphasize that seriousness: "it would be rather awful if the general recognition of his prophetic function should implicate the renunciation of the humor that has endeared him to mankind."[1]

Louis J. Budd's test bore into the core of Twain's comic gifts ought to fatally stall the tendency to renounce the author's humor in preference for some ideological or psychoanalytic thesis about the man. The excerpt I include here from Budd's monograph, *Mark Twain: The Ecstasy of Humor*, identifies with clarity and force the "quintessential Twainian quality"— "an emotional-intellectual drive, an integrative, pleasure-sharing ability to soar above or outside of commonly accepted experience." Twain's point of view, from his early childhood throughout his life and into his old age, was richly, broadly humorous. That point of view provided him with a certain psychological and moral integrity; it carried him through

165

difficult times and shifts in fortune; but most of all, it provided him with a personal satisfaction that Budd properly names "ecstasy."

The remaining selections address more specific aspects of Twain's craft and writing. Don Florence admirably summarizes critical opinion about Clemens's early experimentation with his adopted persona of Mark Twain and notes that this persona acquired "at least some of the flexibility needed to express the range of his humor and his attitudes toward the world." Both Florence and Budd emphasize Twain's playfulness and call into question portrayals of the man as permanently fixated and/or divided against himself. Walter Blair's essay on Twain's "other masterpiece," the blue jay yarn, is a full and rewarding account of this wonderful tale, but it is more than that. Though he restricts himself to a single tale, what Blair has to say about Twain's experience in California, the background of and influences on this story, the author's practiced artistry, and his relation to a tradition of literary humor that stretches back to Aesop make this essay a serviceable introduction to much of Twain's short fiction.

Likewise, Gregg Camfield's provocative reading of "The Facts Concerning the Recent Carnival of Crime in Connecticut" has a wider application for the student of Twain's fiction than the essay's specific subject matter might suggest. Camfield addresses questions of sentimentality, conscience, and the moral sense as they are dramatized in this important story and, in the course of his analysis, touches upon significant and pervasive ingredients in much of Twain later fiction. Susan K. Harris identifies a different, but equally important, element in Twain's fiction: his depiction of women. Twain's portrayal of Eve in the "diaries" of Adam and Eve is exceptional in that the author resists the sort of stereotyping of women that characterizes so much of his fiction. Part of the reason for this, argues Harris, is that the diary form allowed Eve to speak for herself, but another reason is the author's rather belated recognition of "the woman's power to coax the man out of himself, to make him aware that his is not the only consciousness in existence." Because so much of Twain's late fiction deals with solipsistic dream or nightmare, or represents human beings as wholly the product of training, Harris's observation is a tonic reminder that Twain did not give himself over absolutely to that point of view.

Note

1. Howells, *My Mark Twain*, 185.

William Dean Howells

It is easy to say that these new and old sketches by Mr. Clemens are of varying merit; but which, honest reader, would you leave out of the book? There is none but saves itself either by its humor or by the sound sense which it is based on, so that, if one came to reject the flimsiest trifle, one would find it on consideration rather too good to throw away. In reading the book you go through a critical process imaginably very like the author's in editing it; about certain things there can be no question from the first, and you end by accepting all, while you feel that any one else may have his proper doubts about some of the sketches.

The characteristic traits of our friend—he is the friend of mankind—are all here; here is the fine, forecasting humor, starting so far back from its effect that one, knowing some joke must be coming, feels that nothing less than a prophetic instinct can sustain the humorist in its development; here is the burlesque, that seems such plain and simple fun at first, doubling and turning upon itself till you wonder why Mr. Clemens has ever been left out of the list of our *subtile* humorists; here is that peculiar extravagance of statement which we share with all sufficiently elbow-roomed, unneighbored people, but which our English cousins are so good as to consider the distinguishing mark of America humor; here is the incorruptible right-mindedness that always warms the heart to this wit; here is the "dryness," the "breadth"—all the things that so weary us in the praises of him and that so take us with delight in the reading of him. But there is another quality in this book which we fancy we shall hereafter associate more and more with our familiar impressions of him, and that is a growing seriousness of meaning in the apparently unmoralized drolling, which must result from the humorist's second thought of political and social absurdities. It came to Dickens, but the character of his genius was too intensely theatrical to let him make anything but rather poor melodrama of it; to Thackeray, whom our humorists at their best are all like, it came too, and would not suffer him

This review first appeared in the *Atlantic Monthly* December, 1875. It appears as chapter 4 of Howells's *My Mark Twain* (New York: Harper and Brothers, 1910), 120–24.

to leave anything, however grotesque, merely laughed at. We shall be disappointed if in Mr. Clemens's case it finds only some desultory expression, like "Lionizing Murderers" and "A New Crime," though there could not be more effective irony than these sketches so far as they go. The first is a very characteristic bit of the humorist's art; and the reader is not so much troubled to find where the laugh comes in as to find where it goes out—for ten to one he is in a sober mind when he is done. The other is more direct satire, but is quite as subtle in its way of presenting those cases in which murderers have been found opportunely insane and acquitted, and gravely sandwiching among them instances in which obviously mad people have been hanged by the same admirable system.

Nothing more final has been thought of on the subject of a great public, statutory wrong than Mark Twain's petition to Congress asking that all property shall be held during the period of forty-two years, or for just so long as an author is permitted to claim copyright in his book. The whole sense and justice applicable to the matter are enforced in this ironical prayer, and there is no argument that could stand against it. If property in houses or lands—which a man may get by dishonest trickery, or usury, or hard rapacity—were in danger of ceasing after forty-two years, the whole virtuous community would rouse itself to perpetuate the author's right to the product of his brain, and no griping bidder at tax-sales but would demand the protection of literature by indefinite copyright. The difficulty is to condition the safety of real estate in this way; but Mark Twain's petition is a move in the right direction.

We should be sorry to give our readers the impression that they are unconsciously to imbibe political and social wisdom from every page of Mr. Clemens's new book, when we merely wished to point out one of his tendencies. Though there is nearly always sense in his nonsense, yet he is master of the art of pure drolling. The grotesque cannot go further than in that mediæval romance of his where he is obliged to abandon his hero or heroine at the most critical moment simply because he can see no way to get him or her out of the difficulty; and there is a delicious novelty in that ghost-story where the unhappy spectre of the Cardiff Giant is mortified to find that he has been haunting a plaster cast of himself in New York, while his stone original was lying in Albany. "The Experiences of the McWilliamses with the Membranous Croup" is a bit of *genre* romance which must read like an abuse of confidence to every husband and father. These are among the new sketches, though none of them have staled by custom, and the old sketches are to be called so merely for contradistinction's sake. "How I Once Edited an Agricultural Paper," "About Barbers," "Cannibalism in the Cars," "The Undertaker's Chat," "The Scriptural Panoramist," "To Raise Poultry," "A Visit to Niagara" are all familiar favorites, which, when we have read them, we wish merely to have the high privilege of immediately reading over again. We must not leave the famous "Jumping Frog" out of their honorable and pleasant company; it is here in a new effect, first as the "Jumping Frog" in Mark Twain's original English, then in the French of the *Revue des Deux Mondes,* and then in his literal version of the French, which he gives that the reader may see how his frog has been made to appear "to the distorted French eye."

But by far the most perfect piece of work in the book is "A True Story," which resulted, we remember, in some confusion of the average critical mind when it was first published in these pages a little more than one year ago. It is simply the story an old black cook tells of how her children were all sold away from her, and how after twenty years she found her youngest boy again. The shyness of an enlightened and independent press respecting this history was something extremely amusing to see, and one could fancy it a spectacle of delightful interest to the author if it had not had such disheartening features. Mostly the story was described in the notices of the magazine as a humorous sketch by Mark Twain; sometimes it was mentioned as a paper apparently out of the author's usual line; again it was handled non-committally as one of Mark Twain's extravagances. Evidently the critical mind feared a lurking joke. Not above two or three notices out of hundreds recognized "A True Story" for what it was—namely, a study of character as true as life itself, strong, tender, and most movingly pathetic in its perfect fidelity to the tragic fact. We beg the reader to turn to it again in this book. We can assure him that he has a great surprise and a strong emotion in store for him. The rugged truth of the sketch leaves all other stories of slave life infinitely far behind, and reveals a gift in the author for the simple, dramatic report of reality which we have seen equalled in no other American writer.

Louis J. Budd

I am still surprised when some critic declares that Mark Twain had a shallow or fixated mind. His mind was wondrously nimble, was a self-energizing kaleidoscope. More commonly, other critics approach Twain as a divided mind or personality, usually in bi-polar terms. Actually, we're all self-divided—on many points and in more than two ways, but Twain was much more complicated than most of us on this side of sanity. In his psyche those conflicting lines of attitudes and values intersected to form the core of his comic gift.

Last year I finally attended a conference of the International Society for Humor Studies—its tenth—and was dazzled to encounter so many different and stimulating analyses of humor-wit-comedy-laughter. After further reading I have come to one firm conclusion: we won't agree on a unified-field theory—that is, no single theory can cover the entire career of all humorists, all their works, and all the responses of their varying audiences. So I will try merely to get closer to one aspect of Mark Twain, which I find exceptional and even unique.

At the simplest level humor lies in combining divergent lines of experience or reasoning. I feel comfortable in stating that point as a "fact" without going on to grapple with the motives that drive a humorist to play with incongruities, nor will I grapple with the receiver's (humoree's) psychology for responding with at least smiles. I will instead give some test-samples from Twain, such as his comment that "we see through a glass eye darkly" or—evidently an exclamation at breakfast—that "bacon would improve the flavor of an angel." To go on like a stand-up comic who milks a good routine, I add that Twain described someone "as content as an angel full of pie," and Hank Morgan jeered that angels "are always on deck when there is a miracle to the

Delivered at the conference "The State of Mark Twain Studies," at Elmira College Center for Mark Twain Studies, 12–14 August 1993.
Excerpted from Louis J. Budd, *Mark Twain: The Ecstasy of Humor,* Quarry Farm Papers 6(1995):5–10. Reprinted by permission of the Elmira College Center for Mark Twain Studies, Elmira, New York.

fore—so as to get put in the picture, perhaps. Angels are as fond of that as a fire company; look at the old masters." These are just middling samples of his ability to make an incongruous, even clashing association in a way—please note—that compels our laughter rather than puzzlement or disapproval. But I especially like this riff from the new edition by Howard Baetzhold and Joseph McCullough: "For it is easier for a rich man to go through the eye of a camel than for another man to break the Sabbath day and keep it holy."[1]

I don't propose to psychoanalyze why Twain's humor soared above cause and effect conformity. Each of us constantly gets clues that most beliefs and standards are manmade and even arbitrary. However, we find it necessary to focus on day-to-day problems in their given terms; a few persons turn so rigidly focused as to shut out all responsiveness to humor. Most of us try to cope with the daily traps while now and then peeping into the abyss, grinning when Twain writes that "every God has his day." The year before Twain's death he claimed to remember that when he was just seven years old his teacher at Sunday school "had suspicions" that his questioning about Satan "was not reverent."[2] But I don't think psychoanalysis can dig back to Twain's libidinal origins; the results are shaky not only for live subjects but especially for dead geniuses. Twain's personality was so multi-chambered that only his peer—if she or he should bless this earth again—can reenter it fully.

Nor do I propose to engage in the history of abstract ideas though the collision of religious orthodoxy and modern sciences shook up Twain's mind. With great cogency Stanley Brodwin argues that Twain's "profound comic sense had theological roots."[3] Religion aside, Twain shared the shocks of modernization producing a "plurality of social worlds" that in itself "relativizes every one of them. . . . The 'accent of reality' consequently shifts from the objective order of institutions to the realm of subjectivity."[4] However, tens of thousands of intellectuals absorbed these shocks without becoming minor Mark Twains. Sociology aside, they also encountered models of the physical universe that presented it as process rather than fixity, that revolutionized concepts of space and time. In 1873 the idea of "Around the World in Eighty Days" was drastically unsettling.[5] Still, while study of the impact of changing paradigms will help us comprehend Twain's mind, it will leave us far short of his uniqueness.

Tracking Twain's specific reading will not lead us far enough either though Alan Gribben has given us a magisterial accounting of his library with its marginalia.[6] If he read voraciously, so did many of his solemn contemporaries. "Evidently," says Gribben, one of Sam Clemens's "earliest reading experiences" was *Gulliver's Travels.* But all would-be educated westerners knew about Swift's masterpiece yet few of them questioned so whole-heartedly a life supervised and regularized by the first wave of bureaucracy. The more I ponder Twain's genesis the more I appreciate Robert Frost's epigram that, while we circle around and suppose, the "Secret sits in the middle and knows."

Nor, as one last evasion, do I propose to elicit Twain's secret from accessible biographical perspectives though a chain of incongruous experiences surely encouraged his spirit of breaking through the "of course" values and ideas. He grew up as, so he thought, a déclassé Southerner in grubby Hannibal. Early and often he saw death—unexpectedly or senselessly—contradict the promise of normality. Well-rooted in rural primitivism he nevertheless, before the age of twenty, had lived in several major cities. Soon afterward he rose to the prestige of piloting on the Mississippi but suddenly dropped into the hardships of a mining frontier where, wrote W. D. Howells in a review of *Roughing It,* life "must have looked like an extravagant joke." San Francisco of the 1860's was a yet richer laboratory for incongruities, exceeded further by the Sandwich (or Hawaiian) Islands. Coming back East by way of Central America proved almost as startling. Richard Bridgman points out that for Twain traveling "generated the very situations that produce humor: values clashed, perspectives underwent abrupt shifts, and around the next corner, surprise."[7] The tour on the *Quaker City* brought still more surprises, then topped in another way by his honeymoon house in Buffalo, described by himself as "Little Sammy in Fairy Land." Twain, who could have soberly decided that destiny was rewarding him as he deserved, marveled at both the power of chance and the almost unreal combinations it created.

The second half of Twain's life brought almost as many and as deep disjunctions. His teetering between the oral culture that enveloped his childhood and the literacy he embraced so capably was almost replicated when his plebeian nativism interacted with the Euro-British standards of his adopted class in Hartford. During the Grand Tour that the Clemens party made in 1878–79 he encountered the incongruous ghost of a bachelor frolicking with the innocents abroad. The "world" lecture-tour of 1895–96 raised a tide of popularity, even homage, that struck him in humbler moments as bizarre for a boy from a river-town. Old age estranged the white-haired icon still further from that boyhood even as he felt much younger than his public image. These disjunctions certainly help explain the sense of unreality behind much of Twain's late writings. But those writings, we too faintly remember, had a vein and sometimes a central shaft of humor.

My purpose in sketching a biographical or what in my graduate-school days was called a genetic approach is simply to show that I have considered it before deciding for the proposition that Twain's humorous sense sprung from his deepest self and therefore had instinctual energy, was his kind of primal scream. Ignoring his notoriously tricky reminiscences, we can perceive the Twainian quality as soon as he enters the written record through the *Hannibal Journal* owned by his brother. We can already perceive its spontaneity, irreverence, and boldness. We can already perceive its guiding mindset, that core of ego-integrity that carries on through the incipient chaos of the individual's life-arc. This innate quality or attitude, especially its aspect that I will emphasize, kept its strength or reasserted itself to the end of Twain's life. He could feel secure enough psychically to plunge into humor that let down all his defenses or that challenged his own values and ideas.

In fact, I don't perceive Samuel Clemens-Mark Twain as ever fumbling very long for self-identity and, much worse, as never finding it or else losing it near the end. I agree with Carl Van Doren's entry for the *Dictionary of American Biography* over fifty years ago: "His comic energy, while his powers were at their height, was his nature rather than his purpose or weapon." Clive James was, I think, reaching for the same conclusion in the *New Yorker:* "He was democratic all the way down to his metabolism. For Twain, there was no division between democracy and creativity. They were versions of the same thing: exuberance."[8] His humorous élan gave him a rooted strength of selfhood that carried him on through from first to last, absorbing changes, defeats, temptations toward hubris, and his looming death. The state of my own Mark Twain studies is my having come back to this perception, which—I realize—first aroused my interest in him.

By now I should define better the quintessential Twainian quality. Without intricate maneuvering I propose that it is an emotional-intellectual drive, an integrative, pleasure-sharing ability to soar above or outside of commonly accepted experience. Perhaps the plainest yet useful term here would be "play," that is, the blithe toying with ideas and fact that made *The Innocents Abroad* Twain's best-selling book during his lifetime.[9] But we need a more kinetic, dynamic concept; we need the term "ecstasy" to match the élan of self-liberation for arbitrary rules (for example, recall Twain's "don'tcareadams," his name for his white suit), to carry the headiness of cutting through to the malleability of experience, to celebrate the delight of exploding the rigidities of wisdom.[10] In contrast to the mystic's privatized trance, the humorist's transcendent ecstasy is directed outward, is transactional, is made social.

Free-floating perspectives can lead into solipsism. They can also lead to a megalomania that feels only contempt for the conventionally minded, that claims superhuman status. But I can accept those dangers as part of my argument. The destructive perspectives worked as another stimulus, another source of tension that, when defied or mastered, contributed to the constructive force of ecstasy. Ultimately, if Twain suggests that "society itself, and then the universe" are "gigantic hoaxes," he goes on to show them "imposing themselves on credulous man only so long as he will accept them at face value."[11] Even in the "Mysterious Stranger" cycle and especially its culminating or "No. 44" version, Twain conducts both a cosmic dance of ideas and potentially reckless clowning. Now that the latest state of Twain studies explains "No. 44" properly it exhilarates rather than depresses.[12] Unfortunately, the sentimentality of the Adam and Eve sequences distracts current taste from their incorrigible humor, from the fact that Twain's fables about the originary paradoxes of existence always induce some measure of comedy.

To restate my thesis, I contend that Twain's genetic set and early experiences—inward as much as outward, of course—bred an élan that burst through normal boundaries into a sweepingly humorous viewpoint. One side of Twain, as his notebooks show best, registered gross physicality more acceptingly than most of us do. For instance, he could jot down twice the punch-line: "Put your shoes on and give the cheese a chance." In 1903 he rejected an interviewer's cue that he was a latter-day Aristophanes: "But Rabelais! Ah . . . I know Rabelais from the head down to the end of his toes and from his toes to the top of his head. Yes, I know Rabelais, and if I had lived in the fifteenth century I would have been Rabelais" (New York *Evening Journal,* 24 Oct. 1903, p. 2). Twain had that gut awareness that a human spirit encased in heavy, corruptible flesh is inherently, inescapably comic. Less viscerally, his notebooks show fussy attention to running a house, routine shopping, or the nagging decisions and slights that travel entails. In short, he bumped constantly against the world of jagged materiality. His acceptance of, often delight in that world, which included for him a multi-layered social reality, kept his relativism from sinking into a solipsistic vacuum. Susan Harris has stunningly analyzed a different Twain, who escaped from the self by transcending both space and time—again with great mental inventiveness.[13] However, that Twain indulged in humor the least of all.

But Twain just as keenly resisted the burdens of corporeality and of the social framework, from the parlor up through monarchies. He tried some common routes of escape such as mental as well as physical travel. He read histories voraciously and—as Sherwood Cummings has proved in precise detail—learned far more than most amateurs about geology and astronomy, escaping back into deep time or into outer space, which fascinated him with its immensity rather than the symmetries of celestial mechanics. Still, many a contemporary, including humorists, played with such escapes while feeling almost as painfully as he did the gaps between their scientific and their affective worlds. Twain, however, also had moods of resistance when geology and biology looked fanciful rather than provable and therefore verged on solemnly absurd error.

Twain's uniqueness lay in mastering, with a counterpoint of skepticism, the escapes into deep time or space and many others as well, in developing an unmatched repertoire of perspectives beyond commonsense. Collectively, these perspectives brought him—and potentially us—a liberation from ordinary realities. Indeed—soaring beyond liberation—brought an ecstatic sense of triumphing over them. That ecstasy vitalized his most distinctive writings, which like any great intellectual or esthetic artistry, finally transmits a sense of engaged empowerment rather than escape. That irrepressible ecstasy shows highest energy during the 1880s when his family life, his career, and his business affairs were humming fulfillingly, when he completed some of his greatest and therefore most communicatively humorous work, and yet when he was, I believe, beginning to recognize that he would someday die in a still unredeemed world.

Notes

1. In "Adam's Expulsion," p. 114 in *The Bible According to Mark Twain: Writings on Heaven, Eden, and the Flood,* ed. Howard G. Baetzhold and Joseph B. McCullough (Univ. of Georgia Press), 1995.

2. *Is Shakespeare Dead?* (New York: Harper, 1909), p. 25.

3. Among Stanley Brodwin's several brilliant essays see particularly "The Humor of the Absurd: Mark Twain's Adamic Diaries," *Criticism,* 14 (1972), 49–64.

4. Peter L. Berger, Brigitte Berger, and Hansfried Kellner, *The Homeless Mind: Modernization and Consciousness* (New York: Random House, 1973), p. 77.

5. See, more generally, Stephen Kern, *The Culture of Time and Space 1880–1918* (Cambridge: Harvard Univ. Press, 1983); more particularly, Sherwood Cummings, *Mark Twain and Science: Adventures of a Mind* (Baton Rouge: Louisiana State Univ. Press, 1988). Kathleen Walsh's essay in *American Literary Realism 1870–1910*, 21 (1988), 19–28, finds Twain anticipating modern ideas about "arbitrariness of time"; Thomas D. Zlatic's "Mark Twain's View of the Universe," *Papers on Language & Literature*, 27 (1991), 338–55, is admirably learned and penetrating.

6. *Mark Twain's Library: A Reconstruction* (Boston: G. K. Hall, 1980). 2 vols.

7. *Traveling in Mark Twain* (Berkeley: Univ. of California Press, 1987).

8. Clive James, "The Voice of America," *New Yorker*, 14 June 1993, p. 81.

9. Bruce Michelson, "Mark Twain the Tourist: The Form of *The Innocents Abroad*," *America Literature*, 49 (1977), 385–98, states this approach insightfully.

10. Peter L. Berger, *Invitation to Sociology: A Humanistic Perspective* (Garden City, N.Y.: Doubleday, 1963), pp. 136–37, uses "ecstasy" close to the sense I suggest. Robert Polhemus, *Comic Faith: The Great Comic Tradition from Austen to Joyce* (Chicago: Univ. of Chicago Press, 1980), p. 8, develops similarities between "comic euphoria" and "religious ecstasy." Marcel Gutwirth, *Laughing Matter: An Essay on the Comic* (Ithaca: Cornell Univ. Press, 1993), pp. 78–79, discusses a "buoyancy" of "euphoria" and an "effervescence of gaiety and high spirits." Wallace Stevens claims instead for the poet "that occasional ecstasy, or ecstatic freedom of the mind, which is his special privilege"—p. 36 in "The Noble Rider and the Sound of Words," in *The Necessary Angel: Essays on Reality and the Imagination* (New York: Knopf, 1951).

11. Pascal Covici, Jr., *Mark Twain's Humor: The Image of a World* (Dallas: Southern Methodist Univ. Press, 1962), p. 216.

12. Susan Gillman, *Dark Twins: Imposture and Identity in Mark Twain's America* (Berkeley: Univ. of California Press, 1989), argues that No. 44 is "even more exuberantly playful and childlike than either of his surrogates" and points out that Twain himself refers to the "innate frivolities" of his "nature" (p. 163).

13. Susan K. Harris, *"Mark Twain's" Escape from Time: A Study of Patterns and Images* (Columbia: Univ. of Missouri Press, 1982). Intriguingly, in her conclusion Harris senses the same quality I have been discussing: ". . . numerous passages depicting a character flying through outer space indicate the ecstasy offered by the suggestion that his mind, released from the restrictions of the flesh, could collapse time and space and live in an eternity of creative freedom" (p. 159).

Don Florence

We've seen that Twain usually restricts himself to the role of gentleman in the Sandwich Islands letters. In other writings, Twain experiments with defining himself by adopting various other roles, often in sharply limited ways. Branch considers that Twain frequently loses his identity "in a maze of comic poses."[1] But it might be more accurate to suggest that Twain *seeks* an identity, however mistakenly, by experimenting with different ways of restricting himself. That is, Twain seeks definition through restriction, limiting himself to a particular role in a given piece. He takes a particular aspect of his literary personality (say, the sentimental) and renders it, usually in exaggerated form, as though it were *all* that he is (in this case, a sentimentalist). John C. Gerber outlines some of the roles Twain assumes: Twain's "superior poses" (in which he presents himself as superior to the world) include gentleman, sentimentalist, instructor, and moralist; his "inferior poses" (in which he presents himself as helpless) include sufferer, simpleton, and tenderfoot. According to Gerber, each pose gives Twain "psychic support," distancing him from life's anxieties and giving him a limited point of view that "simplified life and made it more tolerable."[2] Gerber is engaging in debatable psychological analysis of Samuel Clemens, not just discussing a literary personality. If we confine ourselves to the persona and implied author, Mark Twain, we see that in adopting a specific role Twain simplifies not only how he presents life but also how he himself is presented. The problem is that such simplification does not do justice. A strategy predicated upon limitation and evasion is not likely to succeed; the sustained, conscious adoption of a set role may seem strained and artificial. Instead of being one natural attitude among many in a dynamic Mark Twain, the pose may become a fixed mask.

Moreover, the poses outlined by Gerber show a dualism between superiority and inferiority. When adopting a "superior pose," Twain sug-

Excerpted from Don Florence, *Persona and Humor in Mark Twain's Early Writings* (Columbia: University of Missouri Press, 1995), 55–61. Reprinted by permission of the University of Missouri Press, and the Curators of the University of Missouri.

gests life is not as bad as it seems and can be mastered; when adopting an "inferior pose," Twain indicates life is much worse than it seems and overpowers one. This dualism, similar to the Twain-Brown duality, shows Twain's debate over life's value. Whenever he becomes enmeshed in this debate, Twain's views tend to polarize and rigidify; whenever he becomes too preoccupied with life's (fixed) "meaning," his humor loses its sportiveness and versatility.

Fortunately, Twain doesn't restrict himself to any given role for long; he does not harden into a permanent, narrow identity. Furthermore, by adopting diverse roles, Twain *is* exploring different ways of looking at the world and playing with possible forms of self-expression. Each role, however unsatisfactory in itself, contributes to a multifaceted and slowly evolving Twain, enabling him to play easily with many viewpoints. Each role lets him test, if in artificial and magnified form, a given perspective or mood. We witness Twain experimenting with himself as a literary personality, though he sometimes limits himself to set roles in these early writings. After all, journalism is by nature episodic and disconnected, without an overall pattern. Even in *The Innocents Abroad*, based on journalistic letters, Twain is occasionally plagued by fragmentation. Such discontinuity can easily lead to the serial adoption of certain roles, with each role controlling a given piece or episode. Only in *Roughing It*, his first book written *as* a book, does Twain become wholly versatile and fluid.

Nevertheless, Twain's experiments in these early pieces indicate well the shape of things to come. Twain suggests how intricate "identity" is and how one may experiment with it for fun or serious purposes. Life is incongruous, and often so are the roles one adopts, as Twain notes when describing a masquerade ball at New York's Academy of Music. He dresses up as a king, but feels like "a highly ornamental butcher"; he remarks on discrepancies everywhere:

> If everybody else felt as solemn and absurd as I did, they have my sympathy. . . . Dukes and princes, and queens and fairies met me at every turn, and I might have managed to imagine myself in a land of enchantment, but for remarks I was constantly overhearing. For instance, I heard Joan of Arc say she would give the world for a mess of raw oysters, and Martin Luther said he didn't feel well, because he had been playing poker for the last forty-eight hours. . . . I even heard the Queen of the Fairies say she wished she had some cheese. These little things have a tendency to destroy the pleasant illusions created by deceptive costumes.[3]

The journalist who would be king had better be careful not to become tripped up in his own playing robes. Twain wrestles, albeit whimsically, with problems of roles and imaginative projections of himself. Poses may let him playfully express or exaggerate various sides of himself, but at what point do poses degenerate into nonsense or, worse yet, render him little better than a poseur? How can Twain be protean yet have integrity? If he does not fit into some conventional niche or assume some set identity, is he in danger of dissipating? Twain tells about being confronted in the Sandwich Islands by a man who is flabbergasted to find that Twain is not a whaling man, a missionary, or a government official (the three primary occupations of white men in the islands). The man asks, "Then, who the mischief are you?"[4] Whether Samuel Clemens was actually beset by such a question is debatable; but Mark Twain presents himself in many narratives as troubled by the question of identity.

A particular identity may, however, undercut itself. In a letter for the *San Francisco Daily Alta California* from New York, Twain comments on P. T. Barnum's museum and simultaneously plays the role of philosopher. Discussing the freakish sights, Twain feels sorry for a monkey whose tail has been bitten off by another monkey and who falls whenever he tries to use his nonexistent tail to grab a beam: "Why cannot he become a philosopher? Why cannot he console himself with the reflection that tails are but a delusion and a vanity at best?"[5] The irony is that the consolations of philosophy may themselves be "but a delusion and a vanity at best." Twain adopts the role of philosopher only to discover that it fails. We recall his discontent with the masquerade ball, where he laments that "Martin Luther" is under the weather after a long bout of poker. The Martin Luther role fails just as surely as the philosopher role. Twain's mood here, he confesses, is "solemn and absurd." Granted, Twain does generate some humor in these comments, but he seems to harden once more into a preoccupation with the merit of life, applying dogmatic tests for "truth" or "reality." The philosopher's position is untrue; "Martin Luther" is unreal. The implicit worry, of course, is that "Mark Twain" is also unreal. And Mark Twain is indeed unreal—there is no such human being. He is but the image that we have of Samuel Clemens. Yet as persona and implied author, Twain may be "real" within the context of his narrative worlds; he conveys the impression of vitality so long as he is dynamic and does not imprison himself within a fixed or arbitrary role. The philosopher fails because he insists upon seeing life only in stoical terms. "Martin Luther" fails because a man puts on a mask and tries to be a character that in no way expresses himself.

A role is a form of play; a pose is an attitude. Any limited form of play, any one attitude, is bound to be inadequate; reality cannot be encompassed by such narrow terms. Furthermore, any role that the player cannot *enter into* or *become* (that is, make a manifestation of himself) is bound to fail even as a partial representation of life. To succeed, Twain must metamorphose into other forms or roles; he must enter and exit each role easily, yet make each role expressive—or creative—of himself. That is, he needs to be a dynamic, highly dramatized literary personality, exhibiting a play of characteristics, each of which can naturally and readily be bodied forth as particular roles or "selves." When Twain projects this variety and does not commit himself to a fixed identity, then he presents himself—and life—richly and humorously.

The past would seem to be the greatest fixity of all: it is supposedly what is dead and done with, what has made and defined (limited) oneself. But Twain renders the past fluid. He produces a burlesque biography of Virginia City Marshal John Perry, altering Perry's past and identity entirely. Twain transmutes Perry into a former Commodore, Commissioner to Japan, inventor of "Perry's Pain Killer," poet, congressman, and, significantly, actor.[6] Twain makes Perry into a cosmos—what he himself is gradually evolving into. Perry becomes an actor with many roles, yet Twain is the stage manager, playing with the identities of others and himself. His creative rewriting of Perry's past anticipates what he will later do with Samuel Clemens's past in works such as *Tom Sawyer*, *Life on the Mississippi*, and *Huckleberry Finn*, as well as in an array of burlesque "autobiographies" of Mark Twain.

Twain begins to play with his Hannibal past in an April 1867 letter for the *Daily Alta California*: "Hannibal has had a hard time of it ever since I can recollect, and I was 'raised' there. First, it had me for a citizen, but I was too young then to really hurt the place." He gives enlivened "reminiscences" of town drunk Jimmy Finn, a scarlet fever epidemic, the new firehouse (which promptly burned down), and the Cadets of Temperance. Considering a current plan to help the town proper by building a railroad to Moberly, Twain doubts its success: "But won't they have to build another road to protect the Moberly? and another and another to protect each enterprise of the kind? A railroad is like a lie—you have to keep building to it to make it stand."[7] Twain makes many of his anecdotes stand by "building" to them. He builds upon Clemens's identity until it can stand as that of Twain; he builds upon the identity of an entire town until it can stand as his town. There is no preoccupation here with facts, fixed roles, or a set identity. Ironically, the more Twain reshapes the Hannibal past, the "truer" it becomes, the more "real" as a town affectionately and humorously "remembered."

In addition to playing with the past, Twain considers various "transcendent figures" (to use Smith's apt term) that suggest ways for him to grow and achieve a measure of mastery. Such figures in Twain's early writings include Judge Shepheard and Detective Rose in the *San Francisco Morning Call* pieces. The most notable example, however, is Captain Edgar (Ned) Wakeman, who will later have other guises and names— Waxman, Blakely, Stormfield—in Twain's writings.[8] Captain Wakeman, an actual person, is described by Twain in a December 1866 letter to the *Daily Alta California:*

> I have been listening to some of Captain Waxman's [Wakeman's] stunning forecastle yarns, and I will do him the credit to say he knows how to tell them. With his strong, cheery voice, animated countenance, quaint phraseology, defiance of grammar and extraordinary vim in the matter of gesture and emphasis he makes a most effective story out of very unpromising materials. There is a contagion about his wholesouled jollity that the chief mourner at a funeral could not resist. He is fifty years old, and as rough as a bear in voice and action, and yet as kind-hearted and tender as a woman. He is a burly, hairy, sun-burned, stormy-voiced old salt, who mixes strange oaths with incomprehensible sailor phraseology and the gentlest and most touching pathos, and is tattooed from head to foot like a Fejee Islander. His tongue is forever going when he has got no business on his hands, and though he knows nothing of policy or the ways of the world, he can cheer up any company of passengers that ever travelled in a ship, and keep them cheered up.[9]

Besides being a superb seaman, Wakeman is a marvelous storyteller whose tall tales and vigorous sea vernacular can absorb and hearten any audience—a feat immensely appealing to a writer and humorist such as Twain. Possessing the easy self-confidence of a sea god, Wakeman has many admirable qualities: he shows his good sense by marrying a runaway young couple; he displays his understanding of human nature by telling of an old woman who was disappointed to find out that a ship was not actually on fire; and, most important, he is a frontier humorist par excellence.[10] In short, Wakeman is a wonderful mixture of wisdom, lively vernacular, and humor. No doubt Twain embellishes Wakeman's character, transforming Wakeman into an Olympian figure and thereby projecting through him his own comic exaggerations, love of the vernacular, and values. Many of the Wakeman characteristics become part of the later Mark Twain. Wakeman also suggests ways Twain may transcend the Twain-Brown dualism. Wakeman is crude, ungrammatical, assertive, and strangely innocent, just like Brown; yet Wakeman is humane, imaginative, and perceptive. In some ways Wakeman is a gigantic child: like Brown and the infant terrors in "Those Blasted Children," he represents yet another Twainian projection of "uncivilized" childhood. He is, however, a child who sees and knows much—a characteristic that will later be incorporated into Huck Finn. Perhaps most important, Wakeman seems unconcerned with set roles or with others' perceptions of him. He is free and various; one attitude melts easily into another. He may be "rough as a bear" yet "kind-hearted and tender as a woman"; he may be "stormy-voiced" yet capable of the "gentlest and most touching pathos." He is not preoccupied with adopting a fixed pose or stance toward his audience. Like life itself, he simply is. He holds forth implicit suggestions of Twain's evolution, for ways to be "whole-souled."

Despite periodic retreats into dualities and fixed roles, Twain evolves into a personality with at least some of the flexibility needed to express the range of his humor and his attitudes toward the world.

Notes

1. Edgar M. Branch, *The Literary Apprenticeship of Mark Twain* (Urbana: University of Illinois Press, 1950), 27.

2. John C. Gerber, "Mark Twain's Use of the Comic Pose," *PMLA* 77 (1962): 297, 301–3. As Blair and Hill note (*America's Humor: From Poor Richard to Doonesbury* [New York: Oxford University Press, 1978], 323), Gerber's idea of "superior" and "inferior" poses corresponds to the ancient Greek concepts of "alazon" (one who pretends to be better than he is) and "eiron" (one who pretends to be less than he is).

3. Mark Twain, *Travels with Mr. Brown*, ed. Franklin Walker and G. Ezra Dane (New York: Alfred A. Knopf, 1940), 120–21.

4. Mark Twain, *Letters from the Sandwich Islands*, ed. G. Ezra Dane (Stanford: Stanford University Press, 1938), 30–31.

5. Twain, *Travels with Mr. Brown*, 118.

6. Mark Twain, *Early Tales and Sketches*, ed. Edgar M. Branch and Robert H. Hirst (Berkeley and Los Angeles: University of California Press, 1979), 1:235–38. For the speculation that Perry may be the model for Buck Fanshaw, see editorial introduction to *Mark Twain of the "Enterprise,"* ed. Henry Nash

Smith and Frederick Anderson (Berkeley and Los Angeles: University of California Press, 1957), 66.

7. Twain, *Travels with Mr. Brown*, 144–46.

8. For a brief discussion of Twain's literary uses of Wakeman, see *Mark Twain's Notebooks and Journals*, ed. Frederick Anderson, Michael B. Frank, and Kenneth M. Sanderson (Berkeley and Los Angeles: University of California Press, 1975), 1:241–43.

9. Twain, *Travels with Mr. Brown*, 22. Twain's sincerity in this homage is shown by his contemporaneous notebook entry, where he declares, "I had rather travel with that old portly, hearty, jolly, boisterous, good-natured old sailor, Capt[.] Ned Wakeman than with any other man I ever came across" (*Notebooks and Journals*, 1:253).

10. Twain, *Travels with Mr. Brown*, 30–33, 23–25, 37–38.

Walter Blair

I. "At His Best and Brightest"

Grizzled Jim Baker, the lone dweller in a deserted California mining camp, begins a story about favorite woodland neighbors by summing up his scientific findings during seven years:

> "There's more *to* a blue-jay than any other creature. He has got more moods, and more different kinds of feelings than other creatures; and mind you, whatever a blue-jay feels, he can put into language. And no mere commonplace language, either, but rattling, out-and-out book-talk—and bristling with metaphor, too—just bristling! And as for command of language—why, *you* never see a blue-jay stuck for a word. No man ever did. They just boil out of him! And another thing: I've noticed a good deal, and there's no bird, or cow, or anything that uses as good grammar as a blue-jay. You may say a cat uses good grammar. Well, a cat does—but you let a cat get excited, once; you let a cat get to pulling fur with another cat on a shed, nights, and you'll hear grammar that will give you the lockjaw. Ignorant people think it's the *noise* which fighting cats make that is so aggravating, but it ain't so; it's the sickening grammar they use. Now I've never heard a jay use bad grammar but very seldom; and when they do, they are as ashamed as a human; they shut right down and leave."[1]

Bernard DeVoto thought "Jim Baker's Blue-Jay Yarn" an interlude in *A Tramp Abroad* (1880), typified Mark Twain's humor in part because of the way it combined fantasy and reality. Baker's furred and feathered friends not only talk but achieve levels of diction, metaphors; and even grammar. But Baker, "a creation from the world of reality," DeVoto says, is born not of fantasy but of "the sharp perception of an individual."

This essay first appeared in *Studies in American Humor* 1 (January 1975) 3:132–47; it has been reprinted in *Essays on American Humor: Blair through the Ages*, ed. Hamlin Hill (Madison: University of Wisconsin Press, 1993), 165–78. Reprinted by permission of *Studies in American Humor*.

"Fantasy," he concludes, "is thus an instrument of realism and the humor of Mark Twain merges into the fiction that is his highest reach."[2]

Critics of several persuasions saw Baker's yarn as what W. E. Henley called it in an early review of *A Tramp Abroad*. Twain "at his best and brightest, . . . delightful as mere reading [and] of a high degree of merit as literature."[3] DeLancey Ferguson, for example, thought it stood out in a book which "contained phrases and passages that were Mark Twain at his best," and added, "were one asked to choose from all Mark Twain's works the most perfect example of the genuine Western tall tale, patiently and skillfully built up . . . the choice would come down at last to this story.[4]

A case can be made for the claim that, just as *Huckleberry Finn* is the greatest of Twain's longer comic works, "Blue-Jay Yarn" is the greatest of the shorter ones. Although it does not have the depth, the scope, or the variety of the novel, it is equally characteristic, and judged on its own terms it is in some ways superior: it has fewer flaws and greater unity. Besides, it is delightfully funny. So it is worth a close look.

The story's background partly accounts for its preeminence and helps one define its genre. Storytelling sessions with some masters of the art in the winter of 1864–65 helped the humorist not only discover the substance of the yarn but rediscover the form that was appropriate for it. Later practice and analysis helped him give the written narrative qualities that—quite rightly—he prized. And literary traditions and models also in important ways contributed to its excellence.

II. Calaveras County Bonanza

During the years before he went West in 1861, Sam Clemens constantly heard stories told well. His mother, an "obscure little woman" with an "enchanted tongue," he called "the most eloquent person" he ever met. Ned, his father's slave, told "The Golden Arm" story which Twain retold year after year to lecture audiences. On the Missouri farm where he spent boyhood summers, he enjoyed his uncle's storytelling; at night in the Quarters he heard Uncle Dan'l "telling the immortal tales which Uncle Remus Harris was to . . . charm the world with, by and by." (Dan'l effectively prepared childish listeners for jimdandy nightmares by unloosing a bloodcurdling ghost story just before he sent them to bed.) During Sam's Wanderjahren, fellow jour printers and steamboatmen were memorable yarnspinners.[5]

He grew up when American humorists were trying to catch in print the substance and the manner of oral yarns. At his printer's case in Hannibal and elsewhere he set up their writings; in his leisure hours he read them. At about the time he went West, however, new styles of writing became fashionable. Many comic journalists replaced rustic yarnspinning with wordplay, topsy-turvy sentences, parodies and burlesques.[6] Writing for the Virginia City *Territorial Enterprise* and for San Francisco newspapers, Twain ground out comedy of the sort currently popular.[7] Throughout the rest of his life, he would often—*too* often—write Phunny Phellow humor of diction. But a visit to the California mining country reacquainted him with the stuff and the style of fireside storytelling that shaped many of his best writings.

Clemens, a twenty-nine-year-old San Francisco journalist, peeved officials by publishing feisty exposés. When he found it expedient to absent himself a while, Jim Gillis, pocket miner out in the area where Baker lived, asked him to be a guest. Between December 4, 1864, and February 25, 1865, the budding author stayed with Gillis and his partner, Jim Stoker, in a Jackass Hill cabin or bunked in a nearby Angel's Camp hotel.

The region once had swarmed with goldseekers, but the rich diggings had played out, and now only a few desultory pocket miners dotted fields, hills, and forests. Clemens did a little pocket mining without luck and was kept from doing more by a rainy season which—even for a state where what natives call Unusual Weather flushes houses down hills—was worse than usual. He, his hosts, and soggy neighbors huddled for hours around the cabin fireplace or the hotel barroom stove. His notebook jottings gripe about endless deluges and the "beans and dishwater" monotonously served by the hotel's French restaurateur. He complains that "4 kinds of soup which he furnishes to customers only on great occasions . . . are popularly known among the Boarders as Hellfire, General Debility, Insanity and Sudden Death." The booze must have been as corrosive: in a plaint that has the poignancy of a personal reminiscence, Clemens holds that a shot of the tavern's straight whiskey "will throw a man a double somerset and limber him up like boiled macaroni before he can set his glass down."[8]

All the same, looking back, he would call this area a "serene and reposeful and dreamy and delicious sylvan paradise" where he had "a fascinating and delightful time." He fondly remembered dates with the Eves of this Eden, a miner's pneumatic daughters whom he called "the Chaparral Quails."[9] More important, every few years during more than four decades, he praised the purveyors of the chief entertainment aside from drinking, the mining camp yarnspinners, analyzed their artistry, and at the top of his form imitated them and retold their stories.

There is support for the guess several scholars have made that the mining country visit, because of the impact of those storytelling orgies in Jim Gillis' Jackass Hill cabin and the Angel's Camp caravanserie, brought a turning point in the author's career. The very first sketch he published after he got back to San Francisco had as its best and chief ingredient a vernacular monologue by one of the Angel's Camp crowd.[10] One evening he told anecdotes to a group of fellow reporters so well that they lost all track of time. Within months he decided that he had a "call" to "drop all trifling . . . & strive for a fame" by cultivating his "talent for humorous writing."[11] Soon after this discovery of his vocation, he published one of the tales that he had heard "around the tavern stove"—"the germ," as he put it, "of my coming good fortune," a piece of writing that "became widely known in America, India, China, England—and the reputation it made for me . . . paid me thousands and thousands of dollars. . . ."[12] The story furnished the chief part of the title of Twain's first book, and though he infrequently revised any piece once it had been printed, he carefully—and substantially—revised this one three times. Other retellings of California mining camp yarns came out in 1865, 1867, 1871, 1880, 1884, 1893, and 1907.[13]

The cream of what turned out to be a bumper crop was the "Blue-Jay Yarn" on eleven pages of *A Tramp Abroad,* published in 1880 when the author paused part way through the writing of *Adventures of Huckleberry Finn.*

The "lovable" personality and the skill of the original teller of this story in the Mother Lode country doubtless helped Twain see its merit. This was Jim Gillis, "gray as a rat, earnest, thoughtful, slenderly educated, slouchily dressed and clay-soiled," but "a gallant creature" whose "styles and bearing could make any costume regal . . . a man, and a whole man." "A much more remarkable person than his family and his intimates ever suspected," Jim in the humorist's opinion was a genius—"a born humorist, and a very competent one" who "would have been a star performer if he had been discovered, and had been subjected to a few years training with a pen." Twain identified Jim, who he thought was the best raconteur in the diggings, as the originator of three of his mining camp tales, though one of them almost certainly was told by Jim's partner. The writer's notebook jottings, his characterizations of the tellers, and his vivid picturings in memoirs and in the stories themselves justify the other attributions.

When inspired, Jim stood with his back to the fire, unleashed his imagination, and spun yarns. Each was a gaudy lie created as he went along but soberly old as "history undefiled." Usually he made his "pard" Stoker the incongruous hero, and Stoker sat smoking, listening solemnly but amiably to his "monstrous fabrications." One of the stories that Twain retold celebrated Stoker's prodigious cat, Tom Quartz, a beast that "had never existed," Twain said, "outside of Jim Gillis's imagination." Another was "Jim Gillis's yarn about the blue jays"—"a charming story, a delightful story, and full of happy fancies."[14] When he theorized about oral storytelling and a writer's adaptation of its ways, he found Jim Gillis a useful teacher.

III. A "High, Delicate Art" Adapted

Twain would call the oral story as Gillis told it "high and delicate art," and would find "no merit in ninety-nine out of a hundred [stories] except the merit put into them by the teller's art."[15]

He deliberately tried to use that art in his books. But he repeatedly said that *written* art had to modify the ways of oral storytelling. If an author merely set down the golden words of a fine storyteller, a funny thing happened on the way to the printer: they turned to dross. Clemens prohibited publication of an interview he gave because quoting talk in print is "an attempt to use a boat on land or a wagon on water."[16]

He decided that careful artistry alone could give printed words the sound of free-and-easy speech. "I amend dialect stuff by talking and talking and *talking* it till it sounds right."[17] Measures like those he took to give painstakingly memorized platform monologues the qualities of off-the-cuff utterances helped him write colloquial passages—"a touch of indifferent grammar flung in here and there, apparently at random" but in fact shrewdly deployed: "heaving in ... a wise tautology"; "sprinkl[ing] in one of those happy turns on something that has previously been said."[18] The chief incongruity in the two-hundred-word opening paragraph of Baker's story—between fulsome praise of book-talk and grammar and abysmal ignorance about both—is made apparent by only four assorted—and strategically placed—grammatical mishaps. And the paragraph illustrates "wise tautology" by reiterating half a dozen times the belief that a jay can express whatever it feels.

Twain lauded Gillis for "build[ing] a story as it goes along, careless of whither it is proceeding, enjoying each fresh fancy as it flashes from the brain." In "How to Tell a Story," he held that the very basis of the American art was "to string incongruities and absurdities together in a wandering and purposeless way."[19] He downgraded jokes with payoff lines, praised stories with "pervasive" humor which, like that of William Dean Howells, "flows softly all around about and over."[20] So his aim was to ape in print the leisurely imagining and inundating humor of Gillis and other experts.

Twain makes "The Blue-Jay Yarn" seem to meander, for one thing, by prefacing it with an apparent unhurried digression of his own, then by having Baker sidle into his monologue as his leisure. The humorist, a continent and an ocean away from the Mother Lode country, strolls into the woods above the Neckar. Soon, remembering German legends that he has been reading about the area, he falls "into a train of dreamy thought about animals which talk, and kobolds, and enchanted folk." Later, lost and alone in the dense silent woods, he fancies that he glimpses some of these creatures in the shadows under the trees.

Suddenly the quiet is shattered by the croak of a raven staring down from a branch at the intruder. A second bird comes along:

> The two sat side by side on the limb and discussed me as freely and
> offensively as two great naturalists might discuss a new kind of bug. . . .
> They called in another friend. This was too much. I saw that they had
> the advantage of me, and so I concluded to get out. . . . They enjoyed
> my defeat as much as any low white people could have done. They
> craned their necks and laughed at me (for a raven *can* laugh, just like a
> man), they squalled insulting remarks after me as long as they could
> see me. . . . When even a raven shouts after you, "What a hat!" "O, pull
> down your vest!" and that sort of thing, it hurts you and humiliates
> you, and there is no getting around it with fine reasoning and pretty
> arguments.[21]

The confrontation leads Twain to recall the man who could understand birds and animals—Jim Baker. Baker's background and some of his opinions are detailed. Only after this preamble—one that at first glance appears to be very loosely related—does Baker's monologue start with the remarks about the great skill with which jays communicate. In a passage a bit longer than the first, and therefore an apparent overelaboration, Jim next argues that "a jay is just as much a human as you be" by mentioning sundry human traits and ("wisely tautological") repeating the claim several times:

You may call a jay a bird. Well, so he is, in a measure—because he's got feathers on him, and don't belong to no church, perhaps; but otherwise he is just as human as you be. And I'll tell you for why. A jay's gifts, instincts, and feelings, and interests, cover the whole ground. A jay hasn't got any more principle than a Congressman. A jay will lie, a jay will steal, a jay will deceive, a jay will betray; and four times out of five, a jay will go back on his solemnest promise. The sacredness of an obligation is a thing which you can't cram into no blue-jay's head. Now on top of all this, there's another thing: a jay can out-swear any gentleman in the mines. You think a cat can swear. Well, a cat can; but you give a blue-jay a subject that calls for his reserve-powers, and where is your cat? . . . Yes, sir, a jay is everything that a man is. A jay can cry, a jay can laugh, a jay can feel shame, a jay can reason and plan and discuss, a jay likes gossip and scandal, a jay has got a sense of humor, a jay knows when he is an ass just as well as you do—maybe better. If a jay ain't human, he better take in his sign, that's all.

The impression that Baker is loquacious is heightened by the introduction here of a different type of comedy. These remarks, proving as they do that his birds are human chiefly by arguing that they are depraved in as many ways as human beings are, have the bite of satire. Twain would have said that Jim's equating of humanity with total depravity, in addition to "wandering in an apparently purposeless way," introduces an important component. "It takes a heap of sense to write good nonsense," he told himself in a note shortly before he wrote the blue-jay yarn.[22] As an oldster, he would marvel at the way his humor outlasted that of more than eighty popular contemporaneous humorists, thus living "forever." ("By forever," he explained, "I mean thirty years.") His explanation: "I have always preached."[23] The humorist was repeating a judgment of his best friend, Howells, who said that "what finally appeals to you in Mark Twain . . . is his common sense."[24]

The way the tale that follows is unfolded reinforces the impression that it wanders since—simple though it is—it (in Twain's phrase) seemingly "fools along and enjoys elaboration" for almost thirteen hundred words. It does not, in fact, detour: each of two parts illustrates a claim Baker makes as he starts his monologue.

Part one: Baker describes the comic doings of some jays around a deserted log house near his cabin. One finds a knothole in the roof and decides to fill it with acorns. Though he dumps in huge numbers, since the house is "just one big room," he fails. The bird becomes increasingly frantic, frustrated, outraged; and his more and more eloquent orations prove that "whatever a blue-jay feels, he can put into language."

Part two: Attracted by his commentaries, first one, then more jays gather and discuss the phenomenon. Finally one learns what the trouble is and announces his discovery. Thereupon greater and greater numbers of birds fly in, study the scene, and jeer about the frustrated jay's mistake. The reactions prove that jays are "just as human as you be." When he makes this uncomplicated fable laughable, Twain proves that the effect of a humorous story depends less upon matter than on manner, in a printed story as well as an oral one, if the author of the printed version adapts oral procedures.

IV. Literary Influences

Writings as well as oral storytellers of course shaped the blue-jay yarn. A beast fable, this narrative is in a genre that had amused audiences, literally, for ages. Even before Aesop, its beginnings, like Aesop himself, are hidden in the mists of antiquity, and from those beginnings to the present, the form has flourished. A few outstanding practitioners were Hesiod, Aristophanes, and Socrates in the ancient world; Chaucer and myriads of anonymous celebrators of Reynard the Fox in the Middle Ages, Robert Henryson and William Caxton in the fifteen century; Francois Rabelais in the sixteenth; Jean de la Fontaine (twelve books; "I use Animals to teach Mankind") and Sir Roger L'Estrange in the seventeenth; Jonathan Swift, John Gay, Gotthold Ephraim Lessing, Bernard Mandeville, Matthew Prior, William Cowper, Johann Woflgang Goethe, and Benjamin Franklin in the eighteenth; Leo Tolstoi, Ivn Krylov, Rudyard Kipling, Trilussa (C. A. Salustra), Guy Wetmore Carryl, and others in the nineteenth.

Since (as scholars have proved) Clemens read widely, he knew several of his remote predecessors in the anthropomorphic field. About the time he wrote Baker's yarn, his reading had helped him remember or discover three Americans working in the genre in the 1880s. As co-editor of a forthcoming anthology—*Mark Twain's Library of Humor* (1888)—he was jotting down in notebooks 15 and 16 lists of possible inclusions. Four times he mentioned George T. Lanigan (1846–86) or his *World's Fables,* and the anthology would include seven of Lanigan's pieces. Twice he named Ambrose Bierce; one entry recalled fables published in a newspaper as many as thirteen years earlier; and the anthology had seven of Bierce's fables, at the time still uncollected. In Bierce's "The Robin and the Woodpecker," the latter bird admits that he does not know why he pecks holes in a dead tree: "Some naturalists affirm that I hide acorns in these pits; others maintain that I get worms out of them." Alert source hunters will notice the bird's theoretical kinship with Baker's blue jay, which dumped acorns into his knothole for reasons that never were clarified. They also may be interested in the fact that at one time when he talked about his story long after he wrote it, Twain called it "a tale of how the poor and innocent *woodpeckers* tried to fill up a house with acorns."[25]

"Uncle Remus (?) writer of colored yarns," another notebook entry, Clemens made before the yarns had appeared between hardcovers and, evidently, before he had learned that the creator's name was Joel Chandler Harris. Clemens and his co-editors included two of Harris' narratives in their anthology; he read Harris' tales to audiences, corresponded with him, swapped stories, arranged meetings, called him "a fine genius," and even tried to get the shy little man to share lecture platforms. It seems possible that partly because he so admired Harris and, like him, as a boy had heard black storytellers tell animal legends, he did well when he exploited what Harris called "that incongruity of animal expression that is just human enough to be humorous" in the "Blue-Jay Yarn."[26]

Several passages in Jim Baker's story are enriched by comic linkings between bird and animal—for instance the jay's discovery of the hole: "He cocked his head to one side, shut one eye and put the other one to the hole, like a possum looking down a jug"; or the doglike gesture showing the jay's puzzlement: "he took a thinking attitude . . . and scratched the back of his head with his right foot." (A kinship—perhaps something more—is indicated when one compares a passage in "Uncle Remus Initiates the Little Boy," the first Uncle Remus story and one included in Twain's anthology: "Den Brer Rabbit scatch on one year wid his off hine-foot sorter jub'usly. . . .") More incongruities are of the sort Harris mentioned—between bird and humans. After he drops the first acorn into the hole, the jay

> was just tilting his head back with the heavenliest smile on his face, when all of a sudden he was paralyzed into a listening attitude and that smile faded gradually out of his countenance like breath off'n a razor,[27] and the queerest look of surprise took its place. . . . He cocked his eye at the hole again, and took a long look; raised up and shook his head;

stepped around to the other side of the hole, and took another look from that side; shook his head again.

His puzzlement grows; so does his anger:

> He fetched another acorn, and done his level best to see what become of it, but he couldn't. . . . Then he begun to get mad. He held in for a spell, walking up and down the comb of the roof and shaking his head and muttering to himself; but his feelings got the upper hand of him, presently, and he broke loose and cussed himself black in the face. I never see a bird take on so about a little thing.

Now he decides that he'll be damned if he doesn't fill that hole if it takes a hundred years, and for two hours and a half, he heaves in acorns without stopping:

> Well at last he could hardly flop his wings, he was so tuckered out. He comes a-drooping down, once more, sweating like an ice-pitcher, drops his acorn in and says, "*Now* I guess I've got the bulge on you by this time!" So he bent down for a look. If you'll believe me, when his head come up again he was just pale with rage. He says, "I've shoveled acorns enough in there to keep the family thirty years, and if I can see a sign of one of 'em, I wish I may land in a museum with a belly full of sawdust in two minutes!"

The culmination of his frantic efforts and of his frustration is accompanied by his greatest flight of eloquence:

> He just had strength enough to crawl up on to the comb an lean his back agin the chimbly, and then he collected his impression and began to free his mind. I see in a second that what I had mistook for profanity in the mines was only just the rudiments, as you may say.

In addition to the animalization or the humanization of birds, the story as Baker tells it amuses because of its comic picturings. Incongruities, as Max Eastman has noticed,[28] are stressed when they are made highly concrete. Twain creates pictures because, as Howells says, "he is the impassioned lover, the helpless slave of the concrete":[29] the jay peering into the knothole, shaking his head, cussing himself black in the face, turning pale with rage, taking a thinking attitude, and leaning his back agin the chimbly attest to this slavery.

Part Three

There are more humanizations and bodyings forth in the second movement of the story. A jay passing by hears the baffled bird "doing his devotions," stops, learns the reason, and calls in other jays:

> They called in more jays; then more and more, till pretty soon the whole region 'peared to have a blue flush about it. There must have been five thousand of them; and such another jawing and disputing and ripping and cussing, you never heard. Every jay in the whole lot put his eye to the hole and delivered a more chuckle-headed opinion about the mystery than the jay that went there before him. They examined the house all over, too.

The figurative comparison to "a blue flush" helps make this vivid, joining earlier figures to give substance and a comic quality to the proceedings and to justify Baker's aperçu that a jay's language, sharing a conspicuous merit with written as well as oral American humor, just bristles with figures of speech. In the final paragraphs, after the old jay solves the mystery and announces his findings, his fellow jays become "a blue cloud," manifest vividly additional human traits, and prove their sense of humor is superior to an owl's:

> They all came a-swooping down like a blue cloud, and as each fellow lit on the door and took a glance, the whole absurdity of the contract that the first jay had tackled hit him home and he fell over backwards suffocating with laughter, and the next jay took his place and done the same.
> Well, sir, they roosted around here on the house-top and the trees for a hour, and guffawed over that thing like human beings. It ain't no use to tell me a blue-jay hasn't got a sense of humor, because I know better. And memory too. They brought jays here from all over the United States to look down that hole, every summer for three years. Other birds too. And they could all see the point, except an owl that come from Nova Scotia to visit the Yo Semite, and he took this thing in on his way back. He said he couldn't see anything funny in it. But then, he was a good deal disappointed about Yo Semite, too.

DeVoto felt that the last sentences "mar the effect of a passage in pure humor" because "they strain toward a joke, escaping from the clear medium of the tale itself into burlesque." Those who have heard an audience respond to the recitation of the sentences by a master—a Hal Holbrook, say—may disagree. Blemish or not, the sentences (as DeVoto adds) are typical of Mark Twain. And their mingling of horseplay with

194

delicate fancifulness is typical of both printed and oral American tall tale humor.

V. "The Principle of Life"

An exchange between Clemens and Joel Chandler Harris indicates that the humorist might well claim that this discussion so far has failed to deal with the chief aim of this story. Clemens had complimented Harris on his picturing of Uncle Remus as he told Negro folktales to a boy on an antebellum Georgia plantation. Harris, as modest as he was shy, protested that the folktales were far more important than characterization: "my relations toward Uncle Remus are similar to those that exist between an almanac maker and a calendar." Nonsense, Clemens answered, "the principle of life" was in the frameworks. The enclosed tales were

> only alligator pears—one merely eats them for the sake of the salad dressing. Uncle Remus is most deftly drawn, and is a lovable and delightful creation; he, and the little boy, and their relations with each other, are high and fine literature, and worthy to live for their own sakes; and certainly the stories are not to be credited with *them*.[30]

Granted that Clemens overstated, he was sincere in praising an achievement that he admired and tried to duplicate: the using of a framework to make up for attritions—over and above those previously discussed—that an oral story suffers when it is reduced to print.

When Clemens refused to let that interviewer publish an accurate transcript of an interview he had granted, he explained that he did so because

> an immense something has disappeared from it. That is its soul . . . everything that gave that body warmth, grace, friendliness and charm and commended it to your affections—or, at least, to your tolerance— is gone and nothing is left but a pallid, stiff and repulsive cadaver.
>
> Such is "talk" almost invariably, as you see it lying in state in an "interview." The interviewer seldom tried to tell one *how* a thing was said; he merely puts in the naked remark and stops there. When one writes for print his methods are very different. . . . He loads, and often overloads, almost every utterance of his characters with explanations and interpretations. . . . Now, in your interview . . . you have not a word of explanation; what my manner was at several points is not indicated.

> Therefore, no reader can possibly know where I was in earnest and when I was joking, or whether I was joking altogether or in earnest altogether. Such a report of a conversation has no value.[31]

A fiction writer, this implies, has the obligation of so representing his listener and his storyteller as to relate them to the story. Somehow, by showing the pair in action and reaction, an artist must clarify such matters as why the one hearkens to a long-winded monologue and why the other gives it the substance and form he does. Somehow, too, the writer must simulate what Twain called "the spontaneity of a personal relation, which contains the very essence of interest."

The "Mark Twain" who listens to the jay story, and enjoys it and repeats it in toto, is characterized by the long first-person account of his ramblings in the Black Forest and his recollection of a faraway friend. He is a relatively complex and ingratiating person—a fact that is made clear when one compares him with the "Mark Twains" who were auditors for a couple of other mining camp storytellings. One of these "Mark Twains," gifted with as little humor, say, as a Canadian owl, is steered by a practical joker into the clutches of a monologist who mercilessly corners him and bores him to death with what he feels are irrelevant maunderings, but which are actually hilarious, before he gratefully escapes. He gives his account because he is outraged. The other "Mark Twain" has his curiosity raised to a fever heat by jocose miners. He therefore listens eagerly to a long-winded chatterbox who barely mentions his subject but spins out (very funny) irrelevancies till whiskey overcomes him, he falls asleep, and his listener at long last learns that he has been hoaxed.[32] By contrast the Black Forest "Mark Twain" has humor and understanding. He relished the "deep and mellow twilight" and the silence of the pine wood; he has enjoyed the German Märchen; he imagines that he glimpses "small flitting shapes here and there down the columned aisles of the forest." When the ravens jaw at him, he can relish their insults and joke about the way "the thing became more and more embarrassing." His amused and amusing account of his adventures has shown why he can hear Jim Baker's monologue with delight, remember it, and at a much later date lovingly repeat it verbatim. He has prepared the reader for his mock-solemn claims that animals talk to each other, that Jim is the one man he has known who can understand them, and whimsical proof: "I knew he could . . . because he told me so himself."

Jim, like his auditor, benefits when compared with his counterparts in the two Mother Lode stories mentioned above. Both of the other storytellers are nonstop babblers simply because they are cursed with total recall and are allergic to relevance. Besides, one of them is "tranquilly, serenely, symmetrically drunk—not a hiccup to mar his voice, not a cloud upon his brain thick enough to obscure his memory." By contrast, Jim is loquacious because he has an appreciative audience; he has endless leisure; and his way of living has given him his awestruck reverence for birds which most normal people find completely unlovable.

The biography of this "middle-aged, simple-hearted miner" shows how he discovered that jays can talk and he can understand them. He has been pushed by solitude into a strange companionship that he fondly recalls and celebrates at length. He "had lived in a lonely corner of California, among the woods and mountains, a good many years, and has studied the ways of his only neighbors, the beasts and the birds." Finally—to put it more bluntly than his compassionate portrayer does— this hermit has become a mite touched in the head. Seemingly random sentences give pertinent evidence: "Seven years ago, the last man in the region but me moved away. There stands his house—been empty ever since. . . ." And a bit later: "Well one Sunday morning I was sitting out here in front of my cabin with my cat, taking the sun, and looking at the blue hills, and listening to the leaves rustling so lonely in the trees. . . ." The statistics, and the pathetic fallacy of "lonely" leaves, are doubly poignant because they are unobtrusive. Equally unstressed is the casual relationship between the recluse's history and (1) a misanthropy that equates the birds' prodigious orneriness with human-ness, and (2) admiration for creatures that eloquently curse a thwarting world and that band together to jeer damfoolishness. Not surprisingly, he fantasizes about these kin-birds, and as DeVoto says, "His patient, explanatory mind actually works before our eyes and no one can doubt him."[33]

Awareness of one of the humorist's favorite devices may help the reader to notice a final touch in his portrayal of Baker. For years, Twain had been making use of counterpoint—repetitions with meaningful modulations: While writing "A Tramp Abroad," he cited one use of the device and its effect. He would, he said, place cheek-by-jowl "a perfectly serious description of 5 very bloody student duels which I witnessed in Heidelberg" and a broadly burlesqued account of a pretentious but completely harmless French duel. "The contrast," he predicted, "will be silent but eloquent comment."[34] Another echoing with variations comes in "Blue-Jay Yarn" when the account of the jeering at "Mark Twain" by raucous ravens is followed by Baker's account of the jeering at the befooled blue jay by other jays. But note the contrast:

Whereas the victim richly elaborates on "Twain's" droll humiliation and abject retreat, Baker says not a word about the mental state, the retorts, or the behavior of his embarrassed protagonist. This chief character, in fact, at this point vanishes from the story. The "silent but eloquent comment" that this contrast suggests is: So completely has Jim Baker identified with a woodland neighbor who, like him, has been defeated and, unlike him, has beautifully and directly voiced his feelings, that he skips any report on the jay's humiliation.

A way of talking, telling a story, thinking and fantasizing that is delightful and funny thus is made probable by a characterization of Jim Baker which is complex enough to encompass a heartwarming touch of pathos.[35]

Notes

1. Mark Twain, *A Tramp Abroad* (Hartford: American Publishing Co., 1880), 36–37. Later quotations also are from 31–42 of this edition.

2. Bernard DeVoto, *Mark Twain's America* (Boston: Little, Brown, 1932), 251.

3. W. E. Henley, *Athenaeum*, April 24, 1880, 529.

4. DeLancey Ferguson, *Mark Twain: Man and Legend* (Indianapolis: Bobbs, Merrill, 1943), 200. Social satire, realistic low life characterization, and highly imaginative fantasy in combinations occur in much American humor.

5. Fred W. Lorch, *The Trouble Begins at Eight* (Ames: Iowa State University Press, 1968), 10–12, gives a good summary.

6. Walter Blair, Introduction, *Native American Humor* (San Francisco: Chandler, 1960), 38–124.

7. Ibid. 147–50; Edgar Branch, *The Literary Apprenticeship of Mark Twain* (Urbana: University of Illinois Press, 1950).

8. Most accounts of the stay are gathered in *Mark Twain's Frontier*, ed. James E. Camp and X. J. Kennedy (New York: Holt, Rinehart and Winston, 1963), 89–136. The notebook jottings are in *Mark Twain's Notebook*, ed. Albert B. Paine (New York: Harper, 1935), 6–8, and Mark Twain, *The Great Landslide Case*, ed. Frederick Anderson and Edgar M. Branch (Berkeley: Friends of the Bancroft Library, 1972), 3–4. Twain assesses the power of Angel's Camp whiskey in "A Unbiased Criticism," *Californian*, March 18, 1865.

9. *Mark Twain in Eruption*, ed. Bernard DeVoto (New York: Harper, 1940), 360; *Mark Twain's Letters*, ed. A. B. Paine (New York: Harper, 1917), 1:170.

10. "An Unbiased Criticism."

11. *My Dear Bro*, ed. Frederick Anderson (Berkeley: Berkeley Albion, 1961). Clemens said that the "high praise" of his writings by Eastern editors brought his decision.

12. *Letters* 1:170.

13. "An Unbiased Criticism" appeared in March 1865. "Jim Smiley and His Jumping Frog," later "The Celebrated [or Notorious] Jumping Frog of Calaveras County," first appeared Nov. 18, 1865, and was frequently reprinted; it was revised in 1867, 1872, and 1875. Versions of "The Great Landslide Case," which the humorist evidently heard told orally for a second time during his pocket mining days, appeared in the Buffalo *Express*, April 2, 1870, and as chapter 34 of *Roughing It* (1872). "Jim Blaine and His Grandfather's Old Ram," chapter 53, and "Dick Baker's Cat," chapter 61, of *Roughing It* were other mining camp tales. The year 1880 brought the blue-jay yarn; 1884 "The Royal Nonesuch," a story originally told, apparently, by Stoker but attributed by Clemens much later to Gillis, in *Adventures of Huckleberry Finn*, Chapter 23; 1893 brought "A Californian's Tale" and 1907 the lecture circuit version of the old ram story. The frog story, the ram story and the blue-jay yarn were included in *Mark Twain's Library of Humor* (1888), an anthology he helped compile.

14. *Eruption* 283–84, 358–66.

15. "How to Tell a Story," *Youth's Companion*, Oct. 3, 1894, rpt in *Literary Essays* (New York, 1899), 7–15; Ernest J. Moyne, "Mark Twain and the Baroness Alexandra Gripenberg," *American Literature*, 45 (Nov. 1973), 376. Two discussions of the humorist's theories about writing and speaking are Sydney J. Krause, "Mark Twain's Method and Theory of Composition," *Modern Philology*, 56 (Feb. 1959), 171–72 and Introduction to *Selected Shorter Writings of Mark Twain*, ed. Walter Blair (Boston: Houghton Mifflin, 1962).

16. *Letters* 2:504.

17. *Mark Twain-Howells Letters*, ed. H. N. Smith and W. M. Gibson (Cambridge: Harvard University Press, 1960), 1:26.

18. "On Speech-Making Reform," *Mark Twain's Speeches* (New York: Harper, 1923), 2–3.

19. Again and again, Twain praised the rambling storyteller and imitated him. The frog story was an example, the ram story a more extreme one. In *Life on the Mississippi* (1883), chapter 13, he gave a sample of the art of Brown, who "could *not* forget anything." Huck tells a rambling history of English royalty in *Adventures of Huckleberry Finn*, chapter 23. In "How to Tell a Story," Twain nominates as "about the funniest thing I ever listened to" James Whitcomb Riley's impersonation of an old farmer "who gets all mixed up and wanders hopelessly round and round" as he tries to tell an ancient joke.

20. "William Dean Howells," *Works* Definitive Edition (New York: 1922–25), 26:228–38.

21. *Tramp Abroad*, 35. The humorist liked these birds so well that, carrying them to India and calling them *Indian* crows, he put them into *Following the Equator* (1897): "If I sat on one end of the balcony, the crows would gather on the railing at the other end and talk about me; . . . they would sit there, in the most unabashed way, and talk about my clothes, and my hair, and my complex-

ion, and probable character and vocation and politics, and how I came to be in India . . . and how I had happened to go unhanged so long . . . and so on, until I could no longer endure the embarrassment of it. . . ."

22. Notebook 14 (1879), Mark Twain Papers, Bancroft Library, University of California, Berkeley.

23. *Eruption* 202.

24. William Dean Howells, "Mark Twain: An Inquiry" (1901), in *My Mark Twain* (New York: Harper, 1910), 182.

25. *Eruption* 361—autobiographical dictation of 1907.

26. *Joel Chandler Harris, Editor and Essayist,* ed. Julia Collier Harris (Chapel Hill: University of North Carolina Press, 1931), 148–49.

27. Cf. Sut Lovingood telling in an 1867 book that Twain reviewed how it was when a rampaging bull smashed into a little bald-headed man: "he jis' disappear'd frum mortul vishun sumhow, sorter like breff frum a lookin-glass." George Washington Harris, *Sut Lovingood's Yarns,* ed. M. Thomas Inge (New Haven: College and University Press, 1966), 110. Twain listed George W. Harris, the author of this book, and its publishers in his notes on American humorists in 1880, and he included one of Sut's stories in his anthology.

28. Max Eastman, *The Enjoyment of Laughter* (New York: Simon and Schuster, 1948), 76–80. Eastman cites as an example a memorable Arizona colloquialism: "He's so stingy he wouldn't pay ten cents to see Christ wrastle a bear."

29. Howells, "Mark Twain: An Inquiry" 179. Twain in turn praised Howells for "translating . . . the vision of the eyes of flesh into words that reproduced their forms and colors."

30. Julia C. Harris, *The Life and Letters of Joel Chandler Harris* (Boston, 1918), 168; *Letters* 2:401–2.

31. *Letters* 2:504–5.

32. The first "Mark Twain" is cornered by Simon Wheeler in the frog story; the second is inveigled into hearing the drunken Jim Blaine tell about his grandfather's ram and many unrelated matters.

33. DeVoto, *Mark Twain's America,* 251. Another "Mark Twain" listens with pleasure to a long story and appreciates its mining camp teller—clearly Jim Baker although here he is called Dick Baker: "Whenever he was out of luck and a little down-hearted, he would fall to mourning over the loss of a wonderful cat he used to own (for where women and children are not, men of kindly impulses take up with pets, for they must love something). And he always spoke of the strange sagacity of that cat with the air of a man who believed in his secret heart that there was something human about it—maybe even supernatural." *Roughing It,* chapter 61.

34. Walter Blair, *Mark Twain and Huck Finn* (Berkeley: University of California Press, 1960), 235–328, passim, treats numerous instances.

35. Brander Mathews, writing about "the immense variety" of Twain's style, writes: "Consider the tale of the Blue Jay . . . wherein the humor is sus-

tained by unstated pathos: what could be better told than this, with every word the right word and in the right place?" "An Appreciation," in Mark Twain, *Europe and Elsewhere* (New York: Harper, 1923), xxviii. In *Mark Twain & "Huck Finn"* 172–78, I have discussed various factors in the humorist's personal situation that caused him to write sympathetically about the misanthropic Jim Baker and the frustrated blue jay.

Gregg Camfield

"The Carnival of Crime" challenges the sentimental model of conscience as a moral sense by suggesting that the conscience is fundamentally at odds with the person it belongs to and is appointed by "higher authority." This challenge is in keeping with the etymology of the word conscience itself, suggesting knowledge of one's self along with God's knowledge of the self. In the older Christian tradition, this knowledge was never for a "natural man" a pleasant knowledge. As Henry James, Sr., put it:

> Conscience is the badge of a fallen nature. It is only after we have eaten of the tree of knowledge of good and evil, that its voice is heard investing us with responsibility. . . . It was never designed as a minister of peace and reconciliation with God, but only as a voice of disunion and menace. It was never designed, according to the apostle, to give a knowledge of righteousness, but only a knowledge of sin, that every mouth might be stopped, and ALL THE WORLD BECOME GUILTY before God.[1]

James essentially repeats the Calvinist line about conscience, that it is a vengeful voice that chastises the natural man for his total depravity. Without conscience, man "must surely have forgotten the very name of God" (145).

The conscience as Clemens depicts it resembles the Calvinist model of conscience in important ways. For one thing, when his conscience is first made visible to him, the narrator has an "incomprehensible sense of being legally and legitimately under his authority," and without doubt the conscience is an external being, in fact a spirit "appointed by authority," rather than an internal sense or intuition. For another, this conscience will not grant any pleasure:

Excerpted from Gregg Camfield, *Sentimental Twain: Samuel Clemens in the Maze of Moral Philosophy* (Philadelphia: University of Pennsylvania Press, 1994), 116–21. Reprinted by permission of the University of Pennsylvania Press.

"Is there any way of satisfying that malignant invention which is called a conscience?"

"Well, none that I propose to tell you my son. Ass! I don't care what act you may turn your hand to, I can straightway whisper a word in your ear and make you think you have committed a dreadful meanness. It is my business—and my joy—to make you repent of everything you do."[2]

Surely this conscience is "a voice of disunion and menace," designed to castigate all human behaviors, whether right or wrong.

Calvinists were concerned, however, not with carnivals of crime, but with the sin to which the flesh is naturally heir. Unlike the Calvinist conscience, the one in Clemens's tale is appointed not to remind man of his fallen state, but to "improve" him and to regulate society. Thus, while this tale's conscience acts the part of a Calvinist conscience, its purpose of "improvement" implies an Arminian conception of salvation by degree through gradual change of behavior. In this purpose, this conscience is distinctly anti-Calvinist and much more in line with either a sentimental or a utilitarian definition of human motivation.

But while the conscience's "purpose . . . is to improve the man" and by improving the man to improve society, consciences

are merely disinterested agents. . . . We obey orders and leave the consequences where they belong. But I am willing to admit this much: we do crowd the orders a trifle when we get a chance, which is most of the time. We enjoy it. We are instructed to remind a man a few times of an error; and I don't mind acknowledging that we try to give pretty good measure. (315)

Here, consciences themselves are motivated by the pleasure principle; hence, while a higher authority may govern their purpose and while that purpose may actually be fulfilled by the actions of consciences—as the list of virtuous people with powerful consciences attests and as the story's conclusion shows the conscienceless narrator indulging in his new business of crime and enjoying it as much as "savage" consciences enjoy harrowing people to suicide—the behavior of consciences themselves is marked by wild moral inconsistency.

The "devilish" egotism of the conscience, according to the narrator, explains this:

I think I begin to see now why you have always been a trifle inconsistent with me. In your anxiety to get all the juice you can out of a sin, you make a man repent of it in three or four different ways. For instance, you found fault with me for lying to that tramp, and I suffered over that. But it was only yesterday that I told a tramp the square truth, to wit, that, it being regarded as bad citizenship to encourage vagrancy, I would give him nothing. What did you do then? Why you made me say to myself, "Ah, it would have been so much kinder and more blameless to ease him off with a little white lie, and send him away feeling that if he could not have bread, the gentle treatment was at least something to be grateful for!" Well, I suffered all day about that. Three days before I had fed a tramp, and fed him freely, supposing it a virtuous act. Straight off you said, "Oh, false citizen, to have fed a tramp!" and I suffered as usual. I gave a tramp work; you objected to it . . . Next I refused a tramp work; you objected to that. Next I proposed to kill a tramp; you kept me awake all night, oozing remorse at every pore. Sure I was going to be right this time, I sent the next tramp away with my benediction; and I wish you may live as long as I do, if you didn't make me smart all night again because I didn't kill him. (316)[3]

Neither the Calvinist nor the sentimentalist version of conscience could account for such absurd inconsistencies as this; this conscience resembles the ego in its purely selfish pursuit of pleasure even in fulfilling its assigned function.

In fact, the parallels between the narrator after he kills his conscience and the conscience itself are striking. The conscience describes himself as the narrator's "most pitiless enemy" (312), showing that, while consciences may force people to have pity for one another, these spirits themselves have none, and implying that all consciences are humankind's collective worst enemy. When the narrator frees himself of his conscience, he, too, loses all compassion for human beings, expressing willingness to kill his Aunt Mary, the person he "loved and honored most in all the world" (302), as readily as people against whom he held grudges. The narrator becomes an enemy to his own kind.

Most important, the conscience repeatedly describes his malignant work as a joy. The biggest conscience in the region so loves his work that "he never sleeps. . . . Night and day you can find him pegging away at Smith, panting with his labor, sleeves rolled up, countenance all alive with enjoyment" (321). The narrator, when free of his conscience at tale's end, similarly develops a profession of deviltry and takes tremendous pleasure from it:

Since that day my life is all bliss. Bliss, unalloyed bliss. . . . I settled all my old outstanding scores, and began the world anew. I killed thirty-eight persons during the first two weeks—all of them on account of ancient grudges. I burned a dwelling that interrupted my view. I swindled a widow and some orphans out of their last cow, which is a very good one, though not a thoroughbred, I believe. I have also committed scores of crimes, of various kinds, and have enjoyed my work exceedingly, whereas it would formerly have broken my heart and turned my hair gray, I have no doubt. (325)

Early in the story, the narrator says that "only a conscience could find pleasure in heaping agony upon a spirit like that" (321), but by story's end the narrator is just as "devilish." One of the implicit answers to Clemens's conundrum, then, is that the conscience reflects all of a human being's "malignant" (316) traits in order to balance them in action.

In killing his conscience, the narrator suddenly transforms his life, much as a conversion experience is said to transform the life of the regenerate. The language here echoes the language of conversion, with the narrator declaring that he "began the world anew" and found himself living a life of "unalloyed bliss." But this is of course a reverse conversion, a conversion from part saint/part sinner to pure sinner. By killing off God's agent of castigation, the natural man frees himself of divine influence and falls into the pure bliss of ego gratification, even tormenting or killing other human beings for the pleasure of making a business of it.[4]

Thus does the story attack utilitarian ideas of morality by suggesting that unbridled ego yields purely evil selfishness; it also seems to attack the Calvinist idea of conscience by conflating it with utilitarian selfishness. If the story did only this, it would endorse the sentimental conception of conscience that so many of Clemens's Hartford neighbors accepted. But he conflates the sentimental conscience with the Calvinist as readily as he identifies Calvinism with selfishness. For one, as I mentioned earlier, this tale does show conscience serving the purpose of public morality. More importantly, the way Clemens shows the conscience as being trained into effectiveness echoes sentimental ideas of developing the moral sense.

The narrator's conscience reveals that it is born with the man, suggesting that it is part of the spiritual equipment of the person, even though a child's conscience is underdeveloped, "thirteen inches high, and rather sluggish, when he was two years old—as nearly all of us are at that age" (321). Consciences can grow either direction from this nascent state, depending both on how well the conscience plays its cards and on how willing the ego is either to acquiesce or to rebel against its proddings:

> Some of us grow one way and some the other. You had a large conscience once; if you've a small conscience now I reckon there are reasons for it. However, both of us are to blame, you and I. You see, you used to be conscientious about a great many things; morbidly so, I may say. . . . Well, I took a great interest in my work, and I so enjoyed the anguish which certain pet sins of yours afflicted you with that I kept pelting at you until I rather overdid the matter. You began to rebel. Of course I began to lose ground, then, and shrivel a little—diminish in statue, get moldy, and grow deformed. The more I weakened, the more stubbornly you fastened on to those particular sins, till at last the places on my person that represent those vices became as callous as shark-skin. (318–19)

The conscience describes other consciences ranging from a microscopic one to a particularly beautiful one so large it needs to live outdoors. Significantly, the narrator's conscience has grown callous, that is, he has lost his sensitivity to the moral character of certain kinds of behavior. In his fanciful way, then, Clemens describes the growth or demise of conscientious behavior as a function of cultivating moral sensitivity, much as sentimental moralists would.

But at the same time that this passage relies on a sentimental definition of conscience, it also challenges the validity of this definition. That the conscience says certain of the narrator's pet sins "afflicted him with anguish" suggests that the feeling of remorse is innate to the human being, while it is the conscience's function simply to bring the remorse to mind. Clemens here hints that there might be a difference between the conscience and the moral sense, though sentimental moralists usually defined them as the same thing.[5] But Clemens found this conception at odds with the operation of conscience as he felt it. In fact, insofar as he accepted the idea that conscience is external to the man, he found no reason that the human being could not have both a conscience and a moral sense. Nevertheless, when the narrator kills his conscience, he kills his sympathy, too. Clemens thus asks whether conscience and the moral sense are indeed the same thing, or whether the conscience is only a necessary external spiritual force needed to activate the moral sense.

Here Clemens's characteristic mode of thinking by juxtaposing conflicting voices and ideas calls into doubt the validity and value of all three definitions of conscience. In his letter to Howells in which he describes the piece, he makes clear the irony of the title by italicizing the word "facts"; the only fact the piece makes clear is that the educated in Hartford, as well as throughout the country, were confused about what motivated moral behavior. His Hartford peers apparently could not solve this conundrum to his satisfaction, because he turned repeatedly to the problem of human motivation throughout his career, especially in *Adventures of Huckleberry Finn,* which he began writing within a few months of presenting his "Facts."

Notes

1. Henry James Sr., *The Nature of Evil* (New York: D. Appleton & Company, 1855), 144–46; hereafter cited parenthetically in the text.

2. "The Facts Concerning the Recent Carnival of Crime in Connecticut," in *Tom Sawyer Abroad, Tom Sawyer, Detective, and Other Stories* (New York: P. F. Collier, n.d.), 316–17; hereafter cited parenthetically in the text.

3. The narrator's similar description of variable remorse when he describes his attendance at a charity sermon is a parody of Benjamin Franklin's account in his *Autobiography* of listening to Whitefield's plea for money. Franklin may very well have been one source of Clemens's knowledge of utilitarianism.

4. As becomes clear in the final paragraph when he declares that he is in the cadaver business.

5. See Joseph Twichell, "The Religious Experience of Children," *The Religious Herald,* December 19, 1878: "Conscience, or if you please, moral sense."

Susan K. Harris

While older women are mother substitutes in Twain's novels about childhood and unmarried young women are moral exemplars, the woman as a celebrated image did not fully evolve until Twain began transforming his image of Livy into a series of loving wives in his fiction. The clearest—and almost the latest—delineation of the ideal woman in Mark Twain's fiction is the character Eve, from the short sketches "Extracts from Adam's Diary" and "Eve's Diary," finished in 1905, only a year after Livy's death. Like other portions of the "Papers of the Adams Family," these sketches were composed at intervals over a decade or more, but they are printed together in the 1917 Harper's edition of Twain's work, probably because they are so obviously a matched pair in conception and mood. They are unusual in Twain's work in that the diary form permits Twain to portray the woman through her own voice as well as from the male protagonist's or omniscient narrator's point of view. In addition, the two voices permit him to use rhetorical fluidity as an index to the progress of Adam and Eve's relationship. Finally, the diaries are unusual in Twain's fiction because sex is clearly one of the attractions the two humans have for each other.

The theme of "Adam's Diary" and "Eve's Diary" concerns Eve's efforts to make Adam aware that, as another human being, her companionship is necessary for his happiness. Only after he recognizes her significance does Adam become truly human himself. Before he accepts her, his self-image is rooted in his janitorial duties and his self-absorption is reflected in his rhetorical brevity. Twain's strategy for developing their relationship is to show how Adam's control over language expands as he comes to understand how much Eve means to him.

Prior to Eve's appearance in Eden, Adam seems to have regarded himself as a faithful watchman, stolidly—and silently—doing his duty; significantly, he initially resents Eve's chatter because "any new and

Excerpted from Susan K. Harris, *Mark Twain's Escape from Time: A Study of Patterns and Images* (Columbia: University of Missouri Press, 1982), 123–28. Reprinted by permission of the author.

strange sound intruding itself here upon the solemn hush of these dreaming solitudes offends my ear."[1] Much of the charm of these pieces comes from Adam's learning to adjust to the "new creature" in his garden; through the course of his diary he evinces his adjustment by gradually relaxing his language, moving from his initial short, clipped clauses to long, lyrical ones. "This new creature with the long hair is a good deal in the way," he begins. "It is always hanging around and following me about. I don't like this; I am not used to company. I wish it would stay with the other animals" ("A&E," p. 343). Perhaps more than any other of Twain's first-person narrators, Adam is paralyzed by his inability to see the other as subject as well as object; he demonstrates his blindness immediately by referring to Eve as "it" until she teaches him to say "she" and "we."

Eve, however, seeks Adam for companionship; unlike him, she is not happy being alone. He thinks she seeks reflections of herself because she is vain: "she fell in the pond yesterday when she was looking at herself in it, which she is always doing," he sourly remarks ("A&E," p. 346); but she claims to go to the pond "for companionship, some one to look at, some one to talk to. It is not enough . . . but it is something, and something is better than utter loneliness" ("A&E," p. 367). Furthermore, Eve encourages Adam to talk more, surmising that his reticence comes from his conviction that "he is not bright, and is sensitive about it and wishes to conceal it. It is a pity that he should feel so, for brightness is nothing; it is in the heart that the values lie. I wish I could make him understand that a loving good heart is riches . . . and that without it intellect is poverty" ("A&E," p. 367). She encourages his slowly expanding vocabulary, knowing that "it show[s] that he possesses a certain quality of perception. Without a doubt that seed can be made to grow, if cultivated."

Since Adam refuses to acknowledge Eve's right to share his life, she sets herself the immediate task of making him notice that she is not the same as the other animals. Twain illustrates Adam's struggle to reject Eve through his terse sentences, his diction, and his hostility toward her implication that he can no longer think of himself as the only intelligent being around. When Eve first appears Adam notes,

> The new creature says its name is Eve. That is all right, I have no objections. Says it is to call it by, when I want it to come. I said it was superfluous, then. The word evidently raised me in its respect; and indeed it is a large, good word and will bear repetition. It says it is not

an It; it is a She. That is probably doubtful; yet it is all one to me; what she is were nothing to me if she would but go by herself and not talk. ("A&E," p. 344)

This passage is significant for the way its language conveys the development of the story's theme. First, Adam's short, choppy sentences convey his unwillingness to engage in conversation with an inferior being; second, he chooses words that will impress Eve with his superiority; third, he insists that Eve's most annoying characteristic is her propensity to talk. Clearly, sound as well as specific words is at issue here, as it is throughout the diaries. Adam resents Eve because she talks; to him; close up; forcing him to answer. Accustomed "only to sounds that are more or less distant from me" ("A&E," p. 343), he resents Eve primarily because she is a sound close to him, one to which he must respond. Adam presents his Eden as a solipsistic universe in which any voice from the outside offends the privacy of his dream; Eve insists that he cease imagining that he is alone and include her in his psychic landscape. One sign of her success is that Adam's smugness is the fist indication that he cares that she notices how smart he is.

Adam's emergence from total self-absorption to awareness of the importance of the other is first evident when he realizes that without Eve he would be lonely. After their Fall, Adam suddenly understands that Eve can compensate for the loss of Eden. "I find she is a good deal of a companion," he remarks. "I see I should be lonesome and depressed without her, now that I have lost my property" ("A&E," p. 349). Furthermore, through his association with Eve, Adam learns that the world, even outside the garden, is beautiful. Whereas originally he perceived only objects that were useful to him he now begins to see objects that stimulate his aesthetic imagination. At once his clauses lengthen; in Twain's mind there seems to be an association between awareness of the significance of others—whether they are other people or simply other aspects of creation—and rhetorical fluidity. Starting with simple adjective-noun combinations—"brown rocks, yellow sand, gray moss"— Adam quickly graduates to metaphor—"the golden islands floating in crimson seas at sunset, the pallid moon sailing through the shredded cloud-rack" ("A&E," p. 373)—language so fluid, especially in contrast to his earlier stop/start sentences, as to indicate a revolution in sensibility. Finally, his appreciation of natural beauty leads Adam to see Eve as the beautiful creature that she is: "Once when she was standing marble-white and sun-drenched on a boulder, with her young head tilted back and her hand shading her eyes, watching the flight of a bird in the sky, I recognized that she was beautiful" ("A&E," p. 373). Having made this leap, Adam suddenly becomes a fully human being, not only knowing that Eve is necessary for companionship but desiring her sexually as well. She, always more ready to articulate her emotions, explicitly attributes her attraction to Adam to his sex, "I love him with all the strength of my passionate nature," she records ("A&E," p. 378). "Merely because he is masculine, I think" ("A&E," p. 380). At the end of his own diary, his language thoroughly relaxed, Adam confesses, "It is better to live outside the Garden with her than inside it without her" ("A&E," p. 356), testimony to the power of sexual companionship to overcome the delights of solitude. While she notes, "I am the first wife; and in the last I shall be repeated," he, at her grave, knows that "wheresoever she was, *there* was Eden" ("A&E," p. 381).

This late piece in many ways summarizes the importance that wives bear in Twain's fiction. Although in many respects Eve simply reflects the popular image of women as being more sociable, more sensitive to the importance of other people, than men, the peculiar twist given that image in Twain's work suggests that for him its significance lay in the woman's power to coax the man out of himself, to make him aware that his is not the only consciousness in existence. As Aunt Polly's efforts to make Tom recognize the vulnerability of others succeed in preparing him to join the community, so Eve's strenuous efforts to make Adam recognize *her* succeed in rescuing him from a solitary paradise that was as sterile as it was ingrown. Twain's "Diaries" are, of course, his version of the fortunate Fall; for all Adam's initial protestations, in retrospect he realizes how lonely it had been to be the only one of his type. Much of his pleasure comes from the fact that with Eve he learns to see aesthetically and to communicate with another being. Within the landscape of his new Eden, she represents the acquisition of truly human emotions and an escape from the paralysis of solitude.

Few of Twain's other late fictional wives have Eve's charm, partly because few are allowed to tell their own stories. Generally wooden, certainly idealized, these characters deserve examination less because they are interesting (on the whole, they are not) than because they reflect the narrators' needs, providing a focus for male emotions that the narrators express in gushing, sentimental terms. As we have already noted, however, sentimental language is one of the means Twain uses to signal the importance of a woman to his characters. Certainly rhetorical fluidity is an index to Adam's sexual and aesthetic development. Similarly, in

Twain's nightmare manuscripts the adulation women evoke indicates the symbolic outlet they offer to men who are often so paralyzed by their troubles or so deeply absorbed in themselves that they have difficulty articulating anything else. Although the women in these stories routinely care for houses and children, their real function is to provide emotional centering for their men. Whether the men accept or reject their women, they are always responding to them; the female figure is often the only secure object in their psychic landscape. One of the objections to Twain's fictional wives always has been that they are stereotypes; unlike the male protagonists, they are rarely allowed to grow and change. But as Carol Christ points out, this is one of the functions of the Angel in Victorian literature; by always being the same, she represents continuity and innocence in a world of flux and corruption.[2] For Twain's protagonists she provides a way to escape not only the anxieties of their public lives but also the anxieties of their private lives.

Notes

1. "Adam's Diary" and "Eve's Diary" in *The $30,000 Bequest* in *The Complete Works of Mark Twain* 18 (New York: Harper and Brothers, 1917), 343; hereafter cited in the text with the abbreviation "A&E."

2. Carol Christ, "Victorian Masculinity and the Angel in the House" in *A Widening Sphere: Changing Roles of Victorian Women*, ed. Martha Vicinus (Bloomington: Indiana University Press, 1977), 146–62. The point, it seems to me, is implicit in Christ's discussion, especially as concerns Tennyson's "isolated maidens."

Chronology

1835	Samuel Langhorne Clemens born November 30 in Florida, Missouri.
1839	Family moves to Hannibal, Missouri.
1847	Father, John Marshall Clemens, dies March 24.
1852	Publishes "The Dandy Frightening the Squatter."
1857	Meets Horace Bixby, who agrees to teach him riverboat piloting.
1858–1859	Apprenticeship as "cub" pilot; receives pilot license April 9, 1859.
1861	Civil War ends his piloting career; travels west with brother Orion to Carson City, Nevada.
1863	Publishes first of his "Carson City Letters" in Virginia City *Territorial Enterprise* under pen name Mark Twain.
1865	"Jim Smiley and His Jumping Frog" published in the New York *Saturday Press* for November 18.
1867	*The Celebrated Jumping Frog of Calaveras County and Other Sketches* published by C. H. Webb. Meets Olivia Langdon.
1869	*The Innocents Abroad* published by American Publishing Company.
1870	February 2, marries Olivia Langdon in Elmira, New York. Son Langdon Clemens born November 7.
1872	*Roughing It* published by American Publishing Company. March 19, daughter Olivia Susan (Susy) born. June 2, Langdon Clemens dies of pneumonia.
1873	*The Gilded Age* (coauthored with Charles Dudley Warner) published by American Publishing Company.
1874	June 8, daughter Clara born. "A True Story" published in November issue of the *Atlantic Monthly*. House in Hartford, Connecticut, completed.

1875 "Old Times on the Mississippi" published in seven installments in the *Atlantic Monthly*. *Mark Twain's Sketches New and Old* published by the American Publishing Company.

1876 *The Adventures of Tom Sawyer* published by the American Publishing Company. "Facts Concerning the Recent Carnival of Crime in Connecticut" published in the June issue of the *Atlantic Monthly*.

1877 December 17, gives the Whittier Birthday Speech in Boston.

1878–1879 Lives abroad in Germany and Italy.

1880 *A Tramp Abroad* published by the American Publishing Company. July 26, daughter Jean born.

1882 *The Prince and the Pauper* and *The Stolen White Elephant, Etc.* published by James R. Osgood.

1883 *Life on the Mississippi* published by James R. Osgood.

1885 *Adventures of Huckleberry Finn* published by Twain's publishing company, Charles L. Webster and Company. "The Private History of a Campaign That Failed" published in December issue of *Century*.

1889 *A Connecticut Yankee in King Arthur's Court* published by Charles L. Webster and Company.

1890 October 27, mother, Jane Lampton Clemens dies. Deeply involved in prospects for the Paige typesetting machine.

1892 *Merry Tales* published by Charles L. Webster and Company.

1893 *The £1,000,000 Bank Note and Other New Stories* published by Charles L. Webster and Company.

1894 Henry Huttleston Rogers superintends Clemens's financial affairs. Assigns Olivia his property, including copyrights. Twain declares bankruptcy. *The Tragedy of Pudd'nhead Wilson and the Comedy of Those Extraordinary Twins* published by American Publishing Company.

1895 Begins around-the-world lecture tour in order to pay creditors.

1896   August 18, daughter Susy dies of meningitis. *Personal Recollections of Joan of Arc* and *Tom Sawyer Abroad, Tom Sawyer, Detective, and Other Stories* published by Harper and Brothers.

1897   *How to Tell a Story and Other Essays* published by Harper and Brothers. *Following the Equator* published by American Publishing Company.

1898   Remaining debts paid in full.

1899   "The Man That Corrupted Hadleyburg" published in December issue of *Harper's Monthly*.

1900   *The Man That Corrupted Hadleyburg and Other Stories and Essays* published by Harper Brothers.

1901   "To the Person Sitting in Darkness" published in the *North American Review* for February and as a pamphlet by the Anti-Imperialist League. Moved to Riverdale-on-the Hudson, New York.

1902   Visits Hannibal, Missouri, for the last time. Receives an honorary degree from the University of Missouri.

1903   *My Debut as a Literary Person and Other Essays and Stories* published by American Publishing Company. Settles in Italy for Olivia's health.

1904   June 5, Olivia Langdon Clemens dies in Italy.

1906   *The $30,000 Bequest and Other Stories* published by Harper and Brothers. *What Is Man?* published anonymously by DeVinne Press.

1907   Receives honorary degree from Oxford University.

1908   Moves into "Stormfield" home in Redding, Connecticut.

1909   *Extract from Captain Stormfield's Visit to Heaven* published as a separate volume by Harper and Brothers. Daughter Jean dies December 24.

1910   Travels to Bermuda; returns April 12. Dies at "Stormfield" April 21. Buried in family plot in Elmira, New York, on April 24.

Selected Bibliography

Primary Works

The American Claimant and Other Stories and Sketches. New York: Harper & Brothers, 1899.

The Bible According to Mark Twain. Edited by Howard G. Baetzhold and Joseph B. McCullough. Athens: University of Georgia Press, 1995.

The Celebrated Jumping Frog of Calaveras County and Other Sketches. New York: C. H. Webb, 1867. "Jim Smiley and His Jumping Frog," "Aurelia's Unfortunate Young Man," "Story of the Bad Little Boy Who Didn't Come to Grief," "Lucretia Smith's Soldier," "Advice for Good Little Girls."

Clemens of the Call: Mark Twain in San Francisco. Edited by Edgar M. Branch. Berkeley and Los Angeles: University of California Press, 1969.

Collected Tales, Sketches, Speeches, & Essays, 1853–1890. Edited by Louis J. Budd. New York: Library of America, 1992.

Collected Tales, Sketches, Speeches, & Essays, 1891–1910. Edited by Louis J. Budd. New York: Library of America, 1992.

Contributions to the Galaxy, 1868–1871, by Mark Twain. Edited by Bruce R. McElderry Jr. Gainesville, Fla.: Scholars' Facsimiles and Reprints, 1961.

[Date, 1601] Conversation As It Was by the Social Fireside in the Time of the Tudors. Privately published, 1880.

A Dog's Tale. New York: Harper & Brothers, 1904. "A Dog's Tale."

A Double-Barrelled Detective Story. New York: Harper & Brothers, 1902.

Early Tales & Sketches, 1851—1864. Edited by Edgar Marquess Branch and Robert H. Hirst. Berkeley and Los Angeles: University of California Press, 1979.

Early Tales & Sketches, 1864–1865. Edited by Edgar Marquess Branch and Robert H. Hirst. Berkeley and Los Angeles: University of California Press, 1981.

Europe and Elsewhere. New York: Harper & Brothers, 1923. "Eve Speaks," "The New Planet," "The War Prayer."

Eve's Diary. New York: Harper & Brothers, 1906.

Extract from Captain Stormfield's Visit to Heaven. New York: Harper & Brothers, 1909. "Extract from Captain Stormfield's Visit to Heaven."

Extracts from Adam's Diary. New York: Harper & Brothers, 1904. "Extracts from Adam's Diary."

Following the Equator: A Journey around the World. Hartford: American Publishing, 1897. "Cecil Rhodes and the Shark," "The Joke That Made Ed's Fortune," "A Story without End."

A Horse's Tale. New York and London: Harper & Brothers, 1907. "A Horse's Tale."

How to Tell a Story and Other Essays. New York: Harper, 1897.

Letters from the Earth. Edited by Bernard DeVoto. New York: Harper & Brothers, 1962.

Life on the Mississippi. Boston: James R. Osgood, 1883. "A Dying Man's Confession," "The Professor's Yarn," "A Burning Brand."

The Man That Corrupted Hadleyburg and Other Stories and Essays. New York: Harper & Brothers, 1900. "The Man That Corrupted Hadleyburg," "Is He Living or Is He Dead?" "The Esquimau Maiden's Romance."

Mark Twain in Eruption: Hitherto Unpublished Pages about Men and Events. Edited by Bernard DeVoto. New York: Capricorn Books, 1940.

Mark Twain of the Enterprise: Newspaper Articles and Other Documents, 1862—1864. Edited by Henry Nash Smith and Frederick Anderson. Berkeley and Los Angeles: University of California Press, 1957.

Mark Twain's Fables of Man. Edited by John S. Tuckey. Berkeley and Los Angeles: University of California Press, 1972. "Little Bessie," "The International Lighting Trust," "The Second Advent," "Randall's Jew Story," "You've Been a Dam Fool, Mary. You Always Was!"

Mark Twain's Mysterious Stranger Manuscripts. Edited by William M. Gibson. Berkeley and Los Angeles: University of California Press, 1969. "No. 44, The Mysterious Stranger," "The Chronicle of Young Satan," "Schoolhouse Hill."

Mark Twain's Own Autobiography: The Chapters from the North American Review. Edited by Michael J. Kiskis. Madison: University of Wisconsin Press, 1990.

Mark Twain's Satires & Burlesques. Edited by Franklin R. Rogers. Berkeley and Los Angeles: University of California Press, 1967.

Mark Twain's Sketches. New York: American News, 1874. "Map of Paris," "The Facts in the Case of the Great Beef Contract."

Mark Twain's Sketches, New and Old. Hartford: American Publishing, 1875. "My Watch," "Experience of the McWilliamses with Membranous Croup," "Some Learned Fables for Good Old Boys and Girls," "A Curious Dream," "A Ghost Story," "How I Edited an Agricultural Paper Once," "Political Economy," "Journalism in Tennessee," "Story of the Good Little Boy Who Did Not Prosper," "A Visit to Niagara," "A Medieval Romance," "A True Story," "Legend of the Capitoline Venus," "Science *vs.* Luck," "Cannibalism in the Cars," "A Mysterious Visit."

Mark Twain's "Which Was the Dream?" and Other Symbolic Writings of the Later Years. Edited by John S. Tuckey. Berkeley and Los Angeles: University of California Press, 1967.

Merry Tales. New York: Charles L. Webster, 1892. "The Private History of a Campaign That Failed," "Luck," "The Invalid's Story," "Mrs. McWilliams and the Lightning."

The £1,000,000 Bank-Note and Other New Stories. New York: Charles L. Webster, 1893. "The £1,000,000 Bank-Note," "Playing Courier."

217

My Début as a Literary Person and Other Essays and Stories. Hartford: American Publishing, 1903. "The Belated Russian Passport," "The Death Disk," "Two Little Tales."

The Mysterious Stranger, A Romance. New York: Harper & Brothers, 1916.

The Mysterious Stranger and Other Stories. New York: Harper & Brothers, 1922. "My Platonic Sweetheart," "The McWilliamses and the Burglar Alarm," "A Fable," "Hunting the Deceitful Turkey."

Punch, Brothers, Punch! and Other Sketches. New York: Slote, Woodman, 1878. "Punch, Brothers, Punch!" "An Encounter with an Interviewer," "The Loves of Alonzo Fitz Clarence and Rosannah Ethelton," "The Canvasser's Tale."

Report from Paradise. Edited by Dixon Wecter. New York: Harper & Brothers, 1952.

Roughing It. Hartford: American Publishing, 1972. "The Facts in the Great Landslide Case," "Buck Fanshaw's Funeral," "Captain Ned Blakely," "Jim Blaine and His Grandfather's Old Ram," "Dick Baker and His Cat," "A Letter from Horace Greeley."

The Stolen White Elephant, Etc. Boston: James R. Osgood, 1882. "The Stolen White Elephant," "The Great Revolution in Pitcairn," "A Curious Experience," "Mrs. McWilliams and the Lightning."

The $30,000 Bequest and Other Stories. New York: Harper & Brothers, 1906. "The $30,000 Bequest," "Was It Heaven? Or Hell?" "Edward Mills and George Benton: A Tale," "The Five Boons of Life," "The Californian's Tale."

Tom Sawyer Abroad, Tom Sawyer, Detective, and Other Stories. New York: Harper & Brothers, 1896.

A Tramp Abroad. Hartford: American Publishing, 1880. "Jim Baker's Blue-Jay Yarn," "The Man Who Put Up at Gadsby's."

Traveling with the Innocents Abroad: Mark Twain's Original Reports from Europe and the Holy Land. Edited by Daniel Morley McKeithan. Norman: University of Oklahoma Press, 1958.

A True Story and the Recent Carnival of Crime. Boston: James R. Osgood, 1877. "Facts concerning the Recent Carnival of Crime in Connecticut."

Secondary Works

Baender, Paul. "The 'Jumping Frog' as a Comedian's First Virtue." *Modern Philology* 60 (February 1963): 192–200.

Baetzhold, Howard G. *Mark Twain and John Bull: The British Connection.* Bloomington: Indiana University Press, 1970.

Baldanza, Frank. *Mark Twain: An Introduction and Interpretation.* Orlando, Fla.: Holt, Rinehart & Winston, 1961.

Bellamy, Gladys. *Mark Twain as a Literary Artist*. Norman: University of Oklahoma Press, 1950.

Blair, Walter. *Native American Humor, 1800–1900*. Rev. ed. Hartford, Conn.: American Book Co., 1960.

———. *Essays on American Humor: Blair through the Ages*. Selected and edited by Hamlin Hill. Madison: University of Wisconsin Press, 1993.

Blair, Walter, and Hamlin Hill. *America's Humor: From Poor Richard to Doonesbury*. New York: Oxford University Press, 1978.

Branch, Edgar M. *The Literary Apprenticeship of Mark Twain, with Selections from His Apprentice Writing*. Champaign: University of Illinois Press, 1950.

———. "Mark Twain: Newspaper Reading and the Writer's Creativity." *Nineteenth-Century Fiction* 37 (March 1983): 576–603.

Brodwin, Stanley. "The Humor of the Absurd: Mark Twain's Adamic Diaries." *Criticism* 14 (1972): 49–64.

———. "Mark Twain's Masks of Satan: The Final Phase." *American Literature* 45 (1973): 206–27.

Budd, Louis J. *Mark Twain: Social Philosopher*. Bloomington: Indiana University Press, 1962.

———. "Mark Twain: Samuel Langhorne Clemens." In *Critical Survey of Short Fiction*, edited by Frank N. Magill. Vol. 6. Salem Press, 1981, 2360–65.

———. *Mark Twain: The Ecstasy of Humor, Quarry Farm Papers* 6. Elmira, N.Y.: Elmira College Center for Mark Twain Studies, 1995.

Camfield, Gregg. *Sentimental Twain: Samuel Clemens in the Maze of Moral Philosophy*. Philadelphia: University of Pennsylvania Press, 1994.

Cardwell, Guy. "Mark Twain's Hadleyburg." *Ohio State Archaeological and Historical Quarterly* 60 (1951): 257–64.

Covici, Pascal, Jr. *Mark Twain's Humor: The Image of a World*. Dallas: Southern Methodist University Press, 1962.

Cox, James M. *Mark Twain: The Fate of Humor*. Princeton, N.J.: Princeton University Press, 1966.

Dolmetsch, Carl. *"Our Famous Guest": Mark Twain in Vienna*. Athens: University of Georgia Press, 1992.

Emerson, Everett. *The Authentic Mark Twain: A Literary Biography of Samuel L. Clemens*. Philadelphia: University of Pennsylvania Press, 1984.

Ensor, Allison. *Mark Twain and the Bible*. Lexington: University of Kentucky Press, 1969.

Ferguson, DeLancey. *Mark Twain: Man and Legend*. Indianapolis: Bobbs Merrill, 1943.

Florence, Don. *Persona and Humor in Mark Twain's Early Writings*. Columbia: University of Missouri Press, 1995.

Foner, Philip. *Mark Twain, Social Critic*. New York: International Publishers, 1958.

Gerber, John C. "Mark Twain's Use of the Comic Pose." *PMLA* 77 (June 1962): 297–304.

Gibson, William M. *The Art of Mark Twain*. New York: Oxford University Press, 1976.

Giddings, Robert, ed. *Mark Twain: A Sumptuous Variety*. Savage, Md.: Barnes and Noble, 1985.

Gribben, Alan. *Mark Twain's Library: A Reconstruction*. 2 vols. Boston: G. K. Hall, 1980.

———. "Those Other Thematic Patterns in Mark Twain's Writings." *Studies in American Fiction* 13 (Autumn 1985): 185–200.

Harris, Susan K. *Mark Twain's Escape from Time: A Study of Patterns and Images*. Columbia: University of Missouri Press, 1982.

———. " 'Hadleyburg': Mark Twain's Dual Attack on Banal Theology and Banal Literature." *American Literary Realism* 16 (Autumn 1983): 240–52.

Hill, Hamlin. *Mark Twain and Elisha Bliss*. Columbia: University of Missouri Press, 1964.

———. *Mark Twain: God's Fool*. New York: Harper & Row, 1973.

Howells, William Dean. *My Mark Twain: Reminiscences and Criticisms*. New York: Harper and Brothers, 1910.

Kaplan, Justin. *Mr. Clemens and Mark Twain*. New York: Simon and Schuster, 1966.

LeMaster, J. R., and James D. Wilson, ed. *The Mark Twain Encyclopedia*. New York: Garland Publishing, 1993.

Long, E. Hudson, and J. R. LeMaster. *The New Mark Twain Handbook*. New York: Garland Publishing, 1985.

Lynn, Kenneth. *Mark Twain and Southwestern Humor*. Boston: Little Brown, 1959.

McMahan, Elizabeth, ed. *Critical Approaches to Mark Twain's Short Stories*. Port Washington, N.Y.: Kennikat Press, 1981.

Macnaughton, William R. *Mark Twain's Last Years as a Writer*. Columbia: University of Missouri Press, 1979.

Michelson, Bruce. *Mark Twain on the Loose: A Comic Writer and the American Self*. Amherst: University of Massachusetts Press, 1995.

Paine, Albert B. *Mark Twain: A Biography*. 3 vols. New York: Harper & Brothers, 1912.

Pettit, Arthur G. *Mark Twain and the South*. Lexington: University of Kentucky Press, 1973.

Rasmussen, R. Kent. *Mark Twain A to Z: The Essential Reference to His Writing*. New York: Facts on File, 1995.

Robinson, Forrest G., ed. *The Cambridge Companion to Mark Twain*. Cambridge: Cambridge University Press, 1995.

Rogers, Franklin R. *Mark Twain's Burlesque Patterns*. Dallas: Southern Methodist University Press, 1960.

Scharnhorst, Gary. "Paradise Revisited: Twain's 'The Man That Corrupted Hadleyburg.' " *Studies in Short Fiction* 18 (Winter 1981): 59–64.

Sloane, David E. E. *Mark Twain as a Literary Comedian*. Baton Rouge: Louisiana State University Press, 1979.

————., ed. *Mark Twain's Humor: Critical Essays*. New York: Garland Publishing, 1993.

Smith, Henry Nash. *Mark Twain: The Development of a Writer*. Cambridge: Harvard University Press, 1962.

Spengemann, William C. *Mark Twain and the Backwoods Angel: The Matter of Innocence in the Works of Samuel L. Clemens*. Kent, Ohio: Kent State University Press, 1966.

Steinbrink, Jeffrey. *Getting to Be Mark Twain*. Berkeley and Los Angeles: University of California Press, 1991.

Stone, Albert B., Jr. *The Innocent Eye: Childhood in Mark Twain's Imagination*. New Haven: Yale University Press, 1961.

Sundquist, Eric J., ed. *Mark Twain: A Collection of Critical Essays*. New York: Prentice Hall, 1994.

Tenney, Thomas A. *Mark Twain: A Reference Guide*. Boston: G. K. Hall, 1977.

Wilson, James D. *A Reader's Guide to the Short Stories of Mark Twain*. Boston: G. K. Hall, 1987.

Wonham, Henry B. *Mark Twain and the Art of the Tall Tale*. New York: Oxford University Press, 1992.

Index

The Author

Tom Quirk is professor of English at the University of Missouri–Columbia. He is the author of many essays on American literature and of three books, *Melville's Confidence Man: From Knight to Knave* (1982), *Bergson and American Culture: The Worlds of Willa Cather and Wallace Stevens* (1990), and *Coming to Grips with Huckleberry Finn* (1994). He is the editor or coeditor of nine other books, including *Writing the American Classics, Biographies of Books*, and *Mark Twain: Tales, Speeches, Essays, and Sketches*. He is currently coediting a Viking Portable edition of American realist and naturalist fiction.

The Editors

Gary Scharnhorst is professor of English at the University of New Mexico, co-editor of *American Literary Realism*, and editor in alternating years of *American Literary Scholarship: An Annual*. He is the author or editor of books about Horatio Alger, Jr., Charlotte Perkins Gilman, Bret Harte, Nathaniel Hawthorne, Henry David Thoreau, and Mark Twain; and he has taught in Germany on Fulbright fellowships three times (1978–79, 1985–86, 1993). He is also the current president of the Western Literature Association and the Pacific Northwest American Studies Association.

Eric Haralson is assistant professor of English at the State University of New York at Stony Brook. He has published articles on American and English literature—with special emphasis on the topic of masculinity—in *American Literature*, *Nineteenth-Century Literature*, the *Arizona Quarterly*, *American Literary Realism*, and the *Henry James Review*, as well as in several essay collections. He is also the editor of *The Garland Encyclopedia of American Nineteenth-Century Poetry*.

ISBN 0-8057-0867-7

90000